The GAA B

Eoghan Corry is a writer and columnist. Three of his previous books on sports history – *Viva, Catch and Kick* and *Kingdom Come* – went to number one in the Irish bestsellers, and his recent book of GAA quotations, *God and the Referee* was also a bestseller. He has formed the storyline of the sports museum in Croke Park and is the former sports, business and features editor of three national newspapers.

The GAA
Book of Lists

Eoghan Corry

HODDER
HEADLINE
IRELAND

Typeset in Garamond and Verdana by Hodder Headline Ireland
Cover design and text design by Anú Design, Tara
Printed and bound in Great Britain by Clays Ltd, St Ives, plc

Hodder Headline Ireland's policy is to use papers that are natural, renewable
and recyclable products and made from wood grown in sustainable forests.
The logging and manufacturing processes are expected to conform to the
environmental regulations of the country of origin.

Hodder Headline Ireland
8 Castlecourt Centre, Castleknock, Dublin 15, Ireland

A division of Hodder Headline
338 Euston Road, London NW1 3BH, England

Contents

Dedicated to my daughter, Constance,

and in memory of
King Milne 1919–2002.

Both of them fascinated by the details behind
the great events of history.

1

GAA Miscellany

There are now associations of sports statisticians and websites dedicated to the terrific trivia that attach themselves to the playing of sports everywhere. GAA has assembled quite a collection of these down the years, largely through the work of an army of amateur historians who set to work reading back through match reports, written memoirs and the oral traditions of the game in the approach to the Association's centenary in 1984. Some of the stories have grown in the telling down the years. Some of the tales have been disputed and some obscured. Like the name of the Dublin player sent off in the 1908 All Ireland final, it may be too late to retrieve the truth behind many of them.

Great Hurlers Who Never Won an All-Ireland

1. Des Foley *(Dublin)*

2. John Delaney *(Laois)*

3. Willie Hogan *(Carlow)*

4. John McGrath *(Westmeath)*

5. Pat Jobber McGrath *(Waterford)*

6. Paddy Molloy *(Offaly)*

7. Christy O'Brien *(Laois)*

8. Gerry O'Malley *(Roscommon)*

9. Joey Salmon *(Galway)*

10. Jimmy Smyth *(Clare)*

11. Johnny Walsh *(Kildare)*

Great Footballers Who Never Won an All-Ireland

1. Kevin Armstrong *(Antrim)*

2. Pat Dunny *(Kildare)*

3. Jim Hannify *(Longford)*

4. Iggy Jones *(Tyrone)*

5. Packie McGarty *(Leitrim)*

6. Peter McGinnity *(Fermanagh)*

7. Sean O'Connell *(Derry)*

8. Mickey Kearins *(Sligo)*

9. Gerry O'Reilly *(Wicklow)*

10. Tom Prendergast *(Laois)*

11. Jimmy Rea *(Carlow)*

5

The Cost of a Corporate Box in Croke Park

Super	Ä450,000
30 seater	Ä410,000
Executive	Ä310,000
Single	Ä240,000

Never Too Old

1. **Pat Leamy** was 53 when he played in the 1951 NHL final against Galway. He had hurled with the American team in the 1932 Tailteann Games.

2. **John T. Power**, the Kilkenny goalkeeper from the 1904–13 period, was 43 when he was recalled for the 1925 All-Ireland hurling semi-final against Galway, despite the fact he hadn't played for 5 years.

3. **Christy Ring** was 43 when a hip injury in the 1963 Railway Cup ended his career after 24 years of championship and provincial hurling. There was speculation he would be recalled for the 1966 All-Ireland hurling final at the age of 46.

4. **Frank Joyce Conlan** was 43 when he played for Kildare in the 1921 Leinster football final.

5. **Larry Hussey Cribben** was 41 when he played for Kildare in the 1919 All-Ireland football final.

Games that Changed Course in the Dying Minutes

1997 Leinster football semi-final
Kildare were leading Meath by 6 points at half-time in extra-time in the Leinster football semi-final when Jody Devine came on as a sub and changed the course of the game with 4 spectacular points.

2. **1994 All-Ireland hurling final**
Limerick were leading by 5 points with 4 minutes to go when Johnny Dooley scored a goal from a 21-yard free. Offaly won by 6 points.

3. **1991 All-Ireland hurling semi-final**
Antrim were leading by 1 point when Kilkenny got a last-minute goal to win 2–18 to 1–19.

4. **1984 Munster hurling final**
Tipperary led by 4 points with 4 minutes to go and Seamus Power opted to send a point over the bar. Back came Tony O'Sullivan and Seanie O'Leary for goals and Cork won by 4 points.

5. **1983 Munster football final**
Kerry were 90 seconds away from nine-in-a-row in Munster when Cork substitute Tadhgie Murphy grabbed on to a free and bustled it into the Kerry goal off the post, for a 1-point win for Cork.

5. **1982 All-Ireland football final**
   Kerry were certainties to win a record five-in-a-row
   All-Ireland titles when they led by 2 points, then
   Offaly substitute Seamus Darby got an opening in
   front of the goal, shot to the net and Kerry
   fumbled the counter-attack for a 1 point Offaly
   victory.

6. **1958 All-Ireland football semi-final**
   Kerry led Derry by 2 points with 2 minutes to go
   when Sean O'Connell scored a shock goal that put
   his county into their first ever final.

7. **1946 All-Ireland football final**
   Roscommon led by 6 points with 3 minutes to go
   when Paddy Burke scored for Kerry. Tom Gega
   O'Connor got another from a defensive mistake 2
   minutes later and the match was drawn. Kerry won
   the replay.

8. **1933 All-Ireland football semi-final**
   Kerry were hunting the record five-in-a-row All-
   Ireland titles but had to travel to Breffni Park to
   meet Cavan. The match was level with 2 minutes to
   go when Vincent McGovern gathered a Patsy
   Devlin pass and booted to the net to put an end to
   Kerry's hopes by 1–5 to 0–5.

9. **1926 All-Ireland football final**

After 29 minutes of the second half between Kildare and Kerry, Bill Gorman scored a dramatic equalising goal and Kerry won the replay by 3 points.

10. **1922 All-Ireland hurling final**

Kilkenny were 3 points down with 3 minutes to go when Paddy Donoghue and Dick Tobin struck for goals. Tipperary came back for an equalising goal but Willie Dwan's shot went over the bar by inches.

11. **1903 All-Ireland football final**

After Dick Fitzgerald's shot for Kerry was saved by Jack Fitzgerald of Kildare, the referee did not give a decision as to whether the goal stood or not and most of the spectators went home unaware of who the new All-Ireland champions were. As it happened, the match had to be replayed twice.

12. **1900 All-Ireland hurling final**

Tipperary forwards were famous for their forward charges, and used them to score 2 goals in the last 6 minutes after they trailed London 0–5 to 0–6. The first was from a free, conceded because the goalkeeper fouled the ball taking it out of a rut, and the second followed from a weak puck-out, Tipperary managed to avoid embarrassment by 5 points.

Replays in GAA Championship Matches

	LF	MF	CF	UF	LH	MH	AI	Total
1990s	17	2	9	12	2	4	3	50
1980s	5	5	4	8	2	3	5	32
1970s	7	2	4	4	3	3	3	28
1960s	4	1	6	5	0	5	1	22
1950s	9	2	1	6	6	0	4	28
1940s	16	2	3	8	0	4	4	37

LF   Leinster football
MF   Munster football
CF   Connacht football
UF   Ulster football
LH   Leinster hurling
MH   Munster hurling
AI   All-Ireland

11

Yellow Bellies

Caesar Colclough of Tintern in south Wexford was
challenged by William III to bring 21 of his best hurlers
to Cornwall to play that county's best 21. Before the
challenge, Colclough held a trial match between 2 local
teams: the Scarroges, from south of the River Scar,
played the Beany Boys, from the prize bean-growing
regions of Forth and Bargy.

Colclough picked his team and brought them to
Cornwall. He gave them a glass of whiskey each and
told them to tie yellow kerchiefs around their waists to
so they would easily recognise each other on the field.
The King of England was heard to shout, 'Well done
yellow bellies', during the course of their victory.

Christy Ring's Finest Performances

1944   *v. Limerick*
Scored a solo-run goal in the final minutes.

1946   *v. Kilkenny*
Scored a solo-run goal just before half-time in
the All-Ireland final.

1956   *v. Limerick*
Scored 3 goals and a point in 10 minutes to
the end of the game, having been closely
marked by Donal Broderick.

1959   *v. Connact*
Scored 4–5 of Munster's 7–11 in the Railway
Cup final, 5 points more than Connacht's total
of 2–6.

1959   *v. Wexford*
Scored 6–4 in a November match at the
Athletics Grounds in Cork at the age of 39.

1962   *Glen Rovers v. Imokilly*
Scored 3 goals in the last 10 minutes.

Comeback Kings of Hurling

16 points – All-Ireland hurling semi-final
Clare (9-4) Galway (4-14)

15 points – 1956 National Hurling League final
Wexford (5–9) v. Tipperary (2–14)

14 points – 1981 Munster hurling semi-final
Limerick (4–10) v. Tipperary (2–16)

12 points – 1927 Munster hurling semi-final
Clare (8–1) v. Waterford (6–8)

11 points – 2001 Munster hurling semi-final
Limerick (4–11) v. Waterford (2–14)

10 points – 1996 Munster hurling final
Limerick (0–19) v. Tipperary (1–16)

10 points – 1981 All-Ireland camogie final
Kilkenny v. Cork

10 points – 1965 Munster hurling championship
Clare (4–8) v. Galway (3–10)

Comeback Kings of Football

13 points – 2005 National Football League
Wexford (2–13) v. Armagh (2–6)

Wide Boys: Wayward Shooting

27 wides – 1960 Munster football final
   Kerry (3–15) v. Waterford (0–8)

25 wides – 2001 Women's Minor football championship
   Sligo (2–9) v. Leitrim (1–13)

24 wides – 2001 Women's football O'Connor Cup
   UCD (2–8) v. IT Tralee (0–5)

23 wides – 1976 Munster semi-final
   Kerry (3–19) v. Waterford (0–6)

23 wides – 1972 Connacht senior football final
   Roscommon(5–8) v. Mayo (3–10)

23 wides – 2001 Sigerson Cup
   Cork IT (5–8) v. Trinity College (0–2)

22 wides – 2000 National Football League
   Longford (1–10) v. Waterford (1–4)

22 wides – 1999 National Football League
   Donegal (0–7) v. Galway (0–14)

22 wides – 1995 Munster hurling semi-final
   Clare (2–13) v. Cork (3–9)

21 wides – 1997 All-Ireland club final
   Athenry (0–14) v. Wolfe Tones (1–8)

21 wides – 1956 All-Ireland football semi-final
   Cork (0–9) v. Kildare (0–5)

21 wides – 2003 All-Ireland hurling quarter-final
   Tipperary (2–16) v. Offaly (2–11)

21 wides – 2003 All-Ireland football semi-final
   Armagh (2–10) v. Donegal (1–9)

21 wides – 2001 National Hurling League
   Galway (0–12) v. Clare (0–9)

The Three Jimmy Cooneys

1900

Jimmy Cooney played for Kilkenny against Tipperary in the All-Ireland football semi-final. He came from the Slate Quarries club near the Tipperary border, and Tipperary objected that he and 4 colleagues actually lived on the Tipperary side of the border. In the All-Ireland final, Jimmy Cooney from Grangemockler played for Tipperary. Yes, the same Jimmy Cooney.

1938

Clare got into the Munster final despite being beaten by Tipperary in Limerick in June by 3–10 to 2–3. On an objection, Tipperary's star midfielder, **Jimmy Cooney** from Carrick-on-Suir, was deemed to be ineligible because he had attended a rugby international. Cooney had been reinstated but, because he had filled a declaration form 10 days before attending the rugby match, Clare questioned his legality. The GAA ruled his declaration could not be accepted on the strange premise that Tipperary had played a challenge match in London on Whit Monday, and that as he had played while suspended and submitted his declaration form while suspended, his county was to be thrown out of the championship.

1998

Clare led Offaly in an All-Ireland semi-final. The referee, **Jimmy Cooney**, blew the whistle for full-time, 2 minutes early. The match was replayed and Offaly subsequently won the All-Ireland championship having suffered 2 defeats in the course of the competition.

The 10 Most Common GAA Team Scores

The lists below are compiled from a sample of 18,500 scorelines recorded at club and inter-county football, hurling, ladies football and camogie matches at all grades in 1998

The figures show 28 per cent of teams failed to score a goal during the course of their fixture; 34 per cent scored 1 goal; 21 per cent scored 2 goals; 10 per cent 3 goals, 4 per cent scored 4 goals; 1.8 per cent scored 5 goals; and 0.7 per cent scored 6 goals.

There were 39 recorded nils, making 0.21 per cent of the total.

1. **1–8**   3.79 per cent

2. **1–9**   3.75 per cent

3. **1–10**   3.51 per cent

4. **1–7**   3.30 per cent

5. **0–8**   2.93 per cent

6. **1–11**   2.88 per cent

7. **0–9**   2.83 per cent

8. **1–6**   2.82 per cent

9. **0–10**   2.80 per cent

10. **0–7**   2.54 per cent

The 10 Most Common GAA Scorelines

1. 1–8 to 1–8

2. 1–9 to 1–9

3. 1–12 to 0–9

4. 1–10 to 1–8

5   1–10 to 1–7

6. 1–9 to 1–7

7   1–9 to 0–11

8. 1–11 to 1–7

9   1–12 to 1–9

10. 1–10 to 1–8

D.J. Carey's Top 10 Hurling Goals

D.J. Carey's career was not over when he selected his Top 10 hurling goals for the TV programme *Breaking Ball* on 3 September 1999.

10. **Kilkenny v. Wexford 1993 Leinster Final replay**
    'A ball came up the Hogan stand sideline, Eamonn Morrissey went out and won it, rounded his man, lost his boot on a wet day and, as he was striking it, I was on the run in and the ball landed in my path. I batted it straight to the net.'

9. **Kilkenny v. Dublin 1998 Leinster championship**
    'A long diagonal ball came in from Michael Kavanagh. It was a great ball for a forward, I was isolated with my man at the edge of the 21. I won the ball, rounded him and shot to the net.'

8. **Kilkenny v. Offaly 1999 Leinster final**
    'This had John Power winning a great ball, beating the defence and taking on a bit of a run. I made my run for goal. He hand-passed it over. I shot straight for goal. It is different from a lot of others, it came off the ground.'

7. **Kilkenny v. Clare 1997 All-Ireland semi-final**
    'Here was a ball I won about 40 yards out. I put it on my hurl and headed for goal. Always at the back of my mind was the defender Anthony Daly. He

eventually pushed me into a corner from which I
had to shoot.'

6. **Kilkenny v. Galway 1997 All-Ireland quarter-final**
'This was a historic game, the first year of the back-
door system. A great long ball came in to Michael
Phelan, he held it up for just the right length of
time. I was going at full pace and continued on. He
laid it off to me. With the fear of being hooked I
just half-batted the ball into the net.'

5. **Kilkenny v. Antrim 1993 All-Ireland semi-final**
'It would be at number one if, on the first
connection, it would have hit the back of the net. I
struck it so well it would have deserved it, but
because it came back and I flicked again, I wouldn't
pick it as my number one.'

4. **Kilkenny v. Offaly 1999 Leinster final**
'Coming up to half-time at the Leinster final, we had
built up a lead, Offaly were bringing it back. Brian
McEvoy won a great ball from the puck-out, twisted
and turned, let in a high ball. I waited my chance.
Possibly, the corner-back and goalkeeper got a bit
mixed up. We don't often score overhead flicks now
and are often criticised for that. I was delighted to
get this one.'

3. **Killkenny v. Clare All-Ireland semi-final 1999**
'This is the goal I would regard as my best quality
finish. This was a very important goal. Denis Byrne

cut in a long long sideline ball. I fielded it, had a
little bit of space, ran through and shot from about
17 yards out. Luckily for us it hit the back of the
net. It was nice to beat the best quality goalkeeper
in the country, Davey Fitzgerald, with that quality of
strike. But it needed to be good.'

2. **Kilkenny v. Cork All Ireland final 1992**

'Normally what I like to do is hit the ball as high as
possible and as hard as possible, but, on this day, to
try to hit a high, hard, wet ball was going to be very
difficult. The thoughts were to hit it low and try
and skid it off the ground. If it hit the ground in
the right place, it was going to be very difficult to
stop because it would skate.'

1. **Kilkenny v. Wexford 1991 Leinster final**

'This was my very first championship game against
Wexford. A ball came out from Eddie O'Connor,
out the field, it broke. I was on the run, picked it
up, kept going with it, gaps opened up. I kept going
and kicked the ball to the net. It will always be my
most memorable goal. It was my first in
championship hurling. But, more importantly, the
timing of it. It came with a few seconds left. They
had no time to come back and score again. A goal
is great in any game. An awful lot of hurling goes
into scoring 3 points. It puts an awful lot of hurling
into one score.'

Controversial Scores that Counted

1. Plunkett Donaghy's goal for Tyrone in the 1986 Ulster final, awarded when the Down goalkeeper, Pat Donnan, was adjudged to have stepped back over the line having caught the ball.

2. Johnny Flaherty's goal in the 1981 All-Ireland hurling final for Offaly against Galway which was said to have been thrown to the net.

3. Matt Ruth's goal in the 1982 Leinster senior hurling final, scored when the ball appeared to have gone wide and was swept back into play by Liam Fennelly.

4. Raymond Cunningham's point for Cavan against Derry in the 1997 Ulster final, which television pictures showed was obviously wide. It was the margin by which Cavan won a first Ulster title in 28 years.

5. Mike Sheehy's opportunist goal in the 1978 All-Ireland final, sent to the net without a whistle for the free, while the referee had his back to the kicker.

6. Seanie Walsh's goal for Kerry against Cork in the 1976 Munster final, kicked with such ferocity that it forced Cork back Brian Murphy to stagger and the umpire thought he crossed the line.

7.   John Quigley's goal for Wexford against Galway in the 1976 All-Ireland hurling semi-final after the referee had blown up for a foul. Even Quigley was surprised when the goal was awarded.

8.   Gerry Murphy's 8th-minute goal for Kerry against Tipperary in the 1999 Munster semi-final, which went outside the post, hit a metal stanchion and rebounded into play. The goal was awarded Kerry won by 1–11 to 0–8.

9.   Richie Bennis' winning point from a 70 in the 1973 Munster hurling final against Tipperary which appeared to veer wide at the last minute but was awarded.

10.   Paddy Loughlin's goal for Kildare against Cavan in the 1928 All-Ireland final, said to have been thrown into the net by many, including the leading sportswriter of the time, P.D. Mehigan.

11.   Padraig Horan's goal for Offaly against Laois in the 1981 Leinster semi-final. It passed outside of the post and under the net, earned Offaly a draw they shouldn't have got. Offaly went on to win the All-Ireland and Laois went back into the background.

12.   Limerick's goal against Kilkenny in the 1980 camogie league semi-final. It passed between the outside of the post and under the net.

And Controversial Scores that Didn't

1. Mick Turley's winning point for Laois against
    Carlow in the 1996 Leinster championship was
    allowed by the referee but quite clearly seen to be
    wide from video evidence. Laois sportingly offered
    to replay the match, which they won.

2. Declan Ryan's point for Tipperary in the 15th
    minute of the 1997 All-Ireland hurling final which
    was flagged wide by the umpire. Tipp lost by a
    point.

3. Pat Fox's goal for Tipperary against Cork in the
    1987 Munster final, it hit the stanchion at back of
    goal and rebounded into play.

4. Tipperary's goal against Galway in the 1988 All-
    Ireland hurling final, sent to the net after a foul.

5. Mayo's third goal against Meath, scored by Liam
    McHale, in the 1988 All-Ireland semi-final, judged
    to have been scored inside the square. It would have
    cut the Meath lead from 4 points to 1 at a crucial
    stage in the second half.

6. Tipperary's goal in the 1987 Munster hurling final
    against Cork which is said to have rebounded from
    a supporting bar behind the goal and back on to the
    field of play.

7. Galway's shot from 40 yards out in the 1985 All-Ireland final from Joe Cooney which seemed to trickle over the end-line before Offaly goalkeeper, Jim Troy, swept it clear. Galway lost by 2 points.

8. Offaly's goal in the same 1985 final where Joe Dooley adamantly denies he was in the square when he scored in the 50th minute.

9. Laois' goal against Offaly in the 1982 Leinster senior hurling semi-final, called back and a penalty awarded instead. Laois drew the semi-final and lost the replay by 9 points.

10. Limerick's goal against Galway after just 2 minutes of the replayed All-Ireland hurling semi-final in 1981, dropped into the square to bounce into the net by Mike Grimes but disallowed. Limerick lost by 5 points.

11. Colman O'Rourke's goal against Kerry, punched in from the edge of the square in the 1976 Munster football final. The match went into extra time, Cork lost and waited 9 years to regain the title.

12. Galway's goal in the 1976 All-Ireland hurling semi-final. John Quigley shot the ball to the net after the referee had blown for a foul, the referee then changed his mind and decided to award the goal.

13. Mossie O'Riordan's goal for Cork hurlers against Tipperary in the first round of the 1949 Munster hurling championship, when his shot rebounded from a stanchion and back on to the field of play with such speed that the umpire did not see it. Tipperary held that it rebounded on to the field from the crossbar. The goal nets were redesigned in 1950.

14. Seán McLaughlin's would-be equalising point for Tyrone against Dublin in injury time in the 1995 All-Ireland final.

15. Nicky English's point after John Commins' clearance was blocked down in the 1987 All-Ireland hurling semi-final, disallowed for a perceived foul on Commins. Galway swept down the field and scored a goal and went on to beat Kilkenny in the All-Ireland final.

16. Nicky English's would-be winning point in the 1991 Munster hurling final against Cork.

Counties Waiting for Success

1. Fermanagh have never won a senior provincial title. They qualified for the All-Ireland semi-final in 2004, for the Ulster final 4 times (1914, 1935, 1945 and 1982), were nominated to play in the All-Ireland semi-final of 1907, and won the McKenna Cup in 1930, 1933 and 1977.

2. Kerry hurlers beat Waterford in 1993, their first win in a Munster senior championship match since 1910, when they beat Waterford by 2–10 to 1–4.

3. Kilkenny footballers have not won a Leinster senior football championship match since 1929 when they beat Louth by 0–10 to 0–4.

4. Leitrim have yet to win an All-Ireland at any grade, although they won the All-Ireland junior 'home' final in 1937 and were Connacht senior football champions in 1927.

5. London have not won a Connacht senior football championship match since beating Leitrim in 1977.

6. Longford are the only county in Leinster never to have won a provincial hurling title at any grade, although they have won special hurling competitions organised on an open-draw basis.

7. Tyrone and Fermanagh hurlers have never won a provincial title at any grade.

8. Ulster hurlers are the only provincial team never to have won at least one Railway Cup. Their shield success in 1987 was their first inter-provincial success. Ulster reached the Railway Cup hurling final with a surprise victory over Leinster in 1945.

9. Wicklow have never won a senior provincial title, although Bray Emmetts won an All-Ireland representing Dublin in 1902. Wicklow were awarded the 1897 Leinster championship for a week but lost to Dublin when the final was eventually played. With Westmeath's victory in 2004, they are the only county in Leinster without a title.

Rules that No Longer Apply

Handpass
Passing with the open hand was legal before 1950 and from 1975–81. It was banned altogether between 1950–75 and is now not allowed for scores unless the ball is propelled with the open hand.

The Ban
From 1906–71, players who played or attended rugby, soccer, hockey or cricket matches could not play Gaelic games.

Forfeit points
In 1888, a forfeit point was awarded when a defender diverted the ball back over his own end-line. A 65 or 45 is awarded in similar circumstances today. They counted if teams were level on goals and points.

Residency
Until 1925, players were compelled to play for the county in which they resided. This caused great debate, particularly with players who returned home at weekends.

Linesman placing ball
Before 1965, the linesman dropped the ball on the sideline for a sideline puck. Until 1985, the linesman was required to place the ball for a sideline kick or puck.

The throw-in
Until 1946, balls were thrown back in when they crossed the sideline.

The 15-player line-up to start the game
At one stage, all the team lined up at the start of the game for the throw-in and sometimes a goal was scored before the goalkeeper got back into position. From 1910, only the 2 midfielders and 6 forwards lined up for the throw-in. From 1965, only the midfielders lined up for the throw-in.

Referee place ball for free
In 1955, players were allowed to place the ball for a free kick themselves.

Goalkeeper not allowed pick up
Until 1960, goalkeepers were not allowed to pick the ball directly from the ground, the same as the other 28 players.

Standing in the square
The parallelogram was introduced in 1910, which brought an end to the 'whipes' whose job was to stand in front of the goal beside the goalkeeper and try for scores.

Record Attendances

All-Ireland Football

All-Ireland senior football final: **90,556**
    1961 final, Down v. Offaly

All Ireland senior football semi-final: **79,383**
    2002 Armagh v. Dublin

All-Ireland senior football quarter-final replay: **79,057**
    2002 Dublin v. Donegal

All-Ireland senior football qualifier: **63,143**
    2003 Donegal v. Tipperary and Armagh v. Dublin

All-Ireland Hurling

All-Ireland senior hurling final: **84,856**
    1954 Cork v. Wexford

All-Ireland senior hurling semi-final: **61,937**
    1996 Wexford v. Galway

All-Ireland senior hurling quarter-final: **46,076**
    2003 Tipperary v. Offaly and Wexford v. Antrim

Women's Football

All-Ireland final: **30,487**
    2002 Mayo v. Monaghan

Camogie

Camogie final: **24,567**
    2004 Tipperary v. Cork

Club Final

Club final: **40,106**
    1999 Crossmaglen v. Ballina and Doora-Barefield
    v. Rathnure

National League

Football final: **70,125**
    1964 Down v. Dublin

Group game: **54,432**
    2003 Dublin v. Armagh

Hurling final: **45,902**
    1956 Wexford v. Tipperary

Connacht

Senior football final: **31,500**
    1965 Galway v. Sligo

Senior football match: **31,500**
    2002 Mayo v Galway

Senior hurling final: **3,000**
  1914 Galway v. Roscommon

Leinster

Senior football match: **82,072**
  2005 Dublin v. Wexford and Kildare v. Laois

Senior football final: **81,025**
  2005 Dublin v. Laois

Senior hurling final: **55,492**
  1997 Wexford v. Kilkenny

Senior hurling match: **52,307**
  1999 Laois v. Kilkenny

Munster

Senior hurling final: **60,177**
  1961 Tipperary v. Cork

Senior hurling match: **45,806**
  1999 Cork v. Waterford

Senior football final replay: **50,235**
  1976 Cork v. Kerry

Senior football match: **43,994**
  1998 Kerry v. Cork

Ulster

Senior football final: **67,136**
>2004 Armagh v. Donegal

Senior football final: **41,000**
>1962 Cavan v. Down

Senior football match: **31,617**
>2002 Armagh v. Tyrone

Senior hurling final: **10,000**
>1993 Antrim v. Down

Others

Second international match: **71,552**
>2002 Ireland v. Australia

GAA tour game abroad: **60,000**
>1931 Kerry v. New York

Railway Cup final: **49,023**
>1959 Munster v. Connacht (hurling) Leinster v.
>Munster (football)

Wembley Tournament: **42,500**
>1963 Kerry v. Cavan and Kilkenny v. Tipperary

Grounds Tournament semi-final: **42,337**
>1963 Dublin v. Kerry

Oireachtas final: **37,227**
    1956 Wexford v. Kilkenny

County final, Cork senior hurling final: **34,151**
    1977 Glen Rovers v. St Finbarr's

Centenary Cup final: **32,480**
    1984 Meath v. Monaghan and Cork v. Laois

Railway Cup football semi-final replay: **20,200**
    1953 Munster v. Ulster

Competitions that No Longer Exist

The Croke Cups
Held between 1896 and 1915 as separate competitions
and now awarded as trophies for the national leagues.
Mayo's first breakthrough came in the football
competition in 1908.

The Ceannaras Tournament
Held for 3 years to raise funds for the GAA
headquarters and an important stepping stone for all 3
winners, Roscommon in 1978, Monaghan in 1979 and
Offaly in 1980.

The Railway Shields
An inter-provincial tournament that lasted until it was
won twice in succession. The football tournament
lasted 3 years and the hurling 4, not before a famous
Munster–Leinster hurling semi-final in 1906 went to 3
meetings.

The Grounds Tournament
Organised between the All-Ireland semi-finalists with
the draws reversed between 1961 and 1973 to raise
funds for ground development. One semi-final in 1963
attracted an attendance of 42,337.

The Wembley Tournament
Between 1958 and 1976 Wembley Stadium was hired by the GAA for an annual festival, peaking in 1963 when 42,500 attended. Sometimes the All-Ireland finalists were invited, occasionally the winners of a tournament at home and, in 1973, the All-Stars.

The St Brendan's Cups
Played between Irish league champions and New York between 1954 and 1960, and won twice by the Americans, the footballers in 1954 and the hurlers in 1958.

The World Cup
Played between New York and the All-Ireland champions between 1967 and 1969, and won by the Irish champions except for one victory by New York hurlers in 1969.

The Open Draw Tournament
Played in 1984 the Centenary Cup, won by Monaghan in 1984 and Kerry in 1985 in football, and by Cork in 1984 in hurling.

The Oireachtas Football Competition
Started in 1941 and won twice by Dublin then once by Roscommon in 1943.

The Tailteann Games

Originally designed as an 'Olympics' of the Celtic nations in commemoration of the sporting festival held in County Meath between 1829 BC and AD 1169. The arrival of the US Olympic team to compete in the 1924 festival in Croke Park created a great stir, particularly the clash between high-jump gold-medalist Harold Osborne and Ireland's Larry Stanley. Eight international hurling matches were played but the tournament was not a success and for the subsequent Tailteann festivals, in 1928 and 1932, international GAA was confined to Ireland v. USA football internationals, both were won by Ireland. The games were discontinued in 1932.

Players Who Won All-Irelands with Two Counties

1. Bobby Beggs *(Galway 1938, Dublin 1942)*

2. Caleb Crone *(Dublin 1942, Cork 1945)*

3. Jack Flavin *(Kerry 1937, Galway 1938)*

4. Oliver Gough *(Wexford 1955, Kilkenny 1963)*

5. Pierce Grace *(Kilkenny 3 Senior hurling 1911–13, Dublin 2 senior football 1906–07)*

6. William Guiry *(Limerick 1896, Dublin 1897)*

7. Garret Howard *(Dublin 2 1924–27, Limerick 3 1921–36)*

8. Mattie Power *(Kilkenny 6 1922–35, Dublin 1927)*

9. William Spain *(Limerick senior hurling 1887, Laois senior football 1889)*

10. Larry Stanley *(Kildare 1919, Dublin 1923)*

Matches that Ended in Disarray

1890 All-Ireland hurling final

Cork captain Dan Lane withdrew his men from the field
because Wexford became too physical. Wexford scored 2
goals at the start of the second half and a Corkman,
playing in his bare feet, had his toe broken by a Wexford
hurl. Cork were later awarded the title.

1890 Munster final

The final between Kerry and Cork ended prematurely
when the ball burst 3 minutes from the end and a
replacement could not be found, the Killorglin men
having neglected to bring a ball.

1892 All-Ireland hurling final

Dublin left the field because a Cork goal, which the
Dubliners thought had gone over the end-line first, was
allowed.

1893 All-Ireland football final

A riot broke out when a Cork player fouled a Wexford
player and several players were injured. Cork refused to
play on and Wexford were awarded the title.

1894 All-Ireland football final

The crowd invaded the field while Cork were leading 1–2
to 0–6 (a goal was worth 5 points at the time), Dublin left

the field. When Cork were asked to replay, they claimed the match and withdrew from the GAA for a year when Dublin were awarded the title.

1899 All-Ireland hurling final
When Wexford could not find a substitute for an injured player, they decided they had enough and walked off the field. They were trailing Tipperary by 3–12 to 1–4 at the time.

1903 All-Ireland football final
Kerry's controversial closing goal (was the Kildare goalkeeper in front of or behind the line when he stopped the ball?) left them 1–4 to 1–3 ahead 5 minutes from the end of a classic final. When the umpires disagreed, it was too much for the 15,000 in attendance at Thurles and they invaded the field.

1908 Croke Cup final
Mayo scored a goal against Kildare and the pitch was invaded, Kildare refused to resume until the pitch was cleared and the referee awarded match and trophy to Mayo. Kildare withdrew from the GAA for a year.

1926 Munster hurling final
Tipperary were leading by 1–2 to nil when the match was abandoned after 16 minutes because the crowd overran the pitch.

1927 Connacht championship

Mayo and Sligo's match lasted just 3 minutes before the crowd invaded. One angry newsman wanted to know why the crowd did not wait until 3 minutes from the end before they invaded and allow everybody to get their money's worth! The referee had changed his mind and disallowed Sligo's goal after Mayo defenders protested and 2 Sligomen – George Higgins and Mickey Noone – left the field in protest. Sligo were disqualified from competition for 12 months.

1928 Railway Cup semi-final

Munster were leading by 1 point, 4 minutes from the end when Ulster took a quick throw-in and scored a goal. Munster refused to kick out the ball, claiming the throw-in should have been awarded to them, walked off the field and were suspended for 6 months.

1930 Munster hurling semi-final

Tipperary v Waterford When Waterford's John and Charles Ware were both sent off they refused to leave the field and after a 12-minute delay the entire team stormed off and refused to continue.

1933 Munster hurling final

Limerick were leading Waterford by 11 points when Waterford player Jim Ware was hit on the head with eight minutes to go and the crowd invaded the pitch to join in a row among the players. Spectator facilities were minimal, and the invasion was almost inevitable because the crush caused the crowd to spill on to the field and there was just one yard between the spectators and the pitch. Limerick were awarded the match.

1936 All Ireland hurling semi-final

Limerick trailed 0-1 to 2-3, then went 4-9 to 2-4 ahead. After Limerick's fourth goal a row erupted at centre-field, blows were struck, the crowd invaded the field and it was some time before Gardai cleared it again. When the dust settled it was discovered that Galway player Healy had been beaten in the melee and badly injured. Galway demanded a Limerick player be sent off, the referee refused, and Galway withdrew in protest.

1938 All-Ireland football final

Galway were leading Kerry in the All-Ireland final when the crowd invaded the field, thinking the final whistle had been blown. It took 10 minutes for the match to be resumed and the Kerry team played out the last 2 minutes with 10 substitutes.

1939 Ulster football final

Play started at 4.15 and was called off at 6.45, the crowd having swept across the field four times in all, on to a steadily shrinking pitch in Castleblayney. When Armagh captain Jim McCullough (was punched by one of the crowd as he was taking a throw-in, a melee followed. The referee abandoned the match when the pitch was not cleared. The replay was staged in Croke Park.

1942 Leinster football semi-final
Carlow led Offaly by six points in a replayed semi-final when the referee blew for full-time ten minutes before time was up by accident. He was threatened by the spectators and when he tried to restart the match Offaly refused to continue and were subsequently suspended for six months.

1948 Ulster football quarter-final
Antrim were leading Donegal when the match at Corrigan Park was abandoned because of a cloudburst.

1960 All-Ireland hurling final
Tipperary played out the last minute with only 12 men because the crowd mistook a free with a minute to go for the final whistle and some of the players went to the dressing rooms.

1966 Camogie semi-final
Dublin against Tipperary in Cahir was chaotic, crowds swamped the field, scores were disputed and nobody was sure who had won when the match ended. The teams were brought to the hotel where it was declared that Dublin had won by a point.

Players Born Outside the County they Played For

1. Martin Carney *(Donegal to Mayo)*

2. Shay Fahy *(Kildare to Cork)*

3. Dave Kavanagh *(Kildare to Offaly)*

4. Ray McCarron *(Luton to Monaghan)*

5. Ogie Moran *(Limerick to Kerry)*

6. John O'Leary *(Wicklow to Dublin)*

7. Tom O'Reilly *(Monaghan to Mayo)*

8. Colm O'Rourke *(Leitrim to Meath)*

9. Ger Power *(Limerick to Kerry)*

10. Stefan White *(Louth to Monaghan)*

Pre-GAA Attempts to Organise Athletics in Ireland

1. **1867** Dublin Amateur Athletics Club

2. **1872** Henry Dunlop's Irish Champion Athletics Club which organised championships

3. **1877** Val Dunbar's Irish National Athletics Committee

4. **1878** Val Dunbar's Irish AAA (disappeared without trace)

5. **1879** Pat Davin's National Athletics Meeting in Balla

6. **1880** Cusack's National Athletics Meeting

7. **1881** Henry Dunlop's Amateur Athletics Association of Ireland

8. **1882** Dublin Athletics Club

GAA Epics

Because of the knockout nature of Gaelic champonships, replays have been part of the romance of the games. In earliest days, a disputed goal or point would be enough to earn a replay. Even today, an offer of a replay has resolved disputes such as that between Laois and Carlow in the 1995 Leinster championship. Games between counties that went to three or more meetings were recalled with affection by players and spectators for years afterwards. The 1991-clash between Dublin and Meath, settled in unlikely fashion with a goal by Meath's Kevin Foley, has grown a mythology all of its own.

6 matches

1925	Sligo v. Roscommon *(football)*

4 matches

1941	Carlow v. Wexford *(football)*
1991	Meath v. Dublin *(football)*

3 matches

1894	Dublin v. Meath *(football)*
1902	Wexford v. Offaly *(football)*
1903	Kildare v. Kilkenny *(football)*

1903	Cavan v. Armagh *(football)*
1903	Kildare v. Kerry *(football)*
1919	Meath v. Louth *(football)*
1925	Galway v. Leitrim *(football)*
1926	Tipperary v. Cork *(hurling)*
1931	Cork v. Kilkenny *(hurling)*
1933	Tyrone v. Antrim *(football)*
1934	Dublin v. Louth *(football)*
1941	Dublin v. Louth *(football)*
1949	Meath v. Louth *(football)*
1954	Kildare v. Carlow *(football)*
1958	Cavan v. Monaghan *(football)*
1964	Roscommon v. Leitrim *(football)*
1965	Cavan v Donegal *(football)*
1979	Wexford v. Carlow *(football)*
1997	Meath v. Kildare *(football)*
1998	Offaly v. Clare *(hurling)*

51

Players Who Missed Penalties at the Canal End

1. Keith Barr missed in the third replay against Meath in 1991 when Dublin were leading.

2. Paul Bealin hit the bar with last kick of the 1997 Leinster championship tie with Meath when Dublin trailed by 3 points.

3. Matt Connor for Offaly, against Dublin in the 1983 Leinster final, shot wide past the right-hand post.

4. Kevin McCabe for Tyrone against Kerry in the 1986 All-Ireland final sent his shot over the bar.

5. Jim McCorry of Armagh against Kerry in the 1953 All-Ireland final.

6. Oisin McConville of Armagh against Kerry in the 2003 All-Ireland final.

7. Eugene McKenna for Tyrone against Dublin in the 1984 All-Ireland semi-final, sent his shot over the bar.

8. Colm O'Rourke for Meath against Dublin in the 1976 Leinster final, sent his shot wide.

9. Jack O'Shea for Kerry against Tyrone in the 1986 All-Ireland final, his shot hit the crossbar and rebounded into play.

10. Charlie Redmond for Dublin against Meath in the last minute of the 1988 Leinster final. He sent his shot over the bar.

11. Charlie Redmond missed early in the 1992 All-Ireland final against Donegal when Dublin were leading.

12. Redmond missed again in the final quarter of the 1994 All-Ireland final against Down.

13. Liam Sammon for Galway against Dublin in the 1974 Leinster final, his penalty was saved and sent for a 50 by Paddy Cullen.

14. Mikey Sheehy for Kerry against Offaly in the 1982 All-Ireland final, his shot was saved by Martin Furlong and cleared.

Cricket: The Other Gaelic Game

The Gaelic Athletic Association is associated with 6
sports – football and hurling played by women and
men, handball and rounders – but in 1982, 2 years
before he became the founding father of the GAA,
Michael Cusack had decided that the game best suited
for the Irish character was cricket.

Cusack's 'Our Boys" column he started in the *Shamrock*
in 1882. He declared that cricket was an Irish game
suitable for young Irish men to play, advising readers
how to play, how to form a club, how to keep the bat,
and urging people to buy Irish stumps, bats and balls.
He continued to write the column until 1901
(concentrating at first on children's games, balloons and
boulders) and then moved to athletics.

The term 'All-Ireland' is derived from the All-England
cricket club. The county clubs that played cricket
formed the basis for the GAA's inter-county structure.
The sport was played on a recreational basis by large
numbers of people in rural Ireland and, by the 1880s,
had developed a county cricket structure parallel to
England's.

Claims were also made that cricket was particularly suited to the Irish people and the 'game of the loop' – Lúb, Lúbán and Lúbóg – described in the heroic literature was a sport that closely resembled cricket. They are all words for 'goal' in Irish, representing an opening, hole or orifice. Cúchulainn is said to have 'defended the hole' in 11th-century manuscripts leading cricket writer Andrew Laing to claim in his 1912 history of the game, *Imperial Cricket*, that that this was the earliest literary reference to cricket and consequently the game was invented in Ireland. 'The idea might arise anywhere, but it was the genius of England which added the stumps, filled up the hole, and carried the implements to perfection.'

All-Ireland Venues No Longer in Use

Ashtown Trotting Grounds
The original venue for the 1893 finals is near where the Phoenix Park Racecourse is today. It was used for harness racing, and when the GAA teams and spectators arrived they found that nobody had arranged for the grass to be cut.

Ballybrit Racecourse
The stand at Ballybrit Racecourse meant that the GAA could provide proper spectator accommodation if they placed a pitch right in front of it, so goalposts were erected there for the 1923 All-Ireland hurling semi-final in which Tipperary beat Galway 3–2 to 1–3.

Birr
The first All-Ireland hurling final was staged at Pat White's field in Birr, behind the scoreboard of the present Birr field.

Clonskeagh
The first All-Ireland football final was played in Byrne's field (the Benburb Club grounds) in Beech Hill halfway between Clonskeagh and Donnybrook, the ground has long since been built over.

Clonturk Park

The major GAA venue of the 1890s, it's in a natural hollow on the banks of the Tolka, opposite where St Patrick's College is today. The housing estate built on the site is called Clonturk Park.

Cork Agricultural Society Grounds

The 1902 finals were staged at the Cork Society Grounds, near where Páirc Uí Chaoimh is today. Several spectators were injured when the roof of a refreshment room collapsed under the weight of the spectators.

Inchicore

St Patrick's GAA club in Inchicore, near the Oblate Church on Tyrconnell Road, was the venue for the 1889 football and hurling finals. Tyrconnell Park housing estate was built over the site of the grounds.

Market's Field, Limerick

Most of the All-Ireland semi-finals involving Munster and Connacht teams took place in Limerick's Market's Field in the 1900s. Mayo footballers and Galway hurlers met Cork teams there on several occasions without success. It later became a soccer ground.

Phoenix Park

The 1893 finals which were fixed for Ashtown were eventually played on the 9 acres area of the Phoenix Park.

Polo Grounds, New York

The triple deck Polo Grounds Stadium was the venue
for the 1947 All-Ireland football final and several
national league finals. The home of the New York
Giants baseball team, the stadium was sold and
demolished for development when the Giants moved
their franchise to San Francisco in 1957.

Unusual Venues for GAA Matches

The frozen Liffey
When frost caused a 6-inch surface of ice over the
Liffey in January 1740, the citizens of Dublin played a
football match on the frozen river.

The lawn in front of Parnell's house
Wicklow GAA fixed its first big tournament for the
lawn in front of Avondale House, as a token of respect
to the nationalist leader. Six half-hour matches between
Wicklow and Wexford clubs were organised and it was
claimed 12,000 were present, although this is unlikely.

Stamford Bridge
The present grounds used by Chelsea soccer club was
the venue for the first inter-provincial hurling match in
1896 between Munster and Leinster and an
international football match in which Ireland beat
England.

Glasgow Celtic Grounds
When Glasgow got home venue against Kilkenny in the
quarter-final of the 1913 All-Ireland hurling
championship, they staged the game at Parkhead. Some
2,000 spectators saw Kilkenny win by 10–6 to 5–2.

Frongoch Prison Camp

After the 1916 Rising, many inter-county footballers were among the thousands interned and imprisoned in Frongoch Prison Camp in Wales. A football competition, the Wolfe Tone Tournament, was held and Kerry, led by Dick Fitzgerald, defeated Louth by 1 point in the final.

The street in front of Croke Park

On Gaelic Sunday, 4 August 1918, the British authorities proscribed all GAA matches. A camogie game was fixed for Croke Park but, when the teams arrived, they found troops guarding the entrance, so they staged their match on the street outside.

The Congo

When the 'Railway Cup' finals were held on St Patrick's Day 1963 at Kolwezi in the Congo between two teams of Irish soldiers on United Nations forces, the scoreboard operator was a little confused about the scoring system. Although A Company beat C Company by 8–3 to 5–10, he reversed the decision: 15 scores to 11.

Rome

A series of matches were held in the 1960s between Aer Lingus teams and clerical students at the Irish College.

Luton Town AFC

Hertfordshire staged their 21st anniversary celebration matches at Kenilworth Road in 1982.

Saudi Arabia

The Almarai Milk Cup was the name of an exotic-sounding tournament staged in March 1985 on the desert planes of Al Khari, 70 kms south of Saudi Arabian capital Riyadh. Irish employees of Masstock supplied the hurlers.

GAA Borders

1. Athlone, in Westmeath, once played in Roscommon and represented Connacht in the 1890 All-Ireland semi-final. The Clan na Gael Club still strays close to the Westmeath border.

2. Ballaghadereen, part of which is officially in Mayo, plays in Galway.

3. Ballinabrackey, largely in Westmeath, play GAA in Offaly.

4. Ballygar play their hurling in Roscommon and their football in Galway. It enabled Mattie McDonagh play minor hurling for Roscommon and football for Galway in the same year.

5. Ballyskenagh from Moneygall Parish played in the North Tipperary championship until the early 1960s, but now play in Offaly.

6. Blessington, in Wicklow, draws part of its playing population from Ballymore Eustace in Kildare.

7. Bray, in Wicklow, formerly played in the Dublin championship and represented Dublin in the 1902 All-Ireland final.

8. Burt, in Donegal, formerly played its hurling in Derry and once contested an Ulster final for Derry.

9. Parts of Drogheda are in Meath.

10. Graiguecullen, in Laois, play their football in Carlow.

11. The Moneygall GAA playing field is in Tipperary. The club plays in Tipperary but half the parish is in Offaly. At one stage in the 1920s, a combined team from Moneygall and Toomevarra played in the North Tipperary championship.

12. Part of the parish of Newry is officially in Armagh, but they play in Down.

13. Riverstown, in Tipperary, play in Offaly.

14. Shinrone, in Offaly, play in Tipperary.

15. Tubber, in Offaly, play in Westmeath.

Famous Sportsmen Who Played GAA

Muhammad Ali whiled away some time in training for a heavyweight boxing fight against Al Blue Lewis in Croke Park in 1972 by playing handball.

Barney Eastwood played minor for Tyrone in the 1948 All-Ireland final before becoming one of the world's premier boxing managers and promoters. He managed in turn Barry McGuigan, Hughie Russell and Dave MacAuley.

Brothers **Bernie and Pat Hartigan** played hurling for Limerick and then competed internationally for Irish athletics teams in the shot putt.

Dick Hearns was a substitute on the Mayo team for the 1932 All-Ireland final and also played with Roscommon, Longford, Donegal, Cork and Dublin. He represented Ireland in amateur boxing and won 173 of the 198 bouts in his career.

Moss Keane played in the Sigerson Cup for UCC before going on to become a rugby international.

Jem Roche played for Wexford in the 1900 Leinster championship and fought Canadian Tommy Burns for the world heavyweight title in 1908.

Mick and Jack Ryan of Rockwell College played Munster championship football for Tipperary and rugby for Ireland in the 1890s.

Dick Spring played for Kerry footballers and also for the hurlers in the 1974–75 National League season while he was a rugby inter-provincial player. He later played at full-back for the Irish rugby team and went into politics, becoming Tánaiste in the 1982–87 coalition government.

Dennis Taylor played minor football for Tyrone before going on to become a professional snooker player and winning the 1985 World Championship.

Jim Stynes played football for Dublin minors and **Sean Wight** who played for Kerry minors went on to successful careers with Melbourne playing Australian Rules football. Stynes won the Brownlow medal and Players Association award in 1989. Tadhg Kennelly of Kerry and Setanta Ó hAilpín of Cork also went to Australia to play Australian Rules.

Padraig Harrington and **Paul McGinley**: Ryder cup golfers both stars in Dublin primary leagues football.

Zin Zan Brooke and **Bernie McCahill**, All-Black rugby internationals played for New Zealand GAA team in the Australasian GAA championships.

Soccer Players who Played GAA

Jimmy Bermingham won an All-Ireland medal with Dublin, won FAI Cup, Leinster Senior Cup, League of Ireland and League of Ireland shield medals, played for Kerry in the 1924 Munster championship and for Bohemians in a record-breaking 1927–28 season.

Tony Grealish, born in London, played Gaelic football at Wembley Stadium long before he first played there in important soccer matches.

Val Harris won an All-Ireland medal with Dublin in 1901, subsequently played for Shelbourne and Everton and was capped 20 times by Irish soccer selectors.

Pat Jennings played Gaelic football until he was 18 and then began a soccer career that brought him to two World Cup finals with Northern Ireland.

John Kirwan won a 1904 medal with Dublin and later won 17 caps when he played with Tottenham Hotspur.

Jimmy Ledwidge won 1898 and 1899 All-Ireland medals for Dublin, then played with Shelbourne and won 2 caps in 1906.

Pat McCann won 1899 and 1901 medals with Dublin and later won 7 caps between 1910 and 1913 when he played for Belfast Celtic and Glenavon.

Kevin Moran won All-Ireland medals with Dublin in 1976 and 1977 before joining Manchester United and going on to a successful international soccer career that brought him to the 1988 European Championship finals.

Martin O'Neill played Gaelic football in Derry and then went on to play for Northern Ireland in two World Cup finals.

Niall Quinn played at corner-forward for Dublin in the 1983 All-Ireland minor hurling final and then went on to play for Arsenal and represent Ireland in the European Championship finals. He returned to play club football for Eadestown in County Kildare

Steve Staunton played Under-16 football for Louth before going on to play for Aston Villa and Liverpool and playing for Ireland in 2 World Cup finals.

Neil Lennon played for Armagh against Derry in the 1987 Ulster minor football final. He later went on to captain Glasgow Celtic.and Northern Ireland before a series of death threats forced him out of the squad in 2002.

GAA Players Who Played Other Sports

Dinny Allen of Cork won an FAI Cup medal with Cork Hibernians in 1973.

Dave Barry of Cork played for the Irish Olympic soccer team in 1987.

Dick Curtis, 1891, 1894 and 1897 All-Ireland medalist with Dublin, was All-Ireland wrestling champion for several years in the 1890s.

Tom Irwin, All-Ireland medalist with Cork hurlers in 1892 and on 1893, 1894 and 1899 beaten football teams, was in line for a cricket cap for Ireland when the ban was introduced in 1905 and he opted to play GAA.

Mickey McDonald of Armagh played Irish League soccer.

Liam McHale was selected for the Irish pre-Olympic basketball squad and was Team West's top scorer in 1987–88.

Brian Mullins of Dublin played for Clontarf rugby club.

Charlie Nelligan played in goal for Home Farm in the 1977–78 season and was considered for an Olympic team place.

John O'Leary of Dublin has been signed as a reserve goalkeeper with Shamrock Rovers.

Billy O'Neill won 2 All-Ireland hurling medals with Cork, turned down a final Irish rugby trial in 1905 because the ban was introduced.

Charlie Paye of Fermoy, a 1911 medalist with Cork, won a Munster Senior Cup medal with Cork Celtic but opted for GAA after the ban was introduced.

Famous Objections

1900 The moving quarrymen

Tipperary claimed that 5 of the Kilkenny football team
who played against them in the All-Ireland semi-final
lived in Tipperary, and were not eligible for Slate
Quarries, the Kilkenny team that had won the Leinster
championship. They then selected the same 5 players
for the Tipperary team that beat Galway in the All-
Ireland final!

1905 The British army reservist

Cork beat Kilkenny by 5–10 to 3–13 but Kilkenny
objected that Cork's goalkeeper was a British army
reservist, and illegal under a 1903 rule. Kilkenny won
the replay 7–7 to 2–9.

1916 Mayo's first final

Mayo beat Cork in the All-Ireland semi-final by 3
points to reach the All-Ireland for the first time, but
had to replay because one of their team had illegally
lined out for a club in Cork. Mayo won again – this
time by 4 points.

1925 Who was living where

The new declaration rule allowed players to declare for
their county of birth, but difficulties arose over Cavan
player J.P. Murphy, living in Mullingar and playing his
club football in Cavan. Cavan were thrown out of the

All-Ireland semi-final after an objection, Cavan counter-objected to a Kerry player who lived in Dublin and Kerry were thrown out. Mayo were awarded the All-Ireland title only to subsequently lose it when Galway beat them in the Connacht final.

1925
Dublin beat Kilkenny by 6–4 to 4–7 in the Leinster hurling final but Kilkenny successfully protested that Dublin's Jim Conroy had played in the Laois championship.

The year of the objection really made its name when the Connacht championship took 11 matches to complete, after 5 draws and 2 objections. Sligo were beaten by Roscommon then objected claiming a disallowed goal of theirs should have been allowed. After 3 draws, Sligo won the 5th match between the teams with a controversial goal (the referee reserved judgement on it until the next council meeting) but Roscommon lodged a successful objection against them. Sligo eventually won by 7 points at the 6th attempt.

1930
Galway defeated Mayo heavily in the Connacht semi-final, but Mayo objected, were granted the match and won the Connacht championship against Sligo. Jimmy Cooney had been banned under the foreign

games rule when his declaration for All-Ireland hurling champions Tipperary was signed. Tipperary were sensationally thrown out of the Munster hurling championship after an objection by Clare.

Six Kildare players gave evidence that they stopped playing when the whistle sounded against Meath, and Meath went on to score a goal. The goal stood and Kildare withdrew from the GAA for 12 months in protest.

1953 The born-outside-the-county objection

Mayo objected to 5 players born outside Roscommon who had helped Roscommon beat Mayo in the Connacht final. The objection continued until the week before the All-Ireland final.

1989 The Tony Keady affair

Galway missed their captain and former hurler of the year Tony Keady because he was deemed to have played illegally in New York. The player was given a 12-month ban, his appeal overturned by the narrow margin of 20 votes to 18 at Central Council, and a subsequent amnesty to illegal players was too late to allow him play in the championship. At one stage, Galway threatened to pull out of the 1989 All-Ireland championship over the affair.

Oops, Wrong Direction

1964

Kit Kehoe came on as a substitute for Celtic in the
replay of their All-Ireland club camogie semi-final
against Glen Rovers, lashed the ball towards the goal
like a bullet, only to learn it was the wrong goal. Luckily
Dublin goalkeeper Eithne Leech saved the goal.

Freak Scores

Barney Rock for Dublin against Galway in the 1983 All-Ireland final

When a Dublin player was having an injury attended to in the square, the goalkeeper sent a kick-out straight to Rock, who immediately landed the ball in the net over the goalkeeper's head.

Padraig Horan's goal in the drawn 1981 Leinster hurling semi-final against Laois

It passed outside the post and went under the net, but was awarded.

Tim Kennelly's point for Cork against Kerry in the 1980 Munster final

Kennelly managed to boot the ball over his own crossbar from 20 yards out!

Mike Sheehy for Kerry against Dublin in the 1978 All-Ireland football final

Scored from a free lofted into the net while Paddy Cullen was arguing with referee Seamus Aldridge.

Jimmy Barry-Murphy for Cork against Kerry in the 1976 Munster final

Goalkeeper Paudie O'Mahoney misdirected a kick-out and sent it straight into Jimmy's hands, alone and unmarked in front of the goal.

Pat Donnellan's goal for Galway against Kerry in the 1963 All-Ireland semi-final

Donnellan was lying injured on the field near the goal. When the ball was passed down, he righted himself, evaded the goalkeeper's tackle and planted the ball in the net. Galway won by 2 points.

Edwin Carolan's point for Cavan against Meath in the drawn 1952 All-Ireland final

The ball seemed to cross the end-line before Carolan retrieved it and kicked back towards the goal. Most people thought he was sending it back to the defender for a kick-out, but when it hit the post and went over the bar, a point was awarded. Cavan won the replay by 4 points.

Packy Boylan's point for Cavan against Kerry in the 1937 All-Ireland football final

The score was recorded on the scoreboard but was disallowed for throwing. Many went home thinking Cavan had won the All-Ireland. In fact, the match ended in a draw, and Cavan lost the replay.

Jack Connolly's goal for Kildare against Kerry in 1903

The ball was played behind the crowd as it moved up the field.

Dick Fitzgerald's goal for Kerry in the same 1903 match

The goal was saved by the Kildare goalkeeper who was then adjudged to have crossed the line.

Founders of the GAA

On 1 November 1884, the following gathered to found the association.

Michael Cusack: Clare-born school teacher, rugby and cricket enthusiast who was also involved in campaigns to revive the Irish language, to reform rules that prevented labourers, artisans and policemen from competing in athletic sports, to have jumping and weight-throwing events included in athletic sports, and, eventually, to revive hurling, handball and the Irish form of football.

Maurice Davin: Champion hammer thrower and world-record holder who became involved in Carrick-on-Suir athletic and rugby club before deciding to join Cusack's campaign to give jumping and weight-throwing more prominence in athletic sports and field games. He drew up the first rules of hurling and football.

John Wyse-Power: Fenian, probably an IRB member, an athletics enthusiast and at the time editor of the *Leinster Leader* in Naas (though shortly after, he joined the *Freeman's Journal*). His widow, Jenny, became a member of the new Irish Senate in 1922.

John McKay: Belfast-born football player and a journalist with the *Cork Examiner*. At the time of the meeting, he was to be instrumental in drawing up rules for Gaelic football.

John K. Bracken: A nationalist building contractor in Templemore, he was not seriously involved in GAA administration afterwards. His son became Minister for Information in Churchill's war cabinet.

P. J. O'Ryan: A young solicitor with offices in Callan and Thurles.

District Inspector Thomas St John McCarthy: An athlete and officer of the Royal Irish Constabulary based in Templemore. Policemen were excluded from athletics as run by the English Athletics Association at the time because they were not 'amateurs'. He was not subsequently involved in the GAA.

Other names associated with the foundation of the GAA by some second-hand press reports are:

John Butler of Ballyhuddy
M. Cantwell of Thurles
Dwyer C. Culhane of Thurles
William Delahunty of Thurles
William Foley of Carrick-on-Suir
Frank Maloney of Nenagh.

GAA Firsts

11 November 1884

First GAA athletics meeting at Toames, near Mallow, 10 days after the association was founded.

15 December 1884

First club to join Cusack's Metropolitan Hurling club in the new association was Clara from County Offaly.

17 January 1885

Killimor defeated Ballinakill by 2 goals to nil in the first hurling match, played before 6,000 spectators at Tynagh, County Galway. It was held the day that the rules for hurling were being drawn up at a meeting in Cork, probably under Killimor Rules! Gort from County Galway and Killanan from County Clare also claim to have played the first hurling match under the rules of the GAA at Gort. Between March and December 1885, 15 hurling matches took place in Galway.

15 February 1885

First football matches were played under the new GAA rules. At Callan, Kilkenny Commercials played Callan. At St Canice's Park in Kilkenny town, 2 town clubs, St Patrick's and St Canice's, met. And in Naas, County

Kildare, Naas played Sallins. All 3 were scoreless draws. In Clare, Whitegate and Ballyanna played a football match in January.

April 1885
First world record by a GAA athlete, J.C. Daly jumped 13.42 metres in what is now known as the triple jump. Within weeks, William Barry, briefly a vice-president of the GAA, set a world hammer record in Tralee and subsequently improved it 8 times in 3 years.

March 1885
Wallsend, Newcastle-upon-Tyne, became the first affiliated club in England.

June 1885
First athletics meeting under GAA rules in the USA held in Boston, the Irish Athletic Club's 'Patron' day.

June 1885
Artane Boys Band played at its first GAA event at a sports in the Corporation Grounds, North Circular Road.

June 1885
GAA athletics meeting in Gaelic Grounds and IAAA meeting at the cricket grounds on same day in Tralee.

Local people supported the GAA meeting. Subsequent IAAA activity was confined to Dublin and Ulster.

October 1885
First GAA athletics championship in Tramore, one of the few provincial venues with a covered stand.

Carmelite, in Terenure, became the first college to affiliate to the GAA.

November 1885
First convention of the GAA brings together representatives from 300 clubs. The GAA won the allegiance of 70 clubs, the IAAA had 30 in their first year, with a further 15 pledging allegiance but not paying affiliation fees. About 150 meetings were staged under GAA auspices. Cusack later described the early growth of the association as being 'like a prairie fire'.

January 1886
The establishment of Wexford's county committee is the first of the new GAA boards.

15 February 1886
First inter-county match between North Tipperary and a Gort/Craughwell selection from South Galway, described

by Michael Cusack as the All-Ireland final, with Cusack as referee and a silver cup for the winners. The hurlers marched side by side through the streets of Dublin to the Clarence Hotel, and then on to the Phoenix Park. There they found that the anxious gatekeeper at the park had locked the gates, forewarned that 'a mob with battering rams' was trying to gain entrance to the Park to attack the Lord Lieutenant's residence. The match was 80 minutes long under the rules of the time, and Tipperary won by the only goal of the game. It was 2 years before points were introduced to cope with the problem of scoreless draws in Gaelic games.

June 1887

The association organised All-Ireland hurling and football championships on a county basis, with champion clubs representing each county. Twelve counties entered, but only 5 competed in the hurling competition and 8 in football.

24 July 1887

The first championship hurling match was played between Meelick of Galway and Castlebridge of Wexford at Dublin's Elm Park. Castlebridge only took up hurling when it became clear Galway would be unable to fulfill a football match between the counties.

21 July 1887

The first football championship match between Dundalk Young Irelands from Louth and Ballyduff Lower from Waterford.

1 April 1888

The first All-Ireland hurling final in Birr between Tipperary and Galway

29 April 1888

The first All-Ireland football final.

GAA World Record Holders

Dan Shanahan of Kilfinane broke the triple jump
record 3 times in a few months in 1886. John Purcell and
O.D. Looney of Macroom pushed the record further
until Shanahan jumped 15.25 metres in 1888 to set a
record that stood until 1909. It was beaten by Dan
Ahearne, whose brother Tim won an Olympic gold in
1908. Ahearne's world record, 15.52 metres, stood for a
further 13 years.

James Mitchell broke the hammer record twice to take
it past the 40-metre mark in 1888. He went to America
with the 'invasion' athletes and never returned, getting a
job as a sportswriter with the *New York Sun*.

John Flanagan of Kilmallock took the hammer record
from Mitchell at the 1895 GAA championships with a
throw of 44.13 metres and went on to break the record
14 times, taking it through the 50-metre mark. His record
was broken by Tom Kiely in 1899 and Matt McGrath in
1907 but Flanagan kept winning it back. He was 41 years
and 160 days old when he broke the record for the last
time with a throw of 56.08 metres, the oldest record
holder in track and field history. He emigrated to the US
in 1897, returned to Ireland in 1911 and lived there until
his death in 1938. His record was surpassed by Matt

McGrath and then, in 1913, by Paddy Ryan of Pallasgreen, whose throw of 57.77 metres lasted as a world record for 25 years.

Tom Kiely of Ballyneale, a nephew of the Davins, took the hammer record from Flanagan for 46 days in 1899. He won the first decathlon gold medal in the Olympic at St Louis in 1904.

Matt McGrath of Nenagh threw a world hammer record of 53.35 m in 1907 and another of 57.10 metres in 1909.

Jim Ryan from Ballyslatteen, New Inn, Tipperary, jumped 6 feet 4.5 inches for a new high jump world record at Tipperary sports in 1895.

Tommy Conneff of Clane ran 4 minutes 17.8 seconds for the mile in 1888, a record that was not broken until 1904. Conneff's world record for the three-quarter mile was not broken until 1931.

Peter O'Connor set a long-jump record of 7.61 metres in Ballsbridge in 1901, breaking his own world record by 4 inches. It stood as a world record for 20 years and as an Irish record until 1990.

GAA Athletic Events that did not Gain International Recognition

1. Standing high jump, long jump and triple jump.

2. Weight-throwing events 'with follow', where the thrower did not have to stay within a circle.

3. The 7-lb hammer (the conventional hammer weighs 16 lbs).

4. Slinging the 56 lbs.

5. The 56 lbs between-the-legs.

6. The 56 lbs over-the-bar, this is not an international event but is still on the Irish national championship programme.

7. Putting the 28-lb, 42-lb and 56-lb weights.

8. Throwing the 7-lb and 14-lb weights from the shoulder.

9. The long jump with weights, where the jumper was allowed to throw a weight behind him to gain extra distance. H. Courtenay once cleared 38 feet 3 inches in this manner, 14 feet longer than Peter O'Connor's world record.

Olympic Medals

The GAA was invited to send an Irish team to compete in the revived Olympics in Athens in 1896, but decided at a Central Council meeting that 'having studied the Olympian games programme no Irish team would be sent, because there were only two events, the shot and the high jump which Irish competitors would be likely to win'. The GAA athletes who competed at early Olympics between 1900 and 1920 did so for the United States or Britain. The exception was Tom Kiely, who had his 1904 medal accredited to Ireland because he paid his own passage to Los Angeles. In 1906, Irish athletes demanded that Ireland be given a separate team status (similar to that accorded to Hungary) but, on the intervention of Prince George of Greece, it was declared they should be part of the British team. Peter O'Connor climbed the flagpole with a green flag after he won a silver medal in the long jump at the intercalated games at Athens in 1906, which are included in this record.

1900

Gold   John Flanagan, hammer

Silver   Pat Leahy of Charleville, high jump

Bronze   Pat Leahy of Charleville, long jump

Peter O'Connor did not compete in the Olympics for political reasons, Ireland would have placed joint 10th of 22 on the medals chart.

1904

Gold   John Flanagan, hammer

        Tom Kiely, decathlon

        Martin Sheridan, discus

        Con Leahy, high jump

        Peter O'Connor, triple jump

Silver   John Flanagan, 56-lb weight throw

        John J. Daly, steeplechase

Bronze   James Mitchel, 56 lbs

Ireland would have placed 5th of 12 on the medals chart.

1906

Gold John Flanagan, hammer

Martin Sheridan, discus

Martin Sheridan, shot put

Silver Con Leahy, triple jump

Peter O'Connor, long jump

John McGough, 1,500 metres

Martin Sheridan, 14-lb stone throw (now defunct)

Martin Sheridan, standing long jump (now defunct)

Martin Sheridan, standing high jump (now defunct)

Ireland would have finished 6th in the medals chart.

GAA athletes requested that an Irish flag be flown after their victories. It was turned down by Greece's Prince George who reputedly said Ireland could have a flag when it had a parliament of its own. Peter O'Connor staged a protest by climbing a flagpole with a green flag while Con Leahy waved another beneath.

1908

Gold	John Flanagan, hammer
	Tim Ahearne, triple jump
	Martin Sheridan, discus
	Martin Sheridan, Greek discus
	Johnny Hayes, marathon
Silver	Con Leahy, high jump
	Denis Horgan, shot put
	Matt McGrath, hammer
Bronze	Con Walsh, hammer
	Martin Sheridan, standing long jump (now defunct)

Ireland would have placed 4th of 23 in the medals chart.

Football and Hurling Olympians

Edmond Barrett: He was born in Listowel and won an All-Ireland hurling medal with London Irish in 1901, an Olympic gold medal on the British tug-of-war team that beat Ireland in the 1908 Olympic final, and a bronze medal for heavyweight wrestling in 1908.

Tommy Corr: He was the last GAA Olympian, he boxed at middleweight in the Los Angeles Olympics and won a 1982 bronze medal in the World Championships at the same weight. Played for Tyrone.

John Flanagan: He was an Olympic gold medalist 1900, 1904 and 1908. He played for Munster hurlers in the first ever inter-provincial against Leinster in 1896. He broke the world hammer record 14 times in all between 1895 and 1911, losing the record only for 2 brief periods to fellow Irishmen Tom Kiely and Matt McGrath of Nenagh.

Tom F. Kiely: He won an early version of the decathlon, the all-round championship, at the 1904 Olympics, having turned down offers from both Britain and America to compete for them, paid his own way, and competed for Ireland. He played in the first hurling inter-provincial for Munster against Leinster in 1896.

Sean Lavin: He was a Mayo All-Ireland finalist of 1922 and the inventor of the toe-to-hand solo-run, became the first sprinter to compete for Ireland at the Olympic Games in 1924.

The Leahy Brothers from Cork: They made history when Pat won a silver in the high jump in Paris in 1900 and finished 4th in the triple jump that year and Con won silver medals in the triple jump in Athens in 1906 and the long jump in London in 1908. In 1906, when the Union Jack was flown to commemorate his victory, Con climbed to the top of the flagpole and replaced it with a green Irish flag.

James Mitchell: He was one of the original GAA invaders, a party of athletes who travelled to America in 1888. He settled down in America and won bronze in the 56-lb weight throw in St Louis in 1904, and came 5th in the hammer and 6th in the discus at the same Olympics.

Peter O'Connor of Wicklow: He jumped an astounding 24 feet 11¾-inch world record in Ballsbridge in 1900. He did not compete in the 1900 Olympics for political reasons but eventually went to on Olympics in 1906 and won a silver medal.

Eamonn O'Sullivan: He was on the Kerry 1932 team that went to the Los Angeles Olympics, Ireland's most successful ever, and finished 4th in the high jump, 4¼ inches behind the Japanese bronze medalist.

Larry Stanley: He was a midfielder on Kildare 1919 and Dublin 1923 All-Ireland winning teams and also national champion high jumper. Stanley competed on the first Irish Olympic team in Los Angeles in 1924 in the high jump.

GAA Rule Changes Down the Years

1885
Original rules, drawn up by Maurice Davin, allow for goals only with 21-a-side teams and different sizes of goal and pitch for football and hurling.

1886
'Points' are introduced after a spate of scoreless draws, initially for driving the ball over the opponents' end-line but later point-posts are erected 21 feet on either side of the goal-posts and 'forfeit points' are conceded by players who drive the ball over their own end-line. Five forfeit points is made equal to a point. Wrestling, permitted in football (one fall decisive), is abolished after protests that the new game was too rough.

1887
The forfeit point is abolished and replaced by a free kick or puck, from 40 yards.

1892
Teams are reduced from 21-a-side to 17-a-side, a goalkeeper, 3 full-backs, 3 half-backs, 4 midfielders or rovers, 3 half-forwards and 3 full-forwards.

A goal is made equal to 5 points.

Champion clubs are allowed to select players from other clubs within the county.

1895
The size of the football is standardised.

Carrying the ball on the hurley is allowed.

Scores direct for a throw-in are banned.

Footballers who get 'bottled up' are to concede a hopped ball.

Linesmen are given flags for the first time to attract the referee's attention and to signal sideline decisions.

Substitutes for injured players, previously allowed only by agreement with the opposing captain, are prohibited.

They became legal, even without the agreement of the opposition, within a short time.

Players sent off by the referee are prohibited from returning to the field of play. This was possible until now with the opposing captain's agreement.

Clubs are made responsible for the conduct of players and supporters.

Referees are permitted to allow scores if the ball is stopped by a spectator before it crosses the line.

1896
A goal is made equal to 3 points.

The height of the crossbar in hurling is reduced from 10½ to 8 feet.

Referees decisions are required in writing at the end of a game.

Referees decisions on the admissibility of scores are decreed to be final and irreversible.

Umpires use colour flags for the first time.

1899
Sideline puck is introduced instead of a throw-in in hurling.

1901
Matches cut short by darkness are to be replayed in full.

Scoring area is reduced to 54 feet.

1903
Scoring area is reduced again, this time to 45 feet.

1909
Proposal that point posts be abolished and goalposts be widened leads to setting up of committee to report on playing rules.

1910
Point posts are abolished and goalposts are fixed at 21 feet apart.

Parallelogram is introduced, players must be outside this area when scoring, instead of outside a 10-yard line as previously was the case.

Goal nets are introduced for all championship matches.

Free pucks awarded for sending the ball across your own end-line are increased from 50 to 70 yards, and free kicks from 40 to 50 yards.

Defenders and goalkeepers are allowed back to their positions before the throw-in, until now even the goalkeeper had to line up for the throw-in.

1913

Teams are reduced from 17-a-side to 15-a-side. Counties are required to register colours.

Players are allowed to fist the ball away while on ground.

Forwards are required to stand 14 yards from a kick-out.

Kick-outs are to be taken from the 21-yard-line after a score, but no players are allowed into the opposing half while their own kick-out is being taken.

Play is allowed to continue where a player is fouled but succeeds in playing on.

Footballers who are grounded are allowed to play the ball on the ground.

A free-out is given when a scorer has been standing in the square.

1923

Numbered jerseys are introduced.

1924

Numbered jerseys are made compulsory for major games.

Programmes for major games are made compulsory.

1925

The 'Declaration rule' is introduced to allow players to declare for their native county although resident elsewhere.

1926

Extra time is made compulsory at replays.

1927

All-Ireland finals and semi-finals are increased to 80 minutes, but a 3-year stay is put on the rule and it is never implemented.

1928

Substitutes are required to be properly attired.

1931

Scores are allowed direct from a sideline puck.

1932

White ball is to be used for All-Ireland finals.

1934
Substitutions are limited to 3 per team.

1935
The size of the pitch is reduced from 170 to 160 yards.
Play is allowed to be extended to allow a free to be
taken.
Raising the ball on the toe for a kick-out is abolished.
Hurlers are not allowed to charge the goalkeeper unless
he is in possession of the ball.

1938
All-Ireland semi-finals are arranged in rotation.

1940
The penalty-kick is introduced in football and semi-
penalty (goalkeeper and two defenders on the line) in
hurling, for fouls in the smaller parallelogram.

1945
Linesmen are allowed to throw in disputed sideline
balls.

Open handpass in football is banned by Central
Council.

1946

Open handpass in football is reinstated by Congress.

Sideline kick ins are introduced instead of throw-ins in football.

Hurling ball is standardised in size, 3½-4½ ounces and 10 inches in circumference.

1948

The first experiments with a rimless hurling ball take place.

1950

The open handpass in football is abolished.

1950–1952

An experiment with a 'hooter' system which times games independently of the referee, the Bogue Clock, proves inconclusive and referees continue to be the sole authority on the length of games. The Bogue Clock remains in use in Gaelic Park, New York.

1954

Full-time training for big matches is banned.

1955

'No stoppage rule' allows play-on after a foul.

Substitutions reaffirmed at a maximum of 3.

Players are allowed to place the ball for their own free. Opponents are required to stand 14 yards from the ball when a free is taken.

1960

Players are allowed to play the ball again when it rebounds from a post.

The goalkeeper is permitted to lift the ball in the square.

1965

Linesman are required to place ball the ball rather than drop it on the line for sideline pucks and kicks.

The throw-in at the start of the match is confined to the 4 midfielders, not the forwards as well.

1970

Play is extended to 80 minutes for All-Ireland finals, semi-finals and provincial finals.

The larger parallelogram is introduced.

1975
Tackling the goalkeeper in the parallelogram is forbidden.

Committing 3 fouls becomes a sending off offence.

The open handpass is reintroduced in football.
All championship matches are to last 70 minutes.

Tackling a player not in possession of the ball (the 'third-man tackle') is banned.

1980
The handpass is retained.

1981
A special congress abolishes the handpass for scores.

1985
Players are allowed to place ball for sideline puck or kick.

1990
Players who are fouled are allowed the option of taking free kicks from the hand.

All sideline kicks are to be taken from the hands.

Players are not permitted to score from the hand while in possession in hurling.

Players are not allowed to make divots while taking kicks from the ground in football or when taking sideline pucks in hurling.

2000
Blood substitutes approved.

Substitutions increased from 3 to 5.

Nicknames of GAA Players and their Real Names

1. Balty Ahearne *(Cork)* – Paddy

2. Gah Ahearne *(Cork)* – Mick

3. Click Brennan *(Sligo)* – Tom

4. Cloney Brennan *(Kilkenny)* – Michael

5. Goggy Brennan *(Kilkenny)* – Martin

6. Ratler Byrne *(Tipperary)* – Mick

7. Red Collier *(Meath)* – Pat

8. Joyce Conlan *(Kildare and Laois)* – Frank

9. Tull Considine *(Clare)* – Turlough

10. Gooch Cooper *(Kerry)* – Colm

11. Eudie Coughlan *(Cork)* – Eugene

12. Goggles Doyle *(Clare)* – John Joe

13. Tull Dunne *(Galway)* – John

14. Chuck Higgins *(Derry)* – Charlie

15. Love Higgins *(Cork)* – Bill

16. Babs Keating *(Tipperary)* – Michael

17. Toots Kelleher *(Cork)* – Denis

18. Wren Kelly *(Kilkenny)* – Jim

19. Beefy Kennedy *(Dublin)* – Paddy

20. Icy Lanigan *(Kilkenny)* – Paddy

21. Fan Larkin *(Kilkenny)* – Philip Francis

22. Bomber Liston *(Kerry)* – Eoin

23. Jobber McGrath *(Westmeath)* – John

24. Hopper McGrath *(Wexford)* – Oliver

25. Hopper McGrath *(Galway)* – Michael

26. Mackey McKenna *(Tipperary)* – John

27. Tyler Mackey *(Limerick)* – John

28. Fox Maher *(Kilkenny)* – Pat

29. Ogie Moran *(Kerry)* – Denis

30. Weeshie Murphy *(Cork)* – Pat

31. Chunky O'Brien *(Kilkenny)* – Liam

32. Hawk O'Brien *(Tipperary)* – Jim

33. Marie O'Connell *(Cork)* – Eddie

34. Gega O'Connor *(Kerry)* – Tom

35.   Hawker O'Grady *(Cork)* – Pat

36.   Doc O'Callaghan *(Roscommon)* – J. P.

37.   Micksie Palmer *(Kerry)* – James

38.   Nipper Shanley *(Leitrim)* – John

39.   Builder Walsh *(Dublin)* – Jim

40.   Link Walsh *(Kilkenny)* – Jim

41.   Drug Walsh *(Kilkenny)* – Dig

42.   Knacker Walsh *(Galway)* – Michael

43.   Shanks Whelan *(Wexford)* – Seamus

Sam Maguire

Sam Maguire from West Cork played for London in the 1900, 1901 and 1903 All-Ireland football finals and went on to become chairman of the GAA in London. A group of Maguire's friends and colleagues commissioned the Dublin firm of Hopkins & Hopkins to design an enlarged replica of the Ardagh Chalice in his honour in 1928, commemorating his work for the infant Irish State after 1919 as much as his deeds on the pitch.

Born in Maulabracka, just outside Dunmanway, County Cork, in 1879, Maguire moved to London to work in the British civil service after he left school. Maguire became Major General and Chief Intelligence Officer in Britain for what was to become, after 1922, the Irish national army. He was eventually captured and imprisoned for running guns between London and Dublin, a crime that of course meant immediate dismissal. He returned to Cork in 1923 and died there 4 years later at the comparatively young age of 47.

His body is buried in the graveyard at St Mary's Church in Dunmanway, and a monument stands to his memory near his home. As the original cup was replaced by a newer model in 1988, Sam Maguire continues to be the name that dominates the dreams of Gaelic footballers everywhere.

The Greatest Hurling Games of All Time: A Random List

Beauty is indeed in the eye of the beholder when it comes to selecting the greatest hurling matches of all time. Previous generations were tempted to select any one of a series, Cork v. Limerick between 1939 and 1944, or the Christy Ring–Nicky Rackard finals of 1954 or 1956. Other games were not necessarily great matches, but great occasions. P. D. Mehigan, the leading GAA writer of his day, wrote that the second of the three matches between Kilkenny and Cork in the 1931 All-Ireland hurling final were the best he had seen. John D. Hickey said the same about the 1958 National Hurling League final between Wexford and Limerick. Pádraig Puirséil nominated Kilkenny's victory over Cork in 1947, a game also regarded by hurling historian Seamus J. Ryan as the day that hurling peaked. A spate of superb matches, especially All-Ireland semi-finals, since the 1990s indicate more recent generations will be staking their own claims for decades to come.

1.   **1907**   Kilkenny v. Cork, All-Ireland final

2.   **1910**   Limerick v. Cork, Munster final

3.   **1922**   Kilkenny v. Tipperary, All-Ireland final

4.   **1927**   Leinster v. Munster, Railway Cup final

5.   **1931**   Cork v. Kilkenny, All-Ireland final first
               replay

6.   **1935**   Kilkenny v. Limerick, National
               Hurling League final

7.   **1940**   Cork v. Limerick, Munster final

8.   **1947**   Cork v. Kilkenny, All-Ireland final

9.   **1956**   Wexford v. Cork, All-Ireland final

10.   **1996**   Limerick v. Tipprary, drawn Munster final

The Greatest Football Games of All Time: A Random List

Changes in the rules, particularly after 1913, 1970 and 1990, transformed Gaelic football into a faster game but, old-timers say, not necessarily a better one. Journalism and memoir suggest that games played shortly after a major rule change are quicker to earn a place in folklore: Dick Fitzgerald rated the 1913 Croke Memorial tournament match as the greatest, similarly many would nominate the Leinster and All-Ireland finals of 1970, when the length of games was extended to 80 minutes leading to freer high-scoring matches, or the 4th match in the 1991 series between Dublin and Meath when the free and sideline ball from the hand had freed up the game.

1. **1894** Tipperary v. Meath, All-Ireland final

2. **1903** Kerry v. Kildare, All-Ireland final replay

3. **1913** Kerry v. Louth, Croke Tournament final

4. **1926** Kerry v. Kildare, drawn All-Ireland final

5. **1938** Kerry v. Galway, drawn All-Ireland final

6. **1977** Dublin v. Kerry, All-Ireland semi-final

7. **1991** Dublin v. Meath, Leinster championship third replay

8.   **1994**   Down v. Derry, Ulster championship first round

9.   **1997**   Meath v. Kildare, Leinster championship first replay

10.   **2005**   Tyrone v. Dublin, drawn All-Ireland quarter-final

Paddy Downey's Most Memorable Matches

In selecting the most memorable games he has seen, in chronological order, Paddy Downey says 'a few of these were not the greatest displays of skill, in either game, but the most memorable for various reasons'.

Hurling

1954	All-Ireland final Cork v. Wexford
1956	All-Ireland final Wesford v. Cork
1959	All-Ireland final Waterford v. Kilkenny (drawn game)
1962	All-Ireland final Tipperary v. Wexford
1972	All-Ireland final Kilkenny v. Cork
1984	Munster final Cork v. Tipperary
1987	Munster final Tipperary v. Cork (replay)
1993	Leinster final Kilkenny v. Wexford (drawn game)
1995	Munster final Clare v. Limerick
2005	All-Ireland semi-final Galway v. Kilkenny

Football

1950	All-Ireland final Mayo v. Louth
1954	All-Ireland final Meath v. Kerry
1955	All-Ireland final Kerry v. Dublin
1956	All-Ireland final Galway v. Cork
1960	All-Ireland final Down v. Kerry
1974	All-Ireland final Dublin v. Galway
1989	All-Ireland final Cork v. Mayo
1975	All-Ireland final Kerry v. Dublin
1977	All-Ireland semi-final Dublin v. Kerry
1982	All-Ireland final Offaly v. Kerry

Owen McCann's Most Memorable Hurling Matches

Veteran journalist Owen McCann wrote: 'Hurling has rewarded me with many stirring games down the years but the more I look back over past matches the more I am convinced that top billing must go to the 1976 All-Ireland final between Cork and Wexford.'

1976 All-Ireland senior final, Cork v. Wexford at Croke Park

This really was one of the great deciders. The Leesiders were 2–2 to no score in arrears after 6½ minutes but, prompted by a regal performance from Pat Moylan at midfield, they powered back in great style. They were on level terms at the break and finished winners by 2–21 to 4–11 in a game in which there were many shining stars on both teams in a splendid exhibition of hurling. However, Moylan was the hero of the day with hurling that was cool, authoritative, invaluable and topped off by 10 golden points.

1994 Leinster senior semi-final, Offaly v. Wexford at Croke Park

A Leinster senior semi-final between Offaly and Kilkenny at Croke Park in 1994 ranks a close second to the 1976 Liam McCarthy Cup tie. There was much to enthuse over in a splendid encounter. A brilliant performance by Brian Whelahan at right half back was a

bright feature of a 4 points success that earned the
Faithful County a first final appearance in 4 years.

Both counties contributed in rich measure to the contest.
Kilkenny battled in typical fashion to advance their quest
for a 4th successive Leinster title but a great defence and
the sharpshooting of the Dooley brothers – Johnny, Billy
and Joe – who scored 2–10 between them, did much to
end the Noreside ambitions.

1996 Munster senior final (draw), Limerick v. Tipperary at Limerick

Two years later, the sharpshooting of Gary Kirby stands
out from a truly classic second half provided by Limerick
and Tipperary when they played a draw in the Munster
final at Limerick. Tipperary looked home and dried at the
interval when they led by 10 points. But what a comeback
by the Shannonsiders! Kirby powered the way with his
points scoring and his 10th in the 70th minute left his
team just a point adrift as the game neared a conclusion.
Then Frankie Carroll rang down the curtain on a pulse-
raising half marked by spirited passages of play by
earning Limerick a draw with a fine point.

1968 All-Ireland senior final, Wexford v. Tipperary at Croke Park

The 1968 All-Ireland senior final was noteworthy for grit,
power, skill and stamina from Wexford as they powered
back from an interval deficit of 8 points to beat
Tipperary in a second half of sheer splendour. Tony

Doran was a real match-winner, with 2–1, as the Model County completed 'mission impossible' in that second half for a 5–8 to 3–12 win. Jack Berry, who scored 2–2, Dan Quigley and Willie Murphy in defence and goalkeeper Pat Nolan were others who did much to orchestrate the first Liam McCarthy Cup win in 8 years.

2002 Munster senior final, Waterford v. Tipperary at Pairc Ui Chaoimh

The Munster senior final of 2002 was another game in which a power-packed finish ensured victory. Waterford were bidding for a first provincial title since 1963 when they lined out against Tipperary at Pairc Ui Chaoimh. A point behind at the interval, they finished in great style, scoring 1–6 without reply in the final 20 minutes to earn a memorable 2–23 to 3–12 win. Ken McGrath went into the game hampered by a shoulder injury, but still strode the scene in majestic fashion with quality hurling and finishing that yielded 7 points, all from play.

1990 All-Ireland senior final, Cork v. Galway at Croke Park

A splendid performance by Joe Cooney and power-packed hurling from Jim Cashman stand out from a thrilling spectacle that was the 1990 Cork–Galway All-Ireland senior final. That game had everything – hurling of the highest standard, skill, some individual performances to marvel at and a superb comeback by Cork, who started outsiders. Cooney, who captained

Galway, was magnificent in the first half and scored
1–6, all but a point from play. He was not quite as
prominent in the second half but still did well and had
a fine game overall. Cork were behind by 1–13 to 1–8
at the break but rallied well, with Cashman at centre
half-back a key figure in prompting an exhilarating
comeback that paid off in a 3-point win.

1989 hurling League tie, Kilkenny v. Offaly at Tullamore

It is often said that hurling is a summer game, but
Kilkenny an Offaly disproved that theory on a February
afternoon in 1989 when they ushered in the resumption
of the National League with a cracking match at
Tullamore. On a day of bitter cold, non-stop rain, and a
pitch that was understandably very heavy, the teams
defied the conditions to provide an excellent match.
Teenager D.J. Carey made a splendid *goalkeeping* debut
for Kilkenny, while Adrian Ronan, who hit 9 points for
the Noresiders. Offaly defenders Pat Delaney and
Aidan Fogarty were commanding figures as the
Noresiders turned an interval deficit of 8 points into an
0–13 to 1–7 win. However, hurling was the real winner
that winter's day.

1989 National League final, Galway v. Tipperary at Croke Park

Tipperary scored 4 goals against Galway in the 1989
National League final at Croke Park, but still lost by 2

points in a magnificent encounter. This was a game that had everything – good in hurling-skilled play, excitement, speed, class, some excellent scores. Indeed Joe Cooney hit one of the best goals in any league final. It was early in the game and he cracked the ball in full flight with power and precision – one of 2 goals by Galway. A game that was a wonderful advertisement for hurling, was also one to remember for Cooney, who finished with 1–7 of his team's total of 2–16 as against Tipperary's 4–8.

1996 All-Ireland minor final draw, Galway v. Tipperary at Croke Park

Minor games are invariably well worth making the effort to get to a ground early. The 1996 All-Ireland Under-18 meeting of Tipperary and Galway certainly proved a wonder aperitif to the Liam McCarthy Cup tie. The Munster champions looked to have the title in the bag when they led by 8 points after 40 minutes yet, at the end, had to rely on 2 late points to earn a draw, 0–20 to 3–11. Two goals by Aidan Poinard and substitute Mark Kerins and the sharpshooting of Eugene Cloonan, who finished with 7 points, did much to prompt the Galway comeback. Midfielder Willie Ryan, forward Eugene O'Neill, scorer of 7 points, and centre half-back John Carroll were the bright stars of Tipperary, who showed a nice line in points scoring with 20 to Galway's 3–11.

1997 All-Ireland senior final, Clare v. Tipperary at Croke Park

The first all-Munster All-Ireland senior final at Croke Park brought Clare and Tipperary into opposition in 1997, a repeat of their clash in the provincial final earlier in the year, which the Banner County won by a goal 1–18 to 0–18. The Liam McCarthy Cup tie was a game worthy of the unique occasion – a gripping encounter with many passages of good hurling, fine displays and a dramatic conclusion. Tipperary trailed by 5 points after 56 minutes, but goals by Liam Cahill and Eugene O'Neill in a 4-minute spell had them a point ahead after 65 minutes. Four minutes later, Clare were back in front by a point and held that lead for a 0–20 to 2–13 win. Midfielders Colin Lynch and Ollie Baker and James O'Connor, who scored 7 points, did much to set the scene for the success.

Owen McCann's Most Memorable Football Games

1994 Ulster senior championship first-round, Derry v. Down at Celtic Park

Derry, who won the All-Ireland senior title for the first time the previous September, and Down provided a fast, free-flowing exhibition of all that is best in the game. The exchanges were thrilling from first to final whistle and there were some splendid individual displays. Derry's hopes of retaining their provincial and national titles were ended when a goal 7 minutes from the end by substitute Ciaran McCabe sealed a memorable 1–14 to 1–12 win for Down. Michael Linden proved a bright star for Down. He teased and tormented the home defence and set the seal on his display by scoring 6 golden points.

1957 National league final, Galway v. Kerry at Croke Park

That was a game of few stoppages, excellent fielding and long kicking and highlighted by a classical display from Galway captain and centre half-back Jack Mahon, a display of the standard of excellence as one could wish to see. Galway won by 1–8 to 0–6.

1996 All-Ireland Vocational Schools title, Donegal v. Kerry at Croke Park

Donegal and Kerry provided early arrivals at headquarters with all that is best in the beautiful game. It was an outstanding encounter, a match to hold its own with the very best in an grade and any code and ended on a dramatic note when Kerry, a point behind, failed in injury-time to earn a draw from a free, 2–13 to 3–9.

1960 All-Ireland senior final, Down v. Kerry at Croke Park

1960 marked Down's debut in a Sam Maguire Cup tie and brought them up against title specialists Kerry. Another bid to bring the trophy across the border for the first time. The final was not a spectacular one, but a super-charged atmosphere, quality displays from a number of players on both sides, keen exchanges and the ever-present sense of history, all contributed to a contest that did justice to the unique occasion. James McCartan and Paddy Doherty were very prominent in fashioning Down's historic 2–10 to 0–8 win.

1987 National Football League final, Dublin v. Kerry at Croke Park

The counties paraded their many talents to superb effect to provide a splendid encounter, with many passages of good football. The Dubs, with a young team, ended the game, that sparkled like the sunshine of that afternoon, 1–11 to 0–11 ahead. A goal by Kieran Duff almost immediately after the start of the second half proved the crucial score.

1982 All-Ireland senior football final, Offaly v. Kerry at Croke Park

This game will not rank as one of the greatest-ever, but the fact that the game had a dramatic ending ensures that it keeps jogging the memory. Despite the threat of rain that eventually materialised, the final was a very keenly contested affair, with fast, open play and some grand individual performances. Kerry, with probably the greatest team of all time, were about the reach the summit of a record five All-Ireland senior titles when substitute Seamus Darby snatched that record from them with a goal virtually on full-time. A fairlytale-like ending to a game that left Offaly winners by 1–15 to 0–17.

1997 All-Ireland minor final, Laois v. Tyrone at Croke Park

Back to the schoolboys and the All-Ireland minor final of 1997 between Laois, who won the title for the first time the previous year, and Tyrone in a traditional

Croke Park curtain-raiser. This was another excellent advertisement for football as an exciting spectator sport. Stephen Kelly, who scored 2–3, was a bright star for Laois, while Declan McCrossan sparkled as Tyrone's captain and centre half-back with his exciting football.

1992 Ulster final, Donegal v. Derry at Clones

This was by no means one of the best-ever. Nevertheless, it still stands out because of Donegal's brilliant against-the-odds second-half performance against the then league champions. The prospects at the interval did not look bright for Donegal. Although they were on level terms at the break, they had a defender dismissed by the referee in the first half and also faced the wind in the second half. However, for a display of courage, commitment and plenty of skill in the second half by Donegal this final ranks as just a little extra special. The gutsy performance turned the key in the door to a 2-point win. Martin McHugh and Declan Bonner were to the fore in forging the success.

2003 Ulster final, Tyrone v. Down at Clones

One of the most thrilling Ulster senior finals and one that featured a splendid second-half comeback. The Mourne County led by 9 points early in the second half, despite being reduced to 14 players in the first half, finished with 4 goals, but still had to settle for a replay. But credit Tyrone for refusing to accept second best. They stuck resolutely to the job on hand and a penalty goal by Peter Canavan and a man-of-the-match display by Brian McGuigan were key factors in earning the O'Neill County a second chance, 1–17 to 4–8.

1987 All-Ireland final, Meath v. Cork at Croke Park

This was a splendid contest, with plenty of good football, keen exchanges and goalmouth thrills. Long-serving campaigners Mick Lyons, Joe Cassells and Colm O'Rourke were very much to the fore in leading the Royals to the promised land after 20 years.

Great Upsets

1989 Antrim v. Offaly
Offaly were 4 points up at half-time. Antrim scored 2–1 in the final 5 minutes to win 4–15 to 1–15 and reach their first final for 46 years. 'It's the greatest day in Antrim's history,' said a jubilant Nelson afterwards.

1993 Kerry v. Waterford
Kerry manager John Meyler ran into then Tipperary manager Babs Keating in Dungarvan the night before the match. 'We'll be playing ye in a fortnight's time,' Meyler assured him. Paul Flynn shot 3–2 in his first championship game, but Kerry held tough for a 4–13 to 3–13 win. 'If we never won another match this would keep me going,' Kerry selector Maurice Leahy said.

1980 Offaly v. Kilkenny
Kilkenny man Diarmuid Healy helped a gifted group of Offaly players marry their skill to newfound belief. Kilkenny led 3–6 to 1–10 at half-time, but Offaly never flinched and ran out 3–17 to 5–10 winners. Padraig Horan's father, Tom, had passed away suddenly during the afternoon, and a great roar went up as he collected and held aloft the trophy.

1992 Clare v. Kerry, Munster football final

Jack O'Shea's last game for Kerry and Seamus Moynihan's first final. John Maughan's Clare team survived a nervy start, led at half-time and grabbed the goals when they needed them to win 2–10 to 0–12. 'There won't be a cow milked in Clare tonight,' said Marty Morrissey on RTÉ.

2003 Monaghan v. Armagh, Ulster football championship

Monaghan's 0–13 to 0–9 victory made their summer, but it ultimately offered a greater springboard to Armagh's. No team had ever won an Ulster title starting from the preliminary round. Without Kieran McGeeney and a handful of regulars, Armagh hit wides past the exposed goal of Monaghan keeper Glenn Murphy.

1957 Waterford v. Kerry, Munster football championship

Four selected players didn't travel to Waterford, leaving Kerry with just 16 to choose from. Legend tells us a few players had a late night before the game. After Tom Cunningham hit the winning point, to put Waterford 2–5 to 0–10 ahead, Paudie Sheehy had a 21-yard free to draw the game – it drifted wide.

1958 Derry v. Kerry, All-Ireland football semi-final

Derry had just won their first Ulster title and only 3 of their players had ever played in Croke Park. Kerry introduced Mick O'Connell and Mick O'Dwyer into a team of veterans. A goal from Sean O'Connell put Derry 4 clear before Tadghie Lyne goaled to pull them back, but Derry held together long enough to come through 2–6 to 2–5.

1990 Cork v. Tipperary, Munster hurling final

Bookies had Cork 4–1 to win the game, but they tore into Tipp. Mark Foley scored a famous 2–7, John Fitzgibbon ripped Tipp's full-back line to shreds and they ran out 4–16 to 2–14 winners. The result led Babs Keating to declare, 'You don't win derbies with donkeys.'

1975 Galway v. Cork, All-Ireland hurling semi-final

With John Connolly, Iggy Clarke and P.J. Molloy in brilliant form, Galway had 3 goals inside 10 minutes. With players like Jimmy Barry-Murphy in their ranks, challenging with Michael Conneely, Cork recovered and trailed 3–7 to 1–6 at half-time. But they could never fully bridge the gap and finished 4–15 to 2–19 behind.

1943 Antrim v Kilkenny

Antrim won by 3–13 to 1–6 in the tight confines of
Corrigan Park where they had already beaten Galway by
7–0 to 6–2. Antrim had played in the senior
championship only because the junior competitions
were suspended during the war. They had even been
beaten by Down in the 1941 Ulster Junior final. Noel
Campbell scored the last-minute goal against Galway,
while Danny McAllister, Kevin Mullan and Kevin
Armstrong scored the goals against Kilkenny.

1912 Antrim v Kerry

Antrim won on the amazing scoreline of 3–5 to 0–2.
Kerry blamed a wedding the day before, but Antrim's
great display in the final suggests this much-vented
legend is only part of the story.

GAA TDs

1. Harry Boland *(Coalition Republic)*

2. Jim Deenihan *(Fine Gael)*

3. John Donnellan *(Fine Gael)*

4. Michael Donnellan *(Fine Gael)*

5. Sean Flanagan *(Fianna Fáil)*

6. Hugh Gibbons *(Fianna Fáil)*

7. Jack Lynch *(Fianna Fáil)*

9. Jack McQuillan *(Clann na Poblachta/Independent)*

10. Eoin O'Duffy *(Fine Gael)*

12. Tom O'Reilly *(Independent)*

13. Dan Spring *(Labour)*

14. Austin Stack *(Sinn Fein)*

15. J.J. Walsh *(Cumann na nGaedhel)*

16. John Wilson *(Fianna Fáil)*

Great Sigerson/Fitzgibbon Myths

The player who said he was studying sums
The famous player (name interchangeable) was playing
illegally on a Sigerson/Fitzgibbon match for a famous
college (name interchangeable) and was asked what he
was studying. He replied 'sums'. It was too good a story
not to be invented.

Nobody got sent off in a Sigerson match before
the 1960s
Not true. Until the 1960s several players were sent off
in Sigerson matches but the press did not report such
things. Denis Philpott was the first recorded sending off
in 1966.

The plans for the original buildings of UCC and
Queen's were mixed up
Not true. The 3 Queen's colleges – Cork, Galway and
Belfast – were designed by different architects in the
1840s.

The base of the Fitzgibbon spent the years 1970–77
in the Corrib
Not true. The base was kept in the attic of a Galway
pub, but turned up in time for Galway to host the
competition in 1977.

UCG won seven-in-a-row in 1942

Not true. There wasn't a Sigerson in the 1942–43
season, though the trophy remained in Galway custody
and they did indeed win six-in-a-row.

Seamus Mallon won a Sigerson medal with
Queen's in 1958

Quite true. But it was not the man who was later
Deputy First Minister in the North. It was another
Seamus Mallon, from a neighbouring parish in Armagh.

Socrates won a Sigerson medal with UCD

Not true. The Brazilian footballer spent a short time
studying with College of Surgeons but didn't kick a
Gaelic football.

Scoring Records

1. Andy Dooric Buckley scored at least 6 goals when Cork beat Kilkenny by 8–9 to 0–8 in the 1903 home All-Ireland final. Other newspaper reports credit him with 7–4.

2. P.J. Riordan of Drombane is said to have scored all but 1 point of Tipperary's total when they beat Kilkenny by 6–8 to 0–1 in the 1895 All-Ireland final.

3. Jimmy Kelly of Kilkenny is said to have scored 7 goals in 30 minutes against Cork in the replay of the 1905 final.

4. Mick Kennedy is credited with 8–1 for Kilkenny against Wexford in the Leinster final of 1916 and with 6–1 by other sources.

5. Nicky Rackard of Wexford got the highest confirmed total in a major game, 7–7 of the 12–17 scored by Wexford against Antrim in the 1954 All-Ireland semi-final.

6. Frank Donnelly of Tyrone scored 5–8 against Fermanagh in the 1959 Dr Lagan Cup, then a division of the National Football League.

7. John Joyce of Dublin scored 5–3 against Longford in the 1960 Leinster championship at Mullingar.

Joyce also forced an own goal in the game as Dublin won by 10–13 to 3–8.

8.   Jimmy Smyth scored 6–4 of Clare against Limerick in 1953.

9.   Nicky Rackard of Wexford scored 6–4 against Dublin in 1954.

10. Christy Ring of Cork scored 6–4 against Wexford in the 1959 National Hurling League.

11. Christy Heffernan of Kilkenny scored 6–4 against Carlow in the 1980 Naitonal Hurling League.

12. Willie Dwyer of Kilkenny and Leinster scored 6–1 against Ulster in the 1962 Railway Cup semi-final.

13. Eddie Keher scored 2–11 for Kilkenny against Tipperary in the 1971 All-Ireland hurling final.

14. Mike Sheehy scored 2-7 for Kerry against Dublin in the 1979 All-Ireland football final.

15. Eddie Keher scored 6-45 in 5 matches in the 1972 hurling championship.

16. Offaly's Paddy Molloy scored 8-15 in 3 hurling matches in 1969.

17. Matt Connor of Offaly scored 5–31 in 4 football matches in 1980.

18. Wicklow's John Timmons scored 4–16 in just 3 football matches in 1957.

19. Martin Kennedy is said to have scored 10 goals in a National Hurling League match. He scored 27 goals in 6 games on the US tour by Tipperary in 1926.

20. Rory Gallagher from Erne Gaels scored 3–9 for Fermanagh against Monaghan in the first round of the Ulster championship in 2001. Peter Donohoe from Cavan held the previous record when he scored 3–5 for Cavan against Tyrone in 1950.

Hurling in Ancient Law

Fragments of law that predate the Brehon Laws of the 7th and 8th centuries, mentioning hurling, may be pre-Christian in origin.

12th century

Meallbhratha (drawing on earlier texts) laid down judgments for 20 games, most of which resembled hurling (injury to an opposing player during a hurling match was punishable).

Leabhar Aicle (drawing on earlier texts) specifies the requirements of players attempting to retrieve a ball (he must seek permission to enter land, must close the gap or gate in the wall, and must cause no damage in retrieving the ball).

Seanchas Mór Commentaries on the Brehon laws of fosterage lay down that it is proper for a king's son to have his camán hooped in bronze, and for lesser subjects to ring theirs in copper. Under Brehon law a camán could not be confiscated.

Hurling in English Legal Texts

1366
Statute of Kilkenny forbade: 'The games which men call hurlings with great clubs of a ball on the ground from which great evils and maims have arisen.'

1527
Statute in archives of the Town of Galway: 'At no tyme to use ne occupye ye hurlinge of ye litill balle with the hookie stickies or staves, nor use no hand balle to play without the walls, but only the great foote balle.'

1578
English-appointed Lord Chancellor William Gerrarde wrote in a letter that the new settlers were 'speaking Irish, playing hurling and copying the customs of the natives'.

1308
John McCrocan, a bystander at a football match from Newcastle Lyons, County Dublin, was charged with accidentally stabbing a player, William Bernard.

Goalkeepers Who Scored

1. Cork goalkeeper James Kelleher from Dungourney
    scored in the 1905 All-Ireland final against
    Kilkenny when his puck-out hopped over the bar.

2. Billy O'Neill scored a goal from a puck-out in the
    1955 All-Army final.

3. Noel Skehan scored a point from a free against
    Galway in the 1982 All-Ireland semi-final.

4. John Hennessy of Emly scored a point direct from
    a puck-out in the 1894 Limerick county
    championship.

5. Galway goalkeeper John Commins became the first
    goalkeeper to score a goal in an All-Ireland final
    when he landed a penalty in the net in the 1986
    final, and did the same again a week later in the All-
    Ireland Under-21 final.

6. Davey Fitzgerald scored a goal from a penalty for
    Clare against Limerick in the 1995 Munster final.

7. Ger Cunningham took a penalty in the 1986 Cork
    County Championship, but didn't make it back in
    time and the opponents scored a goal. Originally, the
    free was from 20 yards out, but when a Galway
    player argued with the referee, it was moved 10 yards
    further on.

Long Kicks

During a Dublin club match **Pat 'Cocker' Daly** is
alleged to have kicked the ball over the railway wall.

Mick 'Gundy' Fitzgerald, playing for Leinster in 1905,
drove a kick over the bar and it rebounded off the
railway wall from all of 85 yards.

138

Famous GAA Pubs

The Premium Level in Croke Park is the best GAA pub
of all – if you can get in – but there are lots of others
to chose from if you can't. A recent trend has been the
shrines to great GAA players and events that crop up in
GAA pubs. Check out the famous Christy Ring wall at
Larry Tompkins' place. The An Fear Rua website
(anfearrua.com) has a good GAA pub guide.

1.   The Big Tree, Parnell Street, Dublin

2.   Seamus Delaney's, Kilkenny

3.   Jamesie Murray's, Knockcroghery

4.   Leeson Lounge, Lower Leeson Street, Dublin

5.   The Orchard, Blackrock, Cork

6.   O'Shea's, Merchant's Quay, Dublin

7.   Tatler Jack's, Killarney

8.   Ciaran Carey's, Dock Road, Limerick

9.   Whelahan's Pub, Birr

10. Any pub in Clones you can get in to on Ulster
     final day

Patrons: Landed Families Who Sponsored Hurling Teams in the 18th Century

Barrington of Cullenagh, County Laois

Barry of Ballinaclough, County Cork

Blake of Menlough, County Galway

Butler of Clanwilliam, County Tipperary

Callaghan of Shanbally, County Tipperary

Carew of Castleboro, County Wexford

Colclough of Duffry Hall, County Wexford

Cosby of Stradbally, County Laois

Cuffe of Desart Court, County Kilkenny

Davies of Blarney, County Cork

Devereux of Carrigmennan, County Wexford

Gregg of Kilcorney, County Clare

Jones of Aghasallagh, County Wicklow

Mathews of Thomastown, County Tipperary

O'Connell of Derrynane, County Kerry

Parsons of Birr, County Offaly

Purcell of Loughmore, County Tipperary

National League

- The winter of 1946–47 was so bad that some teams had not played a single match by April, so the organisers invited the 4 group leaders to play in the semi-finals. Derry beat Clare in the final, while Longford and Wicklow were the beaten semi-finalists.

- Fermanagh were unlikely qualifiers for the 1935 final, having won the McGrath Cup in Ulster.

- Kilkenny's best-ever season in the National Football League was in 1970–71 when they won 4 matches, and lost 3 of the 7 they played in Division 2A. They finished in third place, ahead of Wexford, Clare, Wicklow and Carlow. Since then they have won a total of 8 matches in 27 years, finishing bottom of their section each season except 1994–95, when their 3 points put them ahead of Limerick and London.

- Mayo won the league 6 times in a row, opted out in 1940 to give the others a chance (Connacht rivals Galway beat Meath in the final), and came back to win it in 1941.

- Wicklow won 13 matches in a row as they went straight from Division 4 to Division 2 in 1980–82.

Tours of the USA By GAA Teams

The GAA's only international outlet was the facility to play exhibition matches and games against exile teams in America. Regular GAA exhibitions were played in New York, Boston, Chicago, San Francisco and many smaller cities. The 1947 All-Ireland final was played in the Polo Grounds in New York. The record attendance for a GAA match in the USA was 60,000 to see Kerry play New York in the Yankee Stadium.

1888	Invasion
1926	Tipperary *(hurling)*
1927	Kerry *(football)*
1931	Tipperary *(hurling)*
	Kerry *(football)*
1932	Mayo *(football)*
1933	Kerry *(football)*
1934	Cavan *(football)*
	Kilkenny *(hurling)*
	Galway *(football)*

1935	Limerick (*hurling*)
	Cavan (*football*)
1936	Mayo (*football*)
1937	Laois (*football*)
	Cavan (*football*)
1939	Galway (*football*)
	Kerry (*football*)
1947	Cavan (*football*)
	Kerry (*football*)
1950	Tipperary (*hurling*)
1951	Meath (*football*)
	Galway (*hurling*)
1952	Cork (*football*)
1954	Mayo (*football*)
	Cork (*hurling*)
1956	Dublin (*football*)
	Kerry (*football*)
1957	Cork (*hurling*)

143

Wexford (*hurling*)

Galway (*football*)

Tipperary (*hurling*)

1958   Kilkenny (*hurling*)

Louth (*football*)

1959   Tipperary (*hurling*)

Kerry (*football*)

1960   Waterford (*hurling*)

1962   Down (*football*)

Offaly (*football*)

1963   Mayo (*football*)

1964   Tipperary (*hurling*)

Dublin (*football*)

1965   Galway (*football*)

Tipperary (*hurling*)

1967   Galway (*football*)

Kilkenny (*hurling*)

1968   Tipperary (*hurling*)

        Down (*football*)

        Meath (*football*)

1969   Kerry (*football*)

1970   Cork (*hurling*)

        Kerry (*football*)

1971   Kerry (*football*)

        Selected football team

1972   Derry (*football*)

        Offaly (*football*)

        All Stars to USA, later Toronto, Dubai,
Argentina and Hong Kong.

Penalties

1. In 1940, the penalty kick was introduced in football and semi-penalty (goalkeeper and 2 defenders on the line) in hurling. But the referee at the Leinster junior hurling final became a little confused with the change and, when he awarded a penalty for Meath against Kilkenny, he ordered everybody out except the Kilkenny goalkeeper. The goalkeeper saved the shot regardless!

2. Meath also missed the first penalty to be awarded in the football championship, in the first half of the Leinster final against Laois. Laois had conceded the penalty for charging at the taker of a free that was sent over the bar! Donal Keenan eventually became the first to score a penalty in a provincial final, for beaten Connacht finalists Roscommon against Galway in 1942.

3. The first penalty in an All-Ireland final came in 1948. Padraig Carney scored for Mayo against Cavan, but Cavan still won by a point.

4. In 1944, a potential Carlow breakthrough was foiled when Kerry's Murt Kelly scored a penalty, the first in an All-Ireland football semi-final.

5. In 1953, Kerry were saved when Armagh's Bill McCorry missed a penalty that still haunts the

whole of the north. But Ulster had revenge in 1960 when Paddy Doherty's penalty sent Down 6 points ahead of Kerry and helped change the course of GAA history.

6. In 1961, it was a penalty that was not awarded that caused controversy – Harry Green of Offaly was apparently pulled down in the parallelogram by two Downmen.

7. In 1962, Don Feeley scored a penalty for Roscommon against Kerry but could not prevent one of the greatest whitewashes in history.

8. After the size of the parallelogram was extended in 1970, penalties became more common. Jimmy Keaveney unleashed a Dublin penalty into the top corner of the Kerry net in 1975. Paddy Moriarty of Armagh had 2 against Dublin in 1976, but missed the second. Mike Sheehy scored another for Kerry against Dublin in 1979.

Most One-Sided Hurling Finals

34 points – 1896: Tipperary (8–14) v. Dublin (0–4)

29 points – 1894: Cork (5–10) v. Dublin (2–0)

27 points – 1943: Cork (5–16) v. Antrim (0–4)

27 points – 1921: Cork (6–12) v. Galway (1–0)

26 points – 1918: Limerick (9–5) v. Wexford (1–3)

25 points – 1903: Cork (8–9) v. Kilkenny (0–8)

22 points – 1902: Cork (3–13) v. London (0–0)

24 points – 1893: Cork (6–8) v. Kilkenny (0–2)

20 points – 1941: Cork (5–11) v. Dublin (0–6)

18 points – 1989: Tipperary (4–14) v. Antrim (3–9)

17 points – 1949: Tipperary (3–11) Laois (0–3)

17 points – 1937: Tipperary (3–11) v. Kilkenny (0–3)

The Most One-Sided Hurling Semi-Finals

52 points – 1900: Galway (10–23) v. Antrim (0–1)

44 points – 1954: Wexford (12–17) v. Antrim (2–3)

36 points – 1925: Tipperary (12–9) v. Antrim (2–3)

35 points – 1912: Limerick (11–4) v. Antrim (0–2)

33 points – 1904: Cork (8–18) v. Antrim (2–3)

32 points – 1949: Tipperary (6–18) v. Antrim (0–4)

33 points – 1906: Tipperary (7–14) v. Galway (0–2)

29 points – 1913: Tipperary (10–0) v. Roscommon (0–1)

28 points – 1903: Kilkenny (6–19) v. Antrim (2–3)

28 points – 1948: Dublin (8–13) v. Antrim (2–3)

27 points – 1901: Cork (7–12 v. Galway (1–3)

26 points – 1947: Cork (7–10) v. Antrim (0–5)

26 points – 1972: Cork (7–20) v. London (1–12)

25 points – 1916: Tipperary (8–1) v. Galway (0–0)

24 points – 1915: Cork (6–6) v. Galway (0–0)

24 points – 1923: Limerick (7–4) v. Donegal (0–1)

24 points – 1946: Kilkenny (7–11) v. Antrim (0–7)

24 points – 1984: Cork (3–26) v. Antrim 2–5)

Most One-Sided Football Finals

1889: Tipperary 3–6 Queen's County 0–0
(goal outweighs any number of points)

22 points – 1900 home final: Tipperary 2–17 Galway
0–1

19 points – 1912: Cork 6–6 Antrim 1–2

18 points – 1930: Kerry 3–11 Monaghan 0–2

18 points – 1936: Mayo 4–11 Laois 0–5

17 points – 1979: Kerry 5–11 Dublin 0–9

14 points – 1900: Tipperary 3–7 London 0–2

12 points – 1976: Dublin 5–2 Armagh 3–6

11 points – 1979: Kerry 3–13 Dublin 1–8

10 points – 1902: Dublin 2–8 London 0–4

10 points – 1919: Kildare 2–5 Galway 0–1

9 points – 1908: Dublin 1–10 London 0–4

9 points – 2000: Galway 0–17 Meath 0–8

150

Most One-Sided Football Semi-Finals

27 points – 1901: Cork (4–16) v. Mayo (0–1)

22 points – 1979: Kerry (5–14) v. Monaghan (0–7)

21 points – 1904;: Kerry (4–10) v. Cavan (0–1)

21 points – 1993: Cork (5–15) v. Mayo (0–10)

18 points – 1905: Kildare (4–15) v. Cavan (1–6)

17 points – 1944: Roscommon (5–8) v. Cavan (1–3)

17 points – 1975: Kerry (3–13) v. Sligo (0–5)

16 points – 1902: Dublin (2–12) v. Antrim (0–2)

16 points – 1902: Dublin (4–13) v. Armagh (1–6)

151

16 points – 1976: Kerry (5–14) v. Derry (1–10)

16 points – 1981: Kerry (2–19) v. Mayo (1–6)

15 points – 1913: Wexford (4–4) v. Antrim (0–1)

15 points – 1917: Wexford (6–6) v. Monaghan (1–3)

15 points – 1973: Cork (5–10) v. Tyrone (2–4)

15 points – 2001: Meath (2–14) v. Kerry (0–5)

14 points – 1955: Replay Kerry (4–7) v. Cavan (0–5)

13 points – 1970: Kerry (0–23) v. Derry (0–10)

12 points – 1984: Kerry (2–17) v. Galway (0–11)

11 points – 1983: Dublin (4–15) v. Cork (2–10)

11 points – 1988: Cork (1–14) v. Monaghan (0–6)

11 points – 1987: Replay Cork (0–18) v. Galway (1–4)

Hurling in Heroic Literature

1100

'Táin Bo Culaigne', the story of Cúchulainn (drawing
on two 9th-century texts), the manuscript probably
written by Maolmhuire mac mic Choinn na mBocht in
Clonmacnoise. Cúchulainn introduced himself to the
youths of Emain Mhacha through his hurling prowess,
catching the ball between his legs and carrying it over
the goal. Conchubhuir arrives on the fair green and
finds a hurling match in progress, 50 boys at one end,
Cúchulainn at the other.

'He took his hurley stick of bronze and his silver ball,
and he would shorten his journey with them. He would
strike the ball with the camán and drive it away from
him. Then he would catch his hurling stick and his ball.
He went to the place of assembly of Emainn Mhacha
where the youths were. There were thrice 50 youths led
by Follomain mac Conchubuir at their games on the
green of Emain. The little boy went on to the playing
field in their midst and caught the ball between he legs
when they cast it. Nor did he let it go higher than the
top of his knee nor lower than his ankle. And he
pressed the ball between his two legs. And he carried
the ball away over the goal.'

O'Rabilly translation of 'Táin Bo Culaigne' from The Book
of Leinster (*Dublin, 1970*).

12th century

The Book of Leinster written around 1180 by Aed mac Criomthainn at an Nuachabail, near the townland of Stradbally in Laois. Two unrelated tales in the according hurling with semi-magical status. One tells of a youth captured during a game of hurling on Si Liamhna (Lyon's Hill in County Kildare) who appeals to Patrick for help, and the second concerns an appeal from Caoilte mac Ronain to help find 3 youths captured while playing an annual ritualised match of hurling during the November festival Samhain.

15th century

'Cath Mhaigh Tuireadh Chunga' describes a hurling match that resembles a battle skirmish in 1272 BC, the bodies from which were buried under a mound named Corn an Chluiche.

'Ruad with 27 sons of the courageous Mil sped westwards to the end of Magh Nua to challenge an equal number of the Tuatha de in a hurling match. They dealt many a blow on legs and arms, till their bones were broken and bruised, and fell outstretched on the turf and the match ended.'

15th century

The Toraiocht, the story of Diarmuid and Grainne and their pursuit by Fionn and the Fianna, it was the hurling prowess of Diarmuid that first caught Grainne's eye,

playing on the green at Tara. *The Toraiocht* describes a
match between the Fianna and the Tuatha de Dannaan,
both sides playing for 3 days between the locations of
Listowel and Glenflesk with neither side winning.

'The game was going against the Fianna when you rose
and took his caman from the one nearest you and you
knocked him to the ground. You scored three times
that day against Cairbre and the party of Tara.'

1471

An Leabhar Eoghanach tells of the hurling prowess of the
son of a mythological Ulster chieftain, Muireadhach
Tireach, who scored 30 times in a match against a team
of the King of Leinster's son and later scored 30 times
in a match in Scotland.

1631

'Agallamh na Seanorach' (the story of Oisin and St
Patrick) and 'Cath Fionntra', the Battle of Ventry (a tale
known to have existed in the 10th century) both tell of
the boyhood deeds of Fionn.

Hurling in Bardic Sources

1366
Gofraigh Fionn O Dalaigh's poem which advises
Domhnall Mac Carthaigh that he has to leave aside his
caman now he has acceded to leadership of his clan.

1425
Dubhthaigh mac Eoghada writes he would wish to be
in Carrickfergus to go to the strand to see the hurling.

1550
Lochlainn Og O Dalaigh writes that 3 of the O'Brien
clan had laid down their camans 'which won the game
against the heroes of the land of Far Miague' in favour
of the ivory hilt of the sword.

18th century
The anonymous 'Aird Ti Chuain' recalls the author's
youth spent hurling on the strand.

1780
Brian Merriman from Clare mentions hurling in his epic
poem 'Cuirt an Mhean Oiche': 'ar mhachaire mhin gach
fior-iomana/ag rince, baire, ras is radaireacht.'

1798
The original version of 'Priosuin Cluain Meala', the
croppy boy lies in his cell thinking of his youth, when
'the young active hurlers the field will be sweeping'.

1779
Songs recording hurling in Wexford in the local dialect, Yola, and Carrigmeen by Robert Devereaux, published.

1712
Seamus Dall MacCuarta's 'Iomain na Boinne' describes a match at Fennor, on Slane Castle estate on the banks of the Boyne, on a confined field with predetermined goals.

1740
Redmond Murphy describes a match in Omeath, which was either 8 or 16 a side, in which one of the players was seriously injured and died afterwards.

1720
Matt Concannon describes a six-a-side game between Lusk and Swords at Oxmantown Green.

1806
Fragments of a poem describe a match between Louth and Fermanagh at Inniskeen, County Monaghan, with 12 players a side, plus the captains, and bouts of wrestling to match.

1915
Anonymous song about a mid-19th century match in Annagassan, near Drogheda.

Four Great GAA Punch-Ups

1998 Munster hurlng semi-final: Clare v. Waterford

1996 All-Ireland football final: Meath v. Mayo

1997 Leinster Under-21 final: Dublin v. Offaly

1989 Munster senior hurling championship: Galway v. Tipperary

Tailteann Games Chronology

Mythological References

1829 BC The first celebration of the games.

632 BC The next reference to the games.

Historical References

717 Tailteann games disturbed by Fogartach mac Neill.

772 Thunderstorms caused widespread panic.

774 Disturbed by High King Donnchad Midi.

777 Disturbed when Donnchad Midi defeated Ciannachta.

811 Boycott imposed by the Community of Tallaght in protest against the High King Aed Ingor Oirdnide.

827 Disturbed when the High King Conchobar mac Donnchado slaughtered Gailenga.

889 Last regular celebration by High King Donnchad Donn was disturbed by Muirchertach mac Neill.

927   Games revived by Dub-Oenach nDonnchada.

1007   Revived by Mael Sechnaill II mac Domnaill.

1120   Staged by Toirrdelbach Ua Conchobair.

1169   The last celebration by Ruairi Ua Conchobair.

1806   The last gathering held on 1 August at Teltown
           by locals.

References in *The Book of Leinster* to Oenach Colmain,
festival at the Curragh in Kildare where horses raced on
the open plains

Poem in *The Book of Leinster* commemorating Oenach
Carmain, staged in Wexford during the calends of
August on every third year.

William Wilde's *Beauties of the Boyne and the Blackwater*
(1849): 'Such were the famous assemblies of ancient
Éire. May we live to see them renewed once more in
modern Ireland.'

Handball Chronology

1785   Print illustrating handball (in Monaghan County Museum).

1789   Thomas Buck Whalley won a wager of 100 guineas by playing handball off the walls of Jerusalem.

1790   A court near Rathangan in County Kildare bears the date 1790.

        Jack Fogarty of Carlow first to claim an Irish championship when he beat Kearns of Dublin (in an account by William Farrell).

1798   United Irishman Michael Boylan arrested playing handball in Collon.

1815   Ball-court built in the Royal Belfast Academical Institiute.

1819   Obituary of Corkman John Cavanagh described him as the greatest player of hand-fives in Ireland (*Cork Examiner*, 17 February 1819).

1854   Martin Butler of Kilkenny Ireland's champion ball player.

1870s William Baggs of Tipperary became the first established Irish champion. Baggs introduced the system of 15 or 21-ace championship matches.

1887 Phil Casey beat John Lawlor of Ireland by 5–6 in Cork and 7–0 in New York in 1887.

1902 Mick Egan (USA) beat James Fitzgerald (Ireland) 8–0 in San Francisco for the vacant title.

Oliver Drew from Ireland challenged Egan but Egan's manager refused to hand over the first day's takings and the match was never finished. Drew instead challenged and beat Francois Ordozgotti, pelota champion of France and Spain, for the European title.

1903 Mick Egan beat Ireland's Tim Twohill 7–0 in Jersey and 1–0 in Kanturk.

1909 Alley at the Boot Inn in Ballymun opened.

James Kelly (USA) beat John Joe Bowleys (Ireland) 5–2 in Limerick and 3–0 in Brooklyn to take the vacant world title, the last time it was contested.

1912 Irish Amateur Handball Union established.

1915 Softball game introduced to Ireland.

1924   Irish Amateur Handball Association established.

Americans win handball events at the Tailteann Games in Dublin.

1925   Irish amateur handball association championship.

1930   Irish amateur handball Union disbands.

1929 and **1932** Pelota players tour Ireland.

1957   New York athletic club team toured Ireland.

1964   World handball championships in New York.

1967   World handball championships in Toronto won by Louth born Joey Maher representing Canada.

1970   World handball championship in Croke Park's new 1800-capacity glass-walled alley.

1973   RTE Top Ace television tournament inaugurated.

1974   Handballers from Canada, Ireland and Mexico have competed in the US Handball Association open championships.

1984   World handball championship revived in Croke Park with 40 x 20 and 60 x 30 championships were both held.

1986 World handball championships in Canada.

1988 World handball championships in Australia.

1991 World handball championships in Phoenix, Arizona.

1994 World handball championships in Dublin.

1999 World handball championships in Chicago.

2003 World handball championships in Dublin.

Players Who Won All-Ireland Medals after they had Retired

1. D.J. Carey *(Kilkenny)* retired 1998 won 2000, 2002, 2003 medals.

2. Jimmy Keaveney *(Dublin)* retired 1973 won 1974, 1976, 1977 medals.

3. Brendan Lynskey *(Galway)* retired 1984 won 1987, 1988 medals.

4. Gerry McEntee *(Meath)* retired 1987 won 1988 medal.

5. Mick O'Connell *(Kerry)* retired 1966 won 1969, 1970 medals.

6. Mick O'Dwyer *(Kerry)* retired 1966 won 1969, 1970 medals.

7. Des Ferguson *(Dublin)* retired 1962, won 1963 medal.

8. Jim Kearney *(Meath)* retired 1945, won 1949 medal.

Early GAA Contacts Abroad

The Kentucky Guards Hurling Club

A year after it was founded in Hoboken in 1858, a Grand Council of Irish Hurlers was established in King's County, Brooklyn, to organise 19 wards of the city. There were 3,000 people in the council and Oliver Cotter was elected 'grand scribe'.

The Irish Athletic club in Boston

This was the first American unit to affiliate to the infant GAA and in June 1886 staged the first Gaelic sports in the United States.

Invasion of 1888

Fifty-one of the association's finest athletes went on an exhibition tour across America. Of the travelling party, 17 never returned. Pat Davin's account of the tour was published in 1938.

In America

GAA branches were formed in New York in 1891, and Brooklyn Wolfe Tones beat the Irish Americans in the continent's first hurling final in 1892.

In New York

In 1904, the Irish Counties Athletic Union took control of GAA affairs in New York. It was superseded in 1914 by the New York GAA, which affiliated to the

GAA in Ireland. Chicago had 15-team club league in operation in the 1890s, while Philadelphia, San Francisco and Detroit had GAA organisations from early days. In 1911, a team of Chicago hurlers toured Ireland.

In Australia

Hurling was recorded in Kyneton, and the southwestern Victorian towns of Warranambool and Koroit and Port Fairy in 1881. In 1886, hurling matches were being played under GAA rules and medals for an 1898 final were presented by Larry Foley, bare-knuckle boxing champion of Australia.

Newspaper References to Pre-GAA Hurling

Dublin Flying Post	28 June 1708 and 19 June 1708
London Daily Advertiser	28 September 1747
Dublin Courant	21 May 1748, 31 May 1748, 4 June 1748 and 20 May 1749
Faulkner's Journal	7 June 1748
Finn's Leinster Journal	19 March 1760
Cork Evening Post	4 September 1769
Finn's Leinster	6 July 1768, 30 July 1768, 3 September 1768, 12 July 1769, 29 July 1769, 27 October 1770, 19 July 1776 and 29 August 1780
Dublin Evening Post	12 August 1779
Hibernian Journal	8 October 1792
Universal Advertiser	17 July 1753 and 27 September 1757
Freeman's Journal	4 October 1768
Hoey's Public Journal	14 August 1771
Hibernian Journal	8 October 1792 and 17 October 1792

Newspaper References to Pre-GAA Football

Dublin Courant	23 July 1745
Pue's Occurences	23 August 1746
Universal Advertiser	19 March 1754
Cork Evening Post	3 July 1754
Slater's Public Gazetteer	21 April 1759
Dublin Gazette	28 April 1765
Faulkner's Dublin Journal	15 April 1765 and 12 February 1779
Hibernian Journal	30 April 1774
The Observer	26 February 1792

Michael Cusack

1876   Born in Carron, County Clare.

1874   He first came in contact with handball and rugby football when he came to teach in Blackrock 'French' College.

1877   Set up his own academy.

1870s   The Irish Champion Athletic Club, the City and Suburban Harriers, the Irish Cross Country Association and the Dublin Athletic Club and became involved at committee level in all of them.

1881   Proposed a new body to control Irish athletics in 3 letters to the *Irish Sportsman*.

1882   Gaelic Union for the Preservation and Cultivation of the Irish language was formed in Cusack's Academy, Cusack became first treasurer, from this sprang a *Gaelic Journal*.

1882   Dublin Hurling Club founded by Cusack 'for the purposes of taking steps to re-establish the national game of hurling, so far as is practicable rules shall be framed to make a

transition from hurley to hurling as easy as the superiority of the latter game will permit'. It may have been directly as a result of the journal. It lasted just 4 months and legally disbanded in October 1882.

1883   Dublin Hurling Club became the Metropolitan Hurling Club. The club presented a Challenge Cup to be hurled for between Cusack's Metropolitans and Killimor Club on Ballinasloe Fair Green on Easter Sunday, 1884. The game in Ballinasloe was not a success and Cusack decided to form a national association to draw up rules for hurling.

1884   'A word about Irish athletics', published in the United Irishman.

1 November 1884, Cusack chose this date as a suitable date to found the GAA, as it commemorated the mythical date of the Battle of Cath Gabhra in which the power of the Fianna was said to have been ended in 294 AD.

Sending-Off Incidents in All-Ireland Finals

1887   Unnamed Galway hurler sent off for tripping by Pat McGrath, referee of the first All-Ireland hurling final between Tipperary's Thurles and Galway's Meelick.

1908   Dublin footballer sent off after 25 minutes against London by referee, Martin Conroy.

1914   Clare hurler sent off near end of All-Ireland hurling final against Laois by referee John Lalor (Kilkenny).

1916   Tommy Shanahan (Tipperary) and Dick Grace (Kilkenny) sent off by Waterford referee Willie Walsh in a famous Tipperary v. Kilkenny final. Kilkenny led by 2 points at the time but were beaten by 8.

1943   Cavan's Joe Stafford sent off for striking 10 minutes into the second half by Paddy Mythen (Wexford).

1959   Dick Carroll (Kilkenny) and John Barron (Waterford) sent off as the All-Ireland hurling final entered the last quarter by Limerick referee, G. Fitzgerald.

1961	Tommy Ryan (Tipperary) and Lar Foley (Dublin) sent off by Limerick referee G. Fitzgerald with 15 minutes to go in the All-Ireland hurling final.
1965	Derry O'Shea (Kerry) and John Donnellan (Galway) sent off in the 21st minute of the football final by Mick Loftus (Mayo).
1978	John McCarthy (Dublin) and Charlie Nelligan (Kerry) sent off by Seamus Aldridge of Kildare.
1979	Páidí Ó Sé (Kerry) sent off by Hugh Duggan of Armagh.
1983	A record 4 players – Brian Mullins, Ray Hazley and Ciaran Duff (Dublin) and Tomas Tierney (Galway) – sent off by Antrim referee, John Gough.
1988	Gerry McEntee (Meath) sent off against Cork.
1993	Tony Davis (Cork) sent off against Derry.
1995	Charlie Redmond (Dublin) sent off against Tyrone.
1996	Eamonn Scanlan (Wexford) sent off against Limerick.

173

1996   Liam McHale (Mayo) and Colm Coyle (Meath) sent off in football final replay.

2001   Nigel Nestor (Meath) sent off against Galway.

2003   Diarmaid Marsden (Armagh) sent off against Tyrone by referee Brian White (Wexford).

174

Players Who Returned after Serious Injury

1. Pat Spillane of Kerry, from a 1981–83 ligament
    injury.

2. Colm O'Rourke of Meath, from a 1977 ligament
    injury.

3. Brian Mullins of Dublin, from a badly broken leg
    in 1979.

4. Johnny Culloty of Kerry, back to play in goal after
    a leg injury.

5. Paddy Linden, back to win an Ulster medal after a
    serious car crash.

6. Ambrose Rodgers, from a cruciate ligament injury
    in 1987.

7. Mick O'Dwyer of Kerry, broke both legs in 1968.

The Top 20 GAA Moments

The incidents were selected by an RTÉ panel of journalists, pundits and ex-players, RTÉ viewers selected the order in May 2005.

1. Michael Donnellan's solo run in the 1998 All-Ireland final (**19.4%**).

2. Maurice Fitzgerald's sideline point against the Dubs in 2001 (**17.9%**).

3. Seamus Darby's goal to deny the Kingdom five in a row (**12.1%**).

4. John Fenton's ground-stroke in the 1987 Munster hurling semi-final (**11.6%**).

5. Davy Fitzgerald converts a penalty for Clare in the 1995 Munster final (**7.1%**).

6. Kevin Foley's goal in the epic 1991 Meath–Dublin battle (**4.9%**).

7. D.J. Carey's awe-inspiring point in the 2002 All-Ireland hurling final (**4.5%**).

8. Joe Connolly's victory speech after Galway won the 1980 hurling title (**3%**).

9. Total football as Jack O'Shea's goal helps Kerry win the 1981 final (**2.8%**).

10. Offaly steal victory in 1994's '5-minute final' **(2.6%)**.

11. Mattie McDonagh's goal sees Galway clinch three in a row in 1966 **(2.5%)**.

12. Kerry's Mikey Sheehy lobs Paddy Cullen in the 1978 football decider **(1.9%)**.

13. A bare-footed Babs Keating points for Tipp in the 1971 hurling final **(1.6%)**.

14. An injured Peter Canavan gets his just desserts in 2003 **(1.5%)**.

15. A young Jimmy Barry-Murphy goals for Cork in 1973 **(1.4%)**.

16. Eddie Keher fires 2–9 for the Cats in the 1972 hurling final **(1.3%)**.

17. Paddy Cullen's penalty save in the 1974 football final **(1%)**.

18. Barney Rock's bizarre goal in the 1987 league final **(1%)**.

19. Frank McGuigan's one-man show in the 1984 Ulster football final **(0.9%)**.

20. Offaly fans protest after the premature end to the 1998 All-Ireland hurling semi-final **(0.8%)**.

2

Counties

The GAA has done more than any other organisation to enshrine county identity through its well-supported inter-county competitions. The Angevin empire introduced *comtes* after 1210, after which they gradually replaced dioceses and kingdoms in the Irish landscape. Inter-county hurling matches were already taking place by the 18th century.

The county structure of English cricket was adopted by Irish cricket clubs in the 1850s and many counties formed cricket, polo and tennis clubs under the same organisation. Carlow rugby club and Limerick tennis club are examples of descendants of these original multi-sport county clubs. The GAA brought started organising competition for clubs within counties in 1886, the original county championships, and county teams replaced clubs in All-Ireland competition from 1891 on. After 1900, up to 7 English counties competed in the British leg of the All-Ireland championship. North America, New York, Canada and Europe subsequently became county boards. In 1903, the GAA adopted a proposal from Offaly, that King's County and Queen's County be called Offaly and Laois for GAA purposes. Derry was the last county to organise in 1909. The issue of county identity has interfered with local government attempts to change county boundaries, and is particularly strong in the 6 counties of Northern Ireland, whose counties were replaced by 26 separate civil administrations by the Stormont regime in the 1960s making accurate statistical information much more difficult to compile.

County Nicknames

Antrim	Glensmen, Saffrons
Armagh	Orchard county, Cathedral county
Carlow	Dolmen county, Fighting Cocks, Scallion Eaters
Cavan	Breffni
Clare	Banner county
Cork	Rebel county
Derry	Maiden city, Oakleaf county
Donegal	The Hills, Tirchonaill, O'Donnell county, Herring gutters
Down	Mourne county
Dublin	Liffeysiders, Jackeens
Fermanagh	Maguire county, Lakeland county
Galway	Tribesmen
Kerry	Kingdom
Kildare	Short Grass, Lilywhites, Thoroughbred county
Kilkenny	Cats, Noresiders, Marble county
Laois	O'Moore county, Azurri

Leitrim	Ridge county, Wild Rose county, O'Rourke county
Limerick	Shannonsiders, Treaty county
London	Boys from the county hell
Longford	Slashers
Louth	Wee county
Mayo	Green above the Red, Heather county, Maritime county
Meath	Royal county
Monaghan	Farney, Drumlin county
Offaly	Faithful county
Roscommon	Rossies, Sheep stealers
Sligo	Yeats county, Zebras, Magpies
Tipperary	Premier county
Tyrone	Red Hand, O'Neill county
Waterford	Deise, Suirsiders, Crystal county
Westmeath	Lake county
Wexford	Model county, Yellow Bellies
Wicklow	Garden county

County Colours

Antrim	saffron and white jerseys, white or black shorts
Armagh	orange jerseys, white shorts
Carlow	red, green and yellow
Cavan	royal blue jerseys, white shorts
Clare	saffron and blue
Cork	red jerseys, white shorts
Derry	white with red hoop
Donegal	green and gold
Down	red and black
Dublin	sky-blue jerseys with navy cuffs and shorts
Fermanagh	green and white
Galway	maroon and white
Gloucestershire	red and white
Hertfordshire	blue and gold stripes
Kerry	green with gold hoop, white shorts

Kildare	white jerseys, shorts and socks
Kilkenny	black and amber stripes
Lancashire	saffron
Laois	blue with white hoop
Leitrim	green with gold hoop
Limerick	green jerseys with white cuffs and shorts
London	green jerseys with white cuffs and shorts
Longford	blue and gold
Louth	red with white shorts
Mayo	green with red hoop, white shorts
Meath	green jersey with white shorts
Monaghan	white with blue collar, cuffs and shorts
New York	all white
Offaly	three broad green, white and orange hoops, white shorts
Roscommon	yellow with blue cuffs and collars

Sligo	white with black cuffs and collar, black shorts
Tipperary	blue with gold hoop, white shorts
Tyrone	white with red cuffs and collars, red shorts
Warwickshire	red jerseys with black cuffs and collars, black shorts
Waterford	all white
Westmeath	maroon and white
Wexford	Gold with purple top, white shorts
Wicklow	blue with gold hoop
Yorkshire	blue with wide gold hoop

Counties Ranked by Area

1. **Cork** 2,880 square miles (7,460 sq km, 1,842361 acres)

2. **Galway** 2,293 square miles (5,939 sq km, 1,466,852 acres)

3. **Mayo** 2,084 square miles (5,398 sq km, 796,000 acres)

4. **Donegal** 1,865 square miles (4,830 sq km, 1,333,153 acres)

5. **Kerry** 1,815 square miles (4,701 sq km, 1,161,072 acres)

6. **Tipperary** 1,643 square miles (4,254 sq km, 1,051,042 acres)

7. **Tyrone** 1,260 square miles (3,263 sq km, 806,033 acres)

8. **Clare** 1,231 square miles (3,188 sq km, 787,482 acres)

9. **Antrim** 1,176 square miles (3,046 sq km, 752,298 acres)

10. **Limerick** 1,037 square miles (2,686 sq km, 663,378 acres)

11. **Roscommon** 951 square miles (2,463 sq km, 608,363 acres)

12.	**Down**	945 square miles (2,447 sq km, 604,525 acres)
13.	**Wexford**	908 square miles (2,351 sq km, 580,856 acres)
14.	**Meath**	902 square miles (2,336 sq km, 577,017 acres)
15.	**Derry**	798 square miles (2,067 sq km, 510,488 acres)
16.	**Kilkenny**	796 square miles (2,062 sq km, 509,208 acres)
17.	**Wicklow**	782 square miles (2,025 sq km, 500,252 acres)
18.	**Offaly**	771 square miles (1,998 sq km, 493,216 acres)
19.	**Cavan**	730 square miles (1,891 sq km, 466,987 acres)
20.	**Fermanagh**	724 square miles (1,876 sq km, 463,149 acres)
21.	**Waterford**	710 square miles (1,838 sq km, 454,193 acres)
22.	**Sligo**	693 square miles (1,796 sq km, 443,318 acres)

188

23.	**Westmeath**	681 square miles (1,763 sq km, 435,642 acres)
24.	**Laois**	664 square miles (1,719 sq km, 424,767 acres)
25.	**Kildare**	654 square miles (1,694 sq km, 418,370 acres)
26.	**Leitrim**	589 square miles (1,525 sq km, 376,789 acres)
27.	**Monaghan**	498 square miles (1,291 sq km, 318,575 acres)
28.	**Armagh**	484 square miles (1,253 sq km, 309,619 acres)
29.	**Longford**	403 square miles (1,044 sq km, 257,803 acres)
30.	**Dublin**	356 square miles (922 sq km, 227,736 acres)
31.	**Carlow**	346 square miles (896 sq km, 221,339 acres)
32.	**Louth**	317 square miles (821 sq km, 202,788 acres)

Counties Ranked by Population

1.	**Dublin**	1,122,600
2.	**Antrim**	566,009
3.	**Down**	454,411
4.	**Cork**	448,181
5.	**Derry**	213,035
6.	**Galway**	208,826
7.	**Limerick**	175,529
8.	**Tyrone**	166,516
9.	**Kildare**	163,995
10.	**Armagh**	141,585
11.	**Tipperary**	140,281
12.	**Donegal**	137,383
13.	**Meath**	133,936
14.	**Kerry**	132,424
15.	**Mayo**	117,428
16.	**Wexford**	116,543

17.	**Wicklow**	114,719
18.	**Clare**	103,333
19.	**Louth**	101,802
20.	**Waterford**	101,518
21.	**Kilkenny**	80,421
22.	**Westmeath**	72,027
23.	**Offaly**	63,702
24.	**Laois**	58,732
25.	**Sligo**	58,178
26.	**Cavan**	56,416
27.	**Fermanagh**	54,033
28.	**Roscommon**	53,803
29.	**Monaghan**	52,772
30.	**Carlow**	45,845
31.	**Longford**	31,127
32.	**Leitrim**	25,815

191

Counties Ranked by GAA Clubs

#	County	Clubs
1.	Cork	259
2.	Dublin	211
3.	Wexford	187
4.	Meath	153
5.	Antrim	108
6.	Limerick	107
7.	Clare	88
8.	Galway	86
9.	Laois	85
10.	Offaly	85
11.	Tipperary	82
12.	Kerry	73
13.	Australia	70
14.	Down	70
15.	Kildare	70
16.	North American Board	70
17.	Tyrone	68

18.	**Wicklow**	65
19.	**Donegal**	63
20.	**Derry**	60
21.	**Cavan**	59
22.	**Armagh**	55
23.	**Waterford**	55
24.	**Mayo**	52
25.	**Louth**	51
26.	**Roscommon**	51
27.	**Sligo**	51
28.	**Fermanagh**	50
29.	**Monaghan**	50
30.	**New York**	50
31.	**Westmeath**	48
32.	**Longford**	47
33.	**Kilkenny**	41
34.	**London**	38
35.	**Leitrim**	33

193

194

2

Counties Ranked by Success

	Senior	NL	U-21	Minor	Inter	Junior	Senior B
1. Cork	35	19	20	28	4	23	0
2. Kerry	33	16	9	1	0	15	3
3. Tipperary	29	18	8	7	5	12	1
4. Kilkenny	28	11	8	18	1	9	0
5. Dublin	28	10	1	4	0	8	0
6. Galway	13	11	2	10	2	6	0
7. Wexford	11	4	1	3	2	3	0
8. Limerick	9	11	4	3	1	4	0

	Senior	NL	U-21	Minor	Inter	Junior	Senior B
9. Meath	7	7	1	3	0	10	1
10. Offaly	7	2	1	4	0	2	0
11. Down	5	4	1	3	0	2	0
12. Cavan	5	1	0	2	0	1	0
13. Kildare	4	1	0	0	12	2	3
14. Mayo	3	11	3	6	0	8	0
5. Clare	3	3	0	2	0	2	1
16. Roscommon	2	1	2	3	0	5	1
17. Waterford	2	1	0	2	0	3	0

	Senior	NL	U-21	Minor	Inter	Junior	Senior B
18. Derry	1	5	2	4	0	2	1
19. Tyrone	1	2	0	5	0	1	0
20. Laois	1	2	0	3	0	1	3
21. Donegal	1	0	2	0	0	0	0
22. Armagh	1	0	0	1	0	0	0
23. Louth	1	0	0	2	0	6	1
24. London	1	0	0	0	2	11	0
25. Monaghan	0	1	0	0	0	1	1
26. Longford	0	1	0	0	0	1	0

	Senior	NL	U-21	Minor	Inter	Junior	Senior B
27. Westmeath	0	1	0	1	0	2	3
28. Antrim	0	0	1	0	0	1	4
29. Carlow	0	0	0	0	1	0	1
30. Fermanagh	0	0	0	0	0	1	2
31. Wicklow	0	0	0	0	0	4	1
32. Leitrim	0	0	0	0	0	0	1
33. Sligo	0	0	0	0	0	1	0
34. Warwickshire	0	0	0	0	0	3	0
35. Hertfordshire	0	0	0	0	0	1	0

2

Ground Capacity at County Grounds

Antrim	Casement Park, Belfast	32,500
Armagh	Athletic Grounds	n/a
Carlow	Dr Cullen Park, Carlow	19,000
Cavan	Breffni Park, Cavan	20,000
Clare	Cusack Park, Ennis	24,000
Cork	Páirc Uí Chaoimh, Cork	39,000
Derry	Celtic Park	18,000
Donegal	MacCumhaill Park, Ballybofey	17,500
Down	Pairc Esler, Newry	19,000
Dublin	Parnell Park, Dublin	11,000
Fermanagh	Brewster Park, Enniskillen	18,000
Galway	Pearse Stadium, Galway	35,000
Galway	Tuam Stadium, Tuam	30,000
Kerry	Austin Stack Park, Tralee	14,000
Kerry	Fitzgerald Stadium, Killarney	39,000
Kildare	St Conleth's Park, Newbridge	13,000

Kilkenny	Nowlan Park, Kilkenny	26,300
Laois	O'Moore Park, Portlaoise	27,000
Leitrim	Páirc Sean Mac Diarmada, Carrick-on-Shannon	13,500
Limerick	Gaelic Grounds, Limerick	30,000
Longford	Pearse Park, Longford	12,000
Louth	O'Rahilly's Ground, Drogheda	7,500
Mayo	McHale Park, Castlebar	35,000
Meath	Páirc Tailteann, Navan	29,000
Monaghan	St Tiernach's Park, Clones	36,000
Offaly	O'Connor Park, Tullamore	16,000
Offaly	St Brendan's Park, Birr	11,000
Roscommon	Hyde Park, Roscommon	25,000
Sligo	Markievicz Park, Sligo	13,000
Tipperary	Semple Stadium, Thurles	49,000
Tyrone	Healy Park, Omagh	18,000
Waterford	Fisher's Field, Dungarvan	n/a
Waterford	Walsh Park, Waterford	16,600

Westmeath	Cusack Park, Mullingar	15,000
Wexford	Wexford Park, Wexford	25,000
Wicklow	Aughrim	7,000

Counties Ranked by Registered GAA Teams

1.	**Cork**	2,465
2.	**Tipperary**	1,354
3.	**Dublin**	1,344
4.	**Limerick**	1,177
5.	**Wexford**	1,037
6.	**Galway**	1,029
7.	**Kerry**	831
8.	**Antrim**	740
9.	**Kilkenny**	729
10.	**Waterford**	696
11.	**Kildare**	652
12.	**Meath**	599
13.	**Clare**	592
14.	**Laois**	556
15.	**Mayo**	516

203

Counties Ranked by Adult Football Teams

1.	Cork	442
2.	Dublin	236
3.	Kerry	181
4.	Galway	174
5.	Meath	168
5.	Tipperary	168
7.	Limerick	143
8.	Kildare	136
9.	Mayo	134
10.	Tyrone	133
11.	Wexford	129
12.	Donegal	111
13.	Cavan	110
14.	Waterford	109
15.	Laois	105

205

Counties Ranked by Adult Hurling Teams

1.	**Cork**	348
2.	**Tipperary**	208
3.	**Galway**	159
4.	**Limerick**	158
5.	**Dublin**	136
6.	**Wexford**	134
7.	**Kilkenny**	125
8.	**Waterford**	108
9.	**Clare**	99
10.	**Laois**	83
11.	**Offaly**	74
12.	**Antrim**	67
13.	**Meath**	64
14.	**Westmeath**	42
15.	**Kerry**	36

15.	**Kildare**	36
17.	**Carlow**	32
18.	**Wicklow**	30
19.	**Down**	23
20.	**Roscommon**	22
21.	**Derry**	16
22.	**Armagh**	10
22.	**Longford**	10
22.	**Mayo**	10
25.	**Donegal**	9
25.	**Louth**	9
25.	**Monaghan**	9
28.	**Sligo**	7
28.	**Tyrone**	7
30.	**Fermanagh**	5
30.	**Leitrim**	5
32.	**Cavan**	2

Counties Ranked by Youth Football Teams

1.	**Cork**	903
2.	**Dublin**	588
3.	**Kerry**	484
3.	**Tipperary**	484
5.	**Limerick**	433
6.	**Kildare**	355
7.	**Galway**	350
8.	**Mayo**	344
9.	**Donegal**	334
10.	**Louth**	300
11.	**Antrim**	298
12.	**Tyrone**	289
13.	**Wexford**	267
14.	**Meath**	264
15.	**Kilkenny**	249
16.	**Wicklow**	231

209

Counties Ranked by Youth Hurling Teams

1.	**Cork**	772
2.	**Tipperary**	494
3.	**Limerick**	443
4.	**Wexford**	407
5.	**Dublin**	384
6.	**Galway**	346
7.	**Antrim**	287
7.	**Kilkenny**	287
9.	**Waterford**	259
10.	**Clare**	215
11.	**Wicklow**	179
12.	**Laois**	169
13.	**Offaly**	138
14.	**Kerry**	130
15.	**Kildare**	125

211

County Songs

Less a part of big-match ritual than in the past, county songs evolved from the community singing that was part of match-day ceremonial from the 1930s to the 1950s. The three most famous songs – 'The Banks of My Own Lovely Lee' (Cork), 'Slievenamon' (Tipperary) and 'The Rose of Mooncoin' (Kilkenny) – date from this period.

Some were specially written, 'The Offaly Rover', 'Beautiful Meath' and 'Lovely Leitrim' are of recent origin. 'Bhí sé Lá Pórt Láirge' was voted as the Waterford song by listeners of the local radio station. 'Sliabh Geal gCúa' was the county song in 1957, 'Dungarvan My Home Town' in 1959 and 1963.

GAA staff member Seán O Síocháin wrote rallying songs for Roscommon and Kerry in 1944 but, by and large, the GAA chose songs that could be easily sung by the largest number of supporters.

'Twenty Men From Dublin Town' was Dublin's song until 1963, when it was replaced by 'Molly Malone' in 1974.

'Killarney' was sung for the Kerry team in 1938, in 1940 this was changed to the 'Rose of Tralee' and although 'An Poc ar Bhuile' was sung from the podium by Páidí Ó Sé in 1985, 'the Rose' remains the Kerry song.

'The Men of the West' was shared by Galway, Mayo and Roscommon until the 1950s. 'Galway Bay' replaced 'The Queen of Connemara' as the Galway song after 1955, it was in turn superseded by 'The Fields of Athenry'.

'Boolavogue' replaced 'Kelly from Killane' as the Wexford song in 1955, in turn the 1996 hit 'Dancing at the Crossroads' has increasingly come to replace 'Boolavogue'.

'Paddy Reilly' replaced 'The Flower of Finae' as the Cavan song in 1945. It was temporarily displaced by 'Eileen Og' as the Cavan song in 1948, recently 'My Cavan Girl' has begun to supersede it.

'Roddy McCorley' served Derry in 1958, by 1993 Phil Coulter's 'The Town I Loved so Well' had replaced it.

'Among the Wicklow Hills' has replaced 'Meeting of the Waters' as the Wicklow song.

The Artane Band now brings together the best musicians in the greater Dublin region – the school closed in 1969 and the band went co-ed in September 2002 – and has a designated song for most counties.

Songs for Fermanagh, Longford, Louth and Monaghan are still matters for discussion. 'Tomáil Leanaí in Bhábhdhuin' was the Louth song in 1957 but the 'Turfman From Ardee' has served in recent years.

Antrim	'Green Glens of Antrim'
Armagh	'Boys From the County Armagh'
Carlow	'Follow me up to Carlow'
Cavan	'My Cavan Girl' (formerly 'Come Back Paddy Reilly')
Clare	'My Lovely Rose of Clare'
Cork	'Banks of my Own Lovely Lee'
Derry	'The Town I Love So Well'
Donegal	'Mary From Dungloe'
Down	'Star of the County Down'
Dublin	'Molly Malone'
Fermanagh	'Farewell to Enniskillen'
Galway	'Fields of Athenry (formerly 'Galway Bay')
Kerry	'Rose of Tralee'
Kildare	'Curragh of Kildare'
Kilkenny	'Rose of Mooncoin'
Laois	'Lovely Laois'
Leitrim	'Lovely Leitrim'
Limerick	'Limerick you are a Lady'

Longford	'County Longford' (formerly 'Abbeyshrule')
Louth	'Turfman from Ardee'
Mayo	'Moonlight in Mayo'
Meath	'Beautiful Meath'
Monaghan	'The Town Of Ballybay'
Offaly	'Offaly Rover'
Roscommon	'Men of Roscommon'
Sligo	'Sally Gardens'
Tipperary	'Slievenamon'
Tyrone	'O'Neill's March'
Waterford	'Bhí sé Lá Pórt Láirge'
Westmeath	'Lough Ree oh Lough Ree'
Wexford	'Dancing at the Crossroads' (formerly 'Boolavogue')
Wicklow	'Among the Wicklow Hills' (formerly 'Meeting of the Waters')

Sponsors

Antrim	Bushmills
Armagh	Morgan
Carlow	Stone Developments
Cavan	Kingspan
Clare	*Hurling*: Pat O'Donnell
	Football: M. Donnelly
Cork	ESAT
Derry	Sperrin Metal
Donegal	Donegal Creameries
Down	Canal Court Hotel
Dublin	Arnott's
Fermanagh	Tracey Concrete
Galway	*Football*: Tommy Varden
	Hurling: Supermacs
Kerry	Kerry Group
Kildare	Tegral
Kilkenny	Avonmore

Laois	*Football*: Montague Hotel
	Hurling: Killeshin Hotel
Leitrim	Masonite
Limerick	SW Health Board Drug Campaign
Longford	Longford Arms Hotel
Louth	AIBP
Mayo	Staunton's Intersport
Meath	Kepak
Monaghan	J. G. Kelly
Offaly	Carroll Meats
Roscommon	*Football*: 747 Travel
	Hurling: Casey's Ford
Sligo	Clifford Electrical
Tipperary	Finches
Tyrone	W. J. Dolan
Waterford	*Hurling*: Gain Feeds
	Football: Lawlors Hotel
Westmeath	Greville Arms Hotel
Wexford	Wexford Creamery
Wicklow	Wicklow County Council

3

Catechism of Cliché

A Catechism of Great Football and Hurling Clichés

What counts at this level of the game?
Class.

What sort of road did the two teams travel to the All-Ireland finals?
The long and rocky one.

What sharply descending treatment was accorded the star player left out of the team?
He was dropped.

Or else (more judiciously)?
He got left on the bench.

Despite what?
His unrelenting service to his county.

From which physiological ailment did the team suffer when they failed to score any goals for several matches?
A drought.

What footwear did they manage to leave behind?
Their shooting boots.

And what wise words were they following?

Go for the points and let the goals look after themselves.

Until they indulged in what act of cruelty against our feathered friends?

They broke their duck.

By following which destruction-inducing game plan?

They took the breaks at midfield.

And which numeric balls favoured them?

The 50–50 balls.

Describe the bedclothes of the goalkeeper who did not let in any goals?

He kept a clean sheet.

Did one team win the game?

No, they defeated, routed, annihilated, humiliated, pasted, trounced, squeezed by, or overcame the opposition.

And did the other team lose?

No, they slipped up, collapsed, succumbed, and caved in.

Was the first goal scored at the end of the first half?

Yes, at the psychological moment.

From where was the goal scored?

From the spot.

How did the referee award the penalty?
He had no hesitation.

And what did the kicker do?
He calmly stepped up.

Did he decide where he was going to kick it?
No, he picked his spot.

Did he score?
No, he hammered it into the onion sack.

Or what else?
He booted the leather home.

Past whom?
The hapless custodian.

What act of generosity did he show towards the goalkeeper?
He gave him no chance.

How did the hapless custodian look?
The picture of dejection.

What saccharine taste now affected the taste buds after a previous defeat taste?
It was sweet revenge.

Did the game get rough?
No, hard knocks were given and taken.

Or what else?
It was a hard-fought, physical encounter.

In what penal activity do these teams not indulge?
Taking any prisoners.

At what temperature did the fight start?
Tempers boiled over.

And in what did they indulge themselves?
They indulged in fisticuffs.

And was there a spot of Yiddish algebraic activity?
Yes, a schemozzle in the square.

What sort of scenes resulted?
Scenes that were less than edifying.

To what must it be put down?
A little bit of harmless overenthusiasm.

In whose opinion?
Old timers.

Who cherish what idyllic memory?
The days when men were men.

And did not engage in what long-distance female accoutrements?

Handbags at twenty paces.

To whom did all eyes turn?

The man in the middle.

And what did the referee do?

He reached for the card.

And the player?

He took the long and lonely walk to the dressing room.

And then?

He took an early bath.

How did the player get injured?

He was in the wars.

Was he pushed off the ball?

No, he was unceremoniously bundled off the ball.

And where did he end up?

On the deck.

What happened the injured player?

He was stretchered off.

Of what nature was his loss?
Irreparable.

But he will survive because of how tough he is?
Yes, tough-as-teak.

And after the rain came what happened the pitch?
It turned into a sea of mud.

When did the second goal come?
In the second moiety.

What transaction was involved in scoring?
They opened their account.

And, sticking to finance, what about the other team's account?
They were bankrupt of ideas.

And in what major neglect of their domicile did they partake?
They didn't mind their house.

Was it a low shot?
No, a daisy-cutter.

What did the defenders do to the centre-forward?
They denied him possession at all costs.

But what could he do?

He could take on defences with impunity.

When was the winning goal scored?

As the seconds ticked away.

What distinguished this goal from the others?

It was the match-winner.

Where did that put them?

On the high road to victory.

What did it ruin?

An unblemished record.

What class of agricultural activity were the team engaged in when they scored?

A last-ditch effort.

And what did that do for the game?

It snatched victory from the jaws of defeat.

What effect did this have on the furniture?

It turned the tables.

And why should librarians be worried about it?

It was a turn-up for the books.

Until what part of it was over?

All of it.

Except for what vociferous activity?

Bar the shouting.

What sort of finish was it?

A grandstand finish.

Of what was it typical?

Of all that is best in the game.

How will it be remembered?

As a pulsating, epic encounter between two giants of the game.

What about the losing team?

They fought a gallant rear-guard action.

Did they get tired?

No, they ran out of legs.

And in what did they struggle?

They struggled in vain.

What was not between them?

The puck of a ball.

And what mishaps didn't they get?

They didn't get the breaks.

They played well but for what is there no substitute?
For victory.

On what were the winning fans transported?
They were carried away on a tide of emotion.

But what about the championship as a whole?
It failed to measure up to expectations.

Which All-Ireland championship was won in the end?
The coveted one.

And to where did it bring the winners?
To the pinnacle of the game.

And what did it achieve for the espionage business?
It was a credit to the code.

And now where has the championship gone?
It has gone into the annals.

4

Teams

W ho were the greatest players? Who were the greatest in each position? Since Gaelic football and hurling players started playing in clearly defined zones on the field, selecting all-time teams has become a bit of an obsession among fans. Here is a small ample of some of the teams that were picked by observers of the games and the results of the most exciting team-picking competition of them all, the annual selection of the All-Stars in each position. Watch for that neat trick on the part of selectors down the ages, moving a player to an unfamiliar position to get more than one of their favourites on to the team. It works with the Under-12s, so why not the all stars?

233

Football Team of the Millennium

Selected by a panel in 1999. No one on either of the football or hurling teams predates the 1940s.

1. Dan O'Keefe *(Kerry)*
2. Enda Colleran *(Galway)*
3. Joe Keohane *(Kerry)*
4. Sean Flanagan *(Mayo)*
5. Sean Murphy *(Kerry)*
6. John Joe O'Reilly *(Cavan)*
7. Martin O'Connell *(Meath)*
8. Mick O'Connell *(Kerry)*
9. Tommy Murphy *(Laois)*
10. Sean O'Neill *(Down)*
11. Sean Purcell *(Galway)*
12. Pat Spillane *(Kerry)*
13. Mikey Sheehy *(Kerry)*
14. Tommy Langan *(Mayo)*
15. Kevin Heffernan *(Dublin)*

Hurling Team of the Millennium

1. Tony Reddin *(Tipperary)*
2. John Doyle *(Tipperary)*
3. Nick O'Donnell *(Wexford)*
4. Bobby Rackard *(Wexford)*
5. Paddy Phelan *(Kilkenny)*
6. John Keane *(Waterford)*
7. Brian Whelehan *(Offaly)*
8. Jack Lynch *(Cork)*
9. Lory Meagher *(Kilkenny)*
10. Christy Ring *(Cork)*
11. Mick Mackey *(Limerick)*
12. Jim Langton *(Kilkenny)*
13. Eddie Keher *(Kilkenny)*
14. Ray Cummins *(Cork)*
15. Jimmy Doyle *(Tipperary)*

Hurling Team of the Century (1984)

Nominated by *Sunday Independent* readers and selected by panel of experts including journalists and former players.

1. Tony Reddan *(Tipperary)*
2. Bobby Rackard *(Wexford)*
3. Nick O'Donnell *(Wexford)*
4. John Doyle *(Tipperary)*
5. Jimmy Finn *(Tipperary)*
6. John Keane *(Waterford)*
7. Paddy Phelan *(Kilkenny)*
8. Lory Meagher *(Kilkenny)*
9. Jack Lynch *(Waterford)*
10. Christy Ring *(Cork)*
11. Mick Mackey *(Limerick)*
12. Jimmy Langton *(Kilkenny)*
13. Jimmy Doyle *(Tipperary)*
14. Nicky Rackard *(Wexford)*
15. Eddie Keher *(Kilkenny)*

Hurling Team of the Century Who Have Never Won an All Ireland (1984)

Nominated by *Sunday Independent* readers and selected by panel of experts including journalists and former players.

1. Sean Duggan *(Galway)*
2. Jim Fives *(Waterford)*
3. Noel Drumgoole *(Dublin)*
4. John Joe Doyle *(Clare)*
5. Sean Herbert *(Limerick)*
6. Sean Stack *(Clare)*
7. Colm Doran *(Wexford)*
8. Joe Salmon *(Galway)*
9. Pat Jobber McGrath *(Westmeath)*
10. Jozei Gallagher *(Galway)*
11. Martin Quigley *(Wexford)*
12. Kevin Armstrong *(Antrim)*
13. Jimmy Smyth *(Clare)*
14. Christy O'Brien *(Laois)*
15. Mick Bermingham *(Dublin)*

Football Team of the Century (1984)

Nominated by *Sunday Independent* readers and selected by panel of experts including journalists and former players.

1. Dan O'Keeffe *(Kerry)*
2. Enda Colleran *(Galway)*
3. Paddy O'Brien *(Meath)*
4. Sean Flanagan *(Mayo)*
5. Sean Murphy *(Kerry)*
6. John Joe O'Reilly *(Cavan)*
7. Stephen White *(Louth)*
8. Mick O'Connell *(Kerry)*
9. Jack O'Shea *(Kerry)*
10. Sean O'Neill *(Down)*
11. Sean Purcell *(Galway)*
12. Pat Spillane *(Kerry)*
13. Mike Sheehy *(Kerry)*
14. Tom Langan *(Mayo)*
15. Kevin Heffernan *(Dublin)*

Football Team of the Century Who Have Never Won an All Ireland (1984)

Nominated by *Sunday Independent* readers and selected by panel of experts including journalists and former players.

1. Aidan Brady *(Roscommon)*
2. Willie Casey *(Mayo)*
3. Eddie Boyle *(Louth)*
4. John McKnight *(Armagh)*
5. Gerry O'Reilly *(Wicklow)*
6. Gerry O'Malley *(Roscommon)*
7. Sean Quinn *(Armagh)*
8. Jim Mc Keever *(Derry)*
9. Tommy Murphy *(Laois)*
10. Sean O'Connell *(Derry)*
11. Packie McGarty *(Leitrim)*
12. Michael Kearins *(Sligo)*
13. Charlie Gallagher *(Cavan)*
14. Willie McGee *(Mayo)*
15. Dinny Allen *(Cork)*

Greatest Rounders Players of All-Time

Men

1. Eddie Healey, outfield *(Limekiln, Dublin)* 2002–2004
2. Gary Reilly, 1st base *(Erne Eagles, Cavan)* 1998–2004
3. Damien Mc Ardle, 3rd base *(Erne Eagles, Cavan)* 1998–2004
4. Kevin O'Hagan, shortstop *(Ní Mhíchíl, Derry)* 1997
5. Paul Jennings, pitcher *(Breaffy, Mayo)* 1992–1995
6. Robert Fahy, catcher *(Breaffy, Mayo)* 1992–1995
7. Lawrence Mc Cann, outfield *(Cargin, Derry)* 1987–1989
8. Alan Byrne, catcher *(Lakelands, Dublin)* 1982–1986
9. Tony Davis, 1st base *(Lakelands, Dublin)* 1982–1986

Women

1. Elaine Costello, pitcher *(Limekiln, Dublin)*
    2000–2004
2. Louise Clarke, pitcher *(Bagenalstown, Carlow)*
    2001–2003
3. Tara Corrigan, catcher *(Rathdowney, Laois)*
    1997–2002
4. Bernie Bowe, outfield *(Rathdowney, Laois)*
    1997–2002
5. Fiona Golden, pitcher *(Castlebar, Mayo)* 1992–1996
6. Mary Touhey, catcher *(Castlebar, Mayo)* 1992–1996
7. Deirdre Brennan, catcher *(Donagh, Monaghan)*
    1981–1983
8. Sarah Mc Coy, catcher *(St Ergnats, Antrim)* 1980
9. Barnadette Kelly, catcher *(Erins Own, Antrim)*
    1976–1979

Dick Fitzgerald's Best Players (1914)

Dick Fitzgerald named the 42 best players of his era in his instructional manual *How to Play Gaelic Football*. He included 26 from Kerry, 6 form Kildare, 5 from Cork, 2 each from Louth and Wexford from 1 from Waterford. Kerry had dominated the preceding decade, but though Dublin had 11 titles to Kerry's 5, Dublin didn't merit a single player in his list. Fitzgerald proclaimed 'there were so many great players from Dublin it would be an injustice to pick a few'.

Goalkeepers

Patrick Dillon *(Kerry)*, Dan Mullins *(Kerry)*, Dan Fraher *(Waterford)*, Thomas J Crowley *(Dunmanway, County Cork)*, Jack Fitzgerald *(Kildare)*

Full-Backs

Larry 'Hussey' Cribben *(Kildare)*, Mick Fitzgerald *(Kildare)*, Edmund Wheeler *(Wexford)*, Maurice McCarthy *(Kerry)*, Roddy Kirwan *(Kerry)*, Tom Costelloe *(Kerry)*

Half-Backs

Jim Smith *(Louth)*, Tom Rice *(Kerry)*, Jim Kennelly *(Kerry)*, Mick Mehigan *(Cork)*, Austin Stack *(Kerry)*, Florence O'Sullivan *(Kerry)*

Midfielders
John Buckley *(Kerry)*, Billy Boxer O'Connor *(Kerry)*,
Con Murphy *(Kerry)*, James O'Shea *(Kerry)*

Forwards
Con Clifford *(Kerry)*, Johnny Skinner *(Kerry)*, Jack
Moriarty *(Kerry)*, Denis Doyle *(Kerry)*, John O'Mahoney
(Kerry), Paddy Cahill *(Kerry)*, Denis Breen *(Kerry)*, Thady
O'Gorman *(Kerry)*, Jim O'Gorman *(Kerry)*, John Joe
Rice *(Kerry)*, J. P. O'Sullivan *(Kerry)*, Dr William
O'Sullivan *(Kerry)*, Cornelius O'Sullivan *(Kerry)*, Billy
Mackessy *(Cork)*, Jerry Beckett *(Cork)*, Joe Rafferty
(Kildare), Frank 'Joyce' Conlan *(Kildare)*, Jem Scott
(Kildare), George Campbell *(Louth)*,   Johnny Rossiter
(Wexford)

Referees
Michael F. Crowe *(Dublin)*, J. McDonnell *(Kerry)*, Tom
Irwin *(Cork)*

John D. Hickey's Goalkeepers (1960)

Irish Independent GAA correspondent John D. Hickey selected the greatest goalkeepers of his time in 5-yearly intervals for the 1960 *Our Games Annual*.

Hurling
Tommy Daly *(Dublin* and *Clare)*, Skinny O'Meara *(Tipperary)*, Paddy Scanlon *(Limerick)*, Tom O'Meara *(Tipperary)*, Jimmy O'Connell *(Kilkenny)*, Jim Ware *(Waterford)*, Topny Reddan *(Tipperary)*, Sean Duggan *(Galway)*, Mick Cashan *(Cork)*, Ollie Walsh *(Kilkenny)*, Kevin Matthews *(Dublin)*

Football
Johnny McDonnell *(Dublin)*, Dan O'Keeffe *(Kerry)*, Sean Thornton *(Louth)*, Jack Mangan *(Galway)*, Aidan Brady *(Roscommon)*

Mick Mackey's Defenders (1964)

In an article for the 1964 *Our Games Annual*, Mick
Mackey picked out the best defenders of is playing
career.

Jim Regan *(Cork)*, John Maher *(Tipperary)*, Paddy Byrne
(Kilkenny), Dan Canniffe *(Dublin)*, John Keane
(Waterford), Larry Blake *(Clare)*, Matty Bourke *(Galway)*,
Paddy Clohessy *(Limerick)*

Leinster Camogie Team of Century (2004)

1. Kathleen Tonks *(Wexford)*
2. Liz Neary *(Kilkenny)*
3. Mary Sinnott *(Wexford)*
4. Bridget Doyle, *(Wexford)*
5. Ann Downey *(Kilkenny)*
6. Margaret O'Leary *(Wexford)*
7. Bridie Mc Garry *(Kilkenny)*
8. Kay Coady *(Dublin)*
9. Orla Ni Shiocháin *(Dublin)*
10. Kay Ryder *(Dublin)*
11. Miriam Malone *(Kildare)*
12. Kathleen Mills *(Dublin)*
13. Sophia Brack *(Dublin)*
14. Úna O'Connor *(Dublin)*
15. Angela Downey *(Kilkenny)*

Munster Hurling Team of Millennium (2000)

1. Tony Reddin *(Tipperary)*
2. John Doyle *(Tipperary)*
3. Brian Lohan *(Clare)*
4. Denis Murphy *(Cork)*
5. Jimmy Finn *(Tipperary)*
6. John Keane *(Waterford)*
7. Jackie Power *(Limerick)*
8. Jack Lynch *(Cork)*
9. Phil Grimes *(Waterford)*
10. Jimmy Doyle *(Tipperary)*
11. Mick Mackey *(Limerick)*
12. Christy Ring *(Cork)*
13. Jimmy Smyth *(Clare)*
14. Ray Cummins *(Cork)*
15. Paddy Barry *(Cork)*

Connacht Football Team of the Millennium (2000)

1. Johnny Geraghty *(Galway)*
2. Willie Casey *(Mayo)*
3. Paddy Prendergast *(Mayo)*
4. Sean Flanagan *(Mayo)*
5. Brendan Lynch *(Roscommon)*
6. Gerry O Malley *(Roscommon)*
7. Martin Newell *(Galway)*
8. Padraig Kearney *(Mayo)*
9. Nace O Dowd *(Sligo)*
10. Kevin Winston *(Roscommon)*
11. Sean Purcell *(Galway)*
12. Mickey Kearins *(Sligo)*
13. Tony McManus *(Roscommon)*
14. Tom Langan *(Mayo)*
15. Packie McGarty *(Leitrim)*

Tipperary Hurling Team of the Millennium (2000)

1. Tony Reddan *(Lorrha)*
2. Mickey Byrne *(Sarsfields)*
3. Tony Brennan *(Clonoulty-Rossmore)*
4. John Doyle *(Holycross-Ballycahill)*
5. Jimmy Finn *(Borrisoleigh)*
6. Tony Wall *(Sarsfields)*
7. Tommy Doyle *(Sarsfields)*
8. Mick Roche *(Carrick Davins)*
9. Theo English *(Marlfield)*
10. Jimmy Doyle *(Sarsfields)*
11. Mick Ryan *(Roscrea)*
12. Liam Devaney *(Borrisoleigh)*
13. Paddy Kenny *(Borrisoleigh)*
14. Martin Kennedy *(Kiladangan)*
15. Nicky English *(Lattin-Cullen)*

Galway Football Team of Millennium (2000)

1. Johnny Geraghty
2. Enda Colleran
3. Noel Tierney
4. Tom 'Pook' Dillon
5. John Donnelan
6. Tommy Joe Gilmore
7. Sean Og de Paor
8. John 'Tull' Dunne
9. Mattie McDonagh
10. Cyril Dunne
11. Sean Purcell
12. Seamus Leydon
13. John Keenan
14. Frank Stockwell
15. Brendan Nestor

Galway Hurling Team of Millennium (2000)

1. Seanie Duggan
2. Sylvie Linnane
3. Conor Hayes
4. Mick Dervan
5. Pete Finnerty
6. Sean Silke
7. Iggy Clark
8. Joe Salmon
9. Fr Paddy Gantly
10. Mick King
11. Joe Cooney
12. P. J. Molloy
13. Josie Gallagher
14. John Connolly
15. Noel Lane

P.D. Mehigan's Selections

P.D. Mehigan was the leading GAA journalist from the 1920s to the 1940s and had played hurling for London at the turn of the last century. He wrote several histories of the GAA and was correspondent for the *Cork Examiner*, writing under the pseudonym 'Carbery' and for *The Irish Times* under the byline 'Pato'.

Hurling

1. John Skinny O'Meara *(Tipperary)*
2. Dan Coughlan *(Cork)*
3. Sean Og Hanley *(Limerick)*
4. Mick Derivan *(Galway)*
5. Pat Stakelum *(Tipperary)*
6. James Kelleher *(Cork)*
7. Dick Grace *(Kilkenny)*
8. Lory Meagher *(Kilkenny)*
9. Jim Hurley *(Cork)*
10. Eugene Coughlan *(Cork)*
11. Mick Mackey *(Limerick)*
12. Tom Semple *(Tipperary)*
13. Mattie Power *(Kilkenny)*

14. Martin Kennedy *(Tipperary)*

15. Christy Ring *(Cork)*

(Gaelic Sportsman, 1956)

Football

1. Dan O'Keeffe *(Kerry)*

2. Maurice McCarty *(Kerry)*

3. Joe Barrett *(Kerry)*

4. Pat Prendergast *(Mayo)*

5. John Joe O'Reilly *(Cavan)*

6. Jack Higgins *(Kerry)*

7. Joe Rafferty *(Kildare)*

8. Con Brosnan *(Kerry)*

9. Jack Carvin *(Louth)*

10. Pat Cocker Daly *(Dublin)*

11. Paddy Moclair *(Mayo)*

12. Larry Stanley *(Kildare)*

13. Bill Mackessy *(Cork)*

14. Dick Fitzgerald *(Kerry)*

15. John Joe Sheey *(Kerry)*

Pádraig Puirséil's Selections

Pádraig Puirséil was the leading GAA journalist of his time and *Irish Press* GAA correspondent from the 1950s until 1979. His memory of matches went back to the 1930s.

Hurling

1. Tommy Daly *(Clare)*
2. Bobby Rackard *(Wexford)*
3. Nick O'Donnell *(Wexford)*
4. John Doyle *(Tipperary)*
5. John Keane *(Waterford)*
6. Mick Roche *(Tipperary)*
7. Paddy Phelan *(Kilkenny)*
8. Lory Meagher *(Kilkenny)*
9. Jack Lynch *(Cork)*
10. Josie Gallager *(Galway)*
11. Mick Mackey *(Limerick)*
12. Christy Ring *(Cork)*
13. Jimmy Doyle *(Tipperary)*
14. Nicky Rackard *(Wexford)*
15. Eddie Keher *(Kilkenny)*

(Published in *Our Games Annual* 1979)

Football

1. Tom Bourke *(Mayo)*
2. Jerome O'Shea *(Kerry)*
3. Joe Barrett *(Kerry)*
4. Sean Flanagan *(Mayo)*
5. Sean Murphy *(Kerry)*
6. Jack Higgins *(Kildare)*
7. John Joe O'Reilly *(Cavan)*
8. Padraig Kennedy *(Kerry)*
9. Tommy Murphy *(Laois)*
10. Phelim Murray *(Roscommon)*
11. Sean Purcell *(Galway)*
12. Paul Doyle *(Kildare)*
13. Paddy Moclair *(Mayo)*
14. Paddy McDonnell *(Dublin)*
15. Kevin Heffernan *(Dublin)*

(Published in *Gaelic Weekly*, 1961)

Paddy Downey's Hurling Team

Paddy Downey was GAA correspondent of the *Sunday Mail* and *The Irish Times* for 40 years, and covered all the major GAA occasions between the 1960s and the 1990s. 'I have chosen these teams from the best players I have seen in my time. This does not mean that I disagree with a small number of players chosen as "all time best" on the millennium teams whom I did not see – namely Paddy Phelan (left half-back) and Lory Meagher (midfield) of Kilkenny on the hurling team and Tommy Murphy of Laois (midfield) on the football team,' he said of his list.

1. Tony Reddan *(Tipperary)*
2. Bobby Rackard *(Wexford)*
3. Nick O'Donnell *(Wexford)*
4. John Doyle *(Tipperary)*
5. Jimmy Finn *(Tipperary)*
6. John Keane *(Waterford)*
7. Seán Óg Ó hAilpín *(Cork)*
8. Jack Lynch *(Cork)*
9. Joe Salmon *(Galway)*
10. Jim Langton *(Kilkenny)*
11. Mick Mackey *(Limerick)*
12. Christy Ring *(Cork)*
13. Jimmy Doyle *(Tipperary)*
14. Nick Rackard *(Wexford)*
15. Eddie Keher *(Kilkenny)*

Paddy Downey's Football Team

1. Dan O'Keeffe *(Kerry)*
2. Enda Colleran *(Galway)*
3. Paddy O'Brien *(Meath)*
4. Sean Flanagan *(Mayo)*
5. Sean Murphy *(Kerry)*
6. John Joe O'Reilly *(Cavan)*
7. Martin O'Connell *(Meath)*
8. Mick O'Connell *(Kerry)*
9. Jack O'Shea *(Kerry)*
11. Tony Tighe *(Cavan)*
12. Sean Purcell *(Galway)*
13. Paddy Doherty *(Down)*
13. Mike Sheehy *(Kerry)*
14. Sean O'Neill *(Down)*
15. Kevin Heffernan *(Dublin)*

Con Houlihan's Selections

Legendary *Evening Press* sportswriter Con Houlihan has been attending matches since the 1930s.

Hurling

1. Michael Walsh *(Kilkenny)*
2. Willie O'Connor *(Kilkenny)*
3. Pat Hartigan *(Limerick)*
4. John Horgan *(Cork)*
5. Brian Whelahan *(Offaly)*
6. Anthony Daly *(Clare)*
7. Seán Óg Ó hAilpín *(Cork)*
8. Johnny Dooley *(Offaly)*
9. Frank Kissane *(Kerry)*
10. Christy Ring *(Cork)*
11. Mick Mackey *(Limerick)*
12. Jimmy Barry Murphy *(Cork)*
13. Nicky English *(Tipperary)*
14. Tony Doran *(Wexford)*
15. Johnny Flaherty *(Offaly)*

Football

1. Johnny Culloty *(Kerry)*
2. Páidí Ó Sé *(Kerry)*
3. John O'Keeffe *(Kerry)*
4. Jim Deenihan *(Kerry)*
5. Declan Meehan *(Galway)*
6. Tadhg Crowley *(Cork)*
7. Anthony Rainbow *(Kildare)*
8. Jack O'Shea *(Kerry)*
9. Mick O'Connelly *(Kerry)*
10. Pat Spillane *(Kerry)*
11. Sean Purcell *(Galway)*
12. John Donellan *(Galway)*
13. Mike Sheehy *(Kerry)*
14. Jimmy Keaveney *(Dublin)*
15. John McCarthy *(Dublin)*

259

Raymond Smith's Hurling Selections

Raymond Smith was a Tipperary-born sports journalist who compiled several statistical and historical guides to Gaelic games.

1920–1935

1. Tommy Daly *(Clare)*
2. Eddie 'Marie' O'Connell *(Cork)*
3. Sean Og Murphy *(Cork)*
4. John Joe Doyle *(Clare)*
5. Jim 'Builder' Walsh *(Kilkenny)*
6. Jim Regan *(Cork)*
7. Paddy Phelan *(Kilkenny)*
8. Mick Gill *(Galway)*
9. Lory Meagher *(Kilkenny)*
10. Phil Cahill *(Tipperary)*
11. Mick King *(Galway)*
12. Eugene 'Eudie' Coughlan *(Cork)*
13. Mick 'Gah' Ahearne *(Cork)*
14. Martin Kennedy *(Tipperary)*
15. Mattie Power *(Kilkenny)*

1953–1965

1. Tony Reddan *(Tipperary)*
2. Bobby Rackard *(Wexford)*
3. Nick O'Donnell *(Wexford)*
4. John Doyle *(Tipperary)*
5. Jimmy Finn *(Tipperary)*
6. John Keane *(Waterford)*
7. Tommy Doyle *(Tipperary)*
8. Jack Lynch *(Cork)*
9. Timmy Ryan *(Limerick)*
10. Christy Ring *(Cork)*
11. Mick Mackey *(Limerick)*
12. Jimmy Doyle *(Tipperary)*
13. Jackie Power *(Limerick)*
14. Nicky Rackard *(Wexford)*
15. Tim Flood *(Wexford)*

Seán Óg Ó Ceallacháin's Selections

Seán Óg Ó Ceallacháin was a leading hurler, referee broadcaster and journalist.

Hurling 1940–1980

1. Noel Skehan *(Kilkenny)*
2. Bobby Rackard *(Wexford)*
3. Pat Hartigan *(Limerick)*
4. Tony O'Shaughnessy *(Cork)*
5. Jimmy Finn *(Tipperary)*
6. Ger Henderson *(Kilkenny)*
7. Seamus Cleere *(Kilkenny)*
8. Harry Grey *(Laois* and *Dublin)*
9. Joe Salmon *(Galway)*
10. Christy Ring *(Cork)*
11. Mick Mackey *(Limerick)*
12. Jimmy Langton *(Kilkenny)*
13. Jimmy Doyle *(Tipperary)*
14. Nicky Rackard *(Wexford)*
15. Eddie Keher *(Kilkenny)*

Football 1950–1980

1. Johnny Culloty *(Kerry)*
2. Enda Colleran *(Galway)*
3. Paddy O'Brien *(Meath)*
4. Sean Flanagan *(Mayo)*
5. Sean Murphy *(Kerry)*
6. Kevin Moran *(Dublin)*
7. Joe Lennon *(Down)*
8. Jack O'Shea *(Kerry)*
9. Brian Mullins *(Dublin)*
10. Matt Connor *(Offaly)*
11. Sean Purcell *(Galway)*
12. Pat Spillane *(Kerry)*
13. Mikey Sheehy *(Kerry)*
14. Sean O'Neill *(Down)*
15. Kevin Heffernan *(Dublin)*

Owen McCann's Selections

Owen McCann has been covering Gaelic games since the late 1940s when he started writing for *Empire News*. He has complied several GAA histories and is one of the leading authorities on the statistical history of the games.

Hurling

1. Noel Skehan *(Kilkenny)*
2. Phil 'Fan' Larkin *(Kilkenny)*
3. Pat Hartigan *(Limerick)*
4. John Doyle *(Tipperary)*
5. Brian Whelehan *(Offaly)*
6. Mick Roche *(Tipperary)*
7. Denis Coughlan *(Cork)*
8. Frank Cummins *(Kilkenny)*
9. John Fenton *(Cork)*
10. Nicky English *(Tipperary)*
11. Joe Cooney *(Galway)*
12. Christy Ring *(Cork)*
13. Jimmy Doyle *(Tipperary)*
14. D. J. Carey *(Kilkenny)*
15. Eddie Keher *(Kilkenny)*

Football

1. Thady Turbett *(Tyrone)*

2. Enda Colleran *(Galway)*

3. John O'Keeffe *(Kerry)*

4. Donie O'Sullivan *(Kerry)*

5. Tommy Drumm *(Dublin)*

6. Jack Mahon *(Galway)*

7. Martin O'Connell *(Meath)*

8. Jim McKeever *(Derry)*

9. Jack O'Shea *(Kerry)*

10. Sean O'Neill *(Down)*

11. Sean Purcell *(Galway)*

12. Paddy Doherty *(Down)*

13. Michael Sheehy *(Kerry)*

14. Peter Canavan *(Tyrone)*

15. Kevin Heffernan *(Dublin)*

Peadar O'Brien's Selections

Peadar O'Brien was GAA correspndent of the *Irish Press* from 1979 until the newspaper closed in 1995, and later GAA correspondent of *The Sun*.

Football

1. Dan O'Keeffe *(Kerry)*
2. Enda Colleran *(Galway)*
3. Paddy Prendergast *(Mayo)*
4. Sean Flanagan *(Mayo)*
5. Seamus Moynihan *(Kerry)*
6. Bill Carlos *(Roscommon)*
7. Martin O'Connell *(Meath)*
8. Jim McKeever *(Derry)*
9. Mick O'Connell *(Kerry)*
10. Sean O'Neill *(Down)*
11. Sean Purcell *(Galway)*
12. Mickey Kearins *(Sligo)*
13. Mikey Sheehy *(Kerry)*
14. Peter Canavan *(Tyrone)*
15. Peter McDermott *(Meath)*

Hurling

1. Sean Duggan *(Galway)*

2. Bobby Racklard *(Wexford)*

3. Nick O'Donnell *(Wexford* and *Dublin)*

4. John Doyle *(Tipperary)*

5. Brian Whelahan *(Offaly)*

6. Pat Henderson *(Kilkenny)*

7. T. J. Delaney *(Kilkenny)*

8. Joey Salmon *(Galway)*

9. Frank Cummins *(Kilkenny)*

10. D. J. Carey *(Kilkenny)*

11. Mick Mackey *(Limerick)*

12. Eddie Keher *(Kilkenny)*

13. Jim Doyle *(Tipperary)*

14. Nicky Rackard *(Wexford)*

15. Christy Ring *(Cork)*

267

Tommy Doyle's Hurling Selection

Tomy Doyle selected this time for his biography, *A Lifetime of Hurling* (1955).

1. Tony Reddan *(Tipperary)*
2. Johnny Leahy *(Tipperary)*
3. Sean Og Murphy *(Cork)*
4. John Joe Doyle *(Clare)*
5. John Keane *(Waterford)*
6. Paddy Clohessy *(Limerick)*
7. Paddy Phelan *(Kilkenny)*
8. Jim Hurley *(Cork)*
9. Lory Meagher *(Kilkenny)*
10. Christy Ring *(Cork)*
11. Mick Mackey *(Limerick)*
12. Phil Cahill *(Tipperary)*
13. Eugene 'Eudie' Coughlan *(Cork)*
14. Martin Kennedy *(Tipperary)*
15. Mattie Power *(Kilkenny)*

Jack Lynch's Hurling Selection

Jack Lynch won 6 All-Ireland medals in successive years in the 1940s and later served as Taoiseach 1966–73 and 1977–79.

1. Paddy Scanlon *(Limerick)*
2. Paddy Larkin *(Kilkenny)*
3. Nick O'Donnell *(Wexford)*
4. Willie Murphy *(Cork)*
5. Tommy Doyle *(Tipperary)*
6. John Keane *(Waterford)*
7. Bobby Rackard *(Wexford)*
8. Eugene 'Eudie' Coughlan *(Cork)*
9. Timmy Ryan *(Limerick)*
10. Christy Ring *(Cork)*
11. Mick Mackey *(Limerick)*
12. Jimmy Langton *(Kilkenny)*
13. Eddie Keher *(Kilkenny)*
14. Nicky Rackard *(Wexford)*
15. Josie Gallagher *(Galway)*

1928 Tailteann Games Irish Football Team

Ireland played the USA as part of the Tailteann Games programme. The team was regarded as the best players of the era in each position.

1. John McDonnell *(Dublin)*
2. Tom Shevlin *(Roscommon)*
3. Matt Goff *(Kildare)*
4. Joe Barrett *(Kerry)*
5. Frank Malone *(Kildare)*
6. Jack Higgins *(Kildare)*
7. Paul Russell *(Kerry)*
8. Con Brosnan *(Kerry)*
9. Jim Smith *(Cavan)*
10. Paddy Colleran *(Sligo)*
11. Mick O'Brien *(Dublin)*
12. Paul Doyle *(Kildare)*
13. John Nipper Shanley *(Leitrim)*
14. Paddy McDonnell *(Dublin)*
15. Martin O'Neill *(Wexford)*

J. J. Sheehy *(Kerry)* and Jackie Ryan *(Kerry)* were selected but did not turn out.

1932 Tailteann Games Irish Football Team

1. John McDonnell *(Dublin)*
2. Dee O'Connor *(Kerry)*
3. Joe Barrett *(Kerry)*
4. Luke Colleran *(Sligo)*
5. J. Fane *(Wexford)*
6. Jack Higgins *(Kildare)*
7. Paddy Whitty *(Kerry)*
8. Paddy Martin *(Kildare)*
9. Jim Smith *(Cavan)*
10. Tom Leech *(Galway)*
11. Nicky Walsh *(Wexford)*
12. Jack Delaney *(Laois)*
13. Gerard Courell *(Mayo)*
14. Jackie Ryan *(Kerry)*
15. Martin O'Neill *(Wexford)*

1924 Tailteann Games Irish Hurling Team

1. John 'Junior' O'Mahoney *(Galway)*

2. Mick Derivan *(Galway)*

3. John Joe Hayes *(Tipperary)*

4. Willie Ryan *(Limerick)*

5. Bernie Gibbs *(Galway)*

6. Jim 'Builder' Walsh *(Dublin)*

7. T. Kelly *(Laois)*

8. Dave Murnane *(Limerick)*

9. Denis Ring *(Cork)*

10. Mick Darcy *(Tipperary)*

11. Garret Howard *(Dublin)*

12. Willie Gleeson *(Limerick)*

13. Jack Darcy *(Tipperary)*

14. Jimmy Kennedy *(Cork)*

15. Jimmy Humphries *(Limerick)*

Sub: R. Doherty

1928 Tailteann Games Irish Hurling Team

1. Tommy Daly *(Dublin)*
2. Mick Derivan *(Galway)*
3. Seán Óg Murphy *(Cork)*
4. E. Tobin *(Laois)*
5. Phil Cahill *(Tipperary)*
6. Jim O'Regan *(Cork)*
7. Mick Gill *(Dublin)*
8. John Joe Kinnane *(Limerick)*
9. Eudie Coughlan *(Cork)*
10. Mick King *(Galway)*
11. Jim Builder Walsh *(Dublin)*
12. Garret Howard *(Dublin)*
13. Mattie Power *(Dublin)*
14. Tull Considine *(Clare)*
15. Martin Kennedy *(Tipperary)*

1932 Tailteann Games Irish Hurling Team

1. Tom O'Meara *(Tipperary)*

2. Phil Purcell *(Tipperary)*

3. Eddie O'Connell *(Cork)*

4. John Joe 'Goggles' Doyle *(Clare)*

5. Dinny Barry Murphy *(Cork)*

6. Jim O'Regan *(Cork)*

7. Mickey Cross *(Limerick)*

8. Jim Hurley *(Cork)*

9. Eddy Byrne *(Killkenny)*

10. Mick King *(Galway)*

11. Jim 'Builder' Walsh *(Dublin)*

12. Charlie MacMahon *(Dublin)*

13. Mick 'Gah' Aherne *(Cork)*

14. Mattie Power *(Dublin)*

15. Din O'Neill *(Laois)*

Camogie Team of the Century (2004)

1. Eileen Duffy-O'Mahoney *(Dublin)*
2. Liz Neary *(Kilkenny)*
3. Marie Costine-O'Donovan *(Cork)*
4. Mary Sinnott-Dinan *(Wexford)*
5. Sandy Fitzgibbon *(Cork)*
6. Bridie Martin-McGarry *(Kilkenny)*
7. Margaret O'Leary-Leacy *(Wexford)*
8. Maireád McAtamney-Magill *(Antrim)*
9. Kathleen Mills-Hill *(Dublin)*
10. Linda Mellerick *(Cork)*
11. Pat Moloney-Lenihan *(Cork)*
12. Una O'Connor *(Dublin)*
13. Sophie Brack *(Dublin)*
14. Deirdre Hughes *(Tipperary)*
15. Angela Downey-Browne *(Kilkenny)*

Greatest Handballers of the GAA Era

John Joe Gilmartin *(Kilkenny)*
He was unbeaten in a hardball singles match from 1936 to 1943.

John Ryan *(Wexford)*.
He holds the record, with Gilmartin, of having won four titles in the same year.

Paddy Perry *(Roscommon)*
Perry won eight softball titles in the 1930s.

Pat Kirby *(Clare)*
Kirby won the world 60 x 30 singles championship in Croke Park and became a champion on both sides of the Atlantic.

Joey Maher *(Louth)*
Won the world 40 x 20 championships representing Canada in 1967 and was winner of both the Irish and Canadian titles.

Michael Ducksy Walsh *(Kilkenny)*
Undefeated from 1985 to 1998 in senior singles, and he also won eight All-Ireland titles in the American-sized court, 40 x 20.

Paul Brady *(Cavan)*
Winer fo 2003 world open singles championship.

Ireland's First International Rules Team to Play Australia (1984)

1. Martin Furlong *(Offaly)*
2. Noel Roche *(Clare)*
3. Mick Lyons *(Meath)*
4. Seamus McHugh *(Galway)*
5. Jimmy Kerrigan *(Cork)*
6. Tom Spillane *(Kerry)*
7. P.J. Buckley *(Dublin)*
8. Jack O'Shea *(Kerry)*
9. Shay Fahy *(Kildare)*
10. Barney Rock *(Dublin)*
11. Eoin Liston *(Kerry)*
12. Dermot McNicholl *(Derry)*
13. Colm O'Rourke *(Meath)*
14. Tommy Dwyer *(Carlow)*
15. Matt Connor *(Offaly)*

Subs: Sean Walsh *(Kerry)* Richie Connor *(Offaly)* Liam Tierney *(Longford)* John Costelloe *(Laois)* Liam Hayes *(Meath)* Brian O'Donnell *(Galway)*

Kathleen Mills's Camogie Team of her Era

One of the greatest players in camogie history, and the best known player of her age, she won 15 All-Ireland medals.

1.   Peg Hogg *(Cork)*

2.   Rose Martin *(Dublin)*

3.   Pat Kenny *(Dublin)*

4.   Mary Fitzgeald *(Cork)*

5.   Rose Fletcher *(Dublin)*

6.   T. Griffin *(Tipperary)*

7.   Kay Cody *(Dublin)*

8.   Kay Mills *(Dublin)*

9.   Una O'Connor *(Dublin)*

10. Annette Corrigan *(Dublin)*

11. Ide O'Kiely *(Dublin)*

12. Sophie Brack *(Dublin)*

Joe McDonagh's Team of his Era

1. Noel Skehan *(Kilkenny)*
2. Niall McInenrey *(Galway)*
3. Pat Hartigan *(Limerick)*
4. Brian Murphy *(Cork)*
5. Joe McDonagh *(Galway)*
6. Ger Henderson *(Kilkenny)*
7. Iggy Clarke *(Galway)*
8. John Connolly *(Galway)*
9. Frank Cummins *(Kilkenny)*
10. Billy Fitzpatrick *(Kilkenny)*
11. Jimmy Barry-Murphy *(Cork)*
12. Eddie Keher *(Kilkenny)*
13. Francis Loughnane *(Tipperary)*
14. Tony Doran *(Wexford)*
15. Eamonn Cregan *(Limerick)*

Brendan Fullam's Hurling Selection

Brendan Fullam is the author of several histories of the
GAA and has done invaluable work in compiling an
oral history of the memoirs of great players. He
compield this list for *The Throw-In: The GAA and the Men
Who Made It* (Wolfhound, 2004).

1. Ollie Walsh *(Kilkenny)*
2. Jimmy Brohan *(Cork)*
3. Pat Hartigan *(Limerick)*
4. Willie O'Connor *(Kilkenny)*
5. Pat Stakelum *(Tipperary)*
6. Billy Rackard *(Wexford)*
7. Phil Grimes *(Waterford)*
8. John Fenton *(Cork)*
9. Johnny Dooley *(Offaly)*
10. Joe Cooney *(Galway)*
11. Tom Cheasty *(Waterford)*
12. D.J. Carey *(Kilkenny)*
13. Oliver Hopper McGrath *(Wexford)*
14. Tony Doran *(Wexford)*
15. Eamonn Cregan *(Limerick)*

Justin McCarthy's Team of his Era

Picked for inclusion in Brendan Fullam's *Legends of the Ash* (Merlin, 1997).

1. Seamus Durack *(Clare)*
2. Phil Fan Larkin *(Kilkenny)*
3. Pat Hartigan *(Limerick)*
4. Denis Murphy *(Cork)*
6. Seamus Cleere *(Kilkenny)*
7. Dan Quigley *(Wexford)*
8. Ger Loughnane *(Clare)*
9. Justin McCarthy *(Cork)*
10. Mick Roche *(Tipperary)*
11. Eamonn Cregan *(Limerick)*
12. Willie Walsh *(Cork)*
13. Jimmy Doyle *(Tipperary)*
14. Charlie McCarthy *(Cork)*
15. Tony Doran *(Wexford)*
16. Eddie Keher *(Kilkenny)*

Jack Mahon's Football Team of his Era

Galway All-Ireland medallist Jack Mahon published the team of his era in the *Gaelic Weekly* of 30 March 1968.

1. Johnny Geraghty *(Galway)*
2. Enda Colleran *(Galway)*
3. Paddy Prendergast *(Mayo)*
4. Sean Flanagan *(Mayo)*
5. Sean Murphy *(Kerry)*
6. Gerry O'Malley *(Roscommon)*
7. Stephen White *(Louth)*
8. Padraig Carney *(Mayo)*
9. Mick O'Connell *(Kerry)*
10. Sean O'Neill *(Down)*
11. Sean Purcell *(Galway)*
12. Paddy Doherty *(Down)*
13. Ollie Freaney *(Dublin)*
14. Tom Langan *(Mayo)*
15. Kevin Heffernan *(Dublin)*

John D. Hickey's Hurling Selection from his Lifetime

The long-serving *Irish Indepndent* GAA correspondent, John D. Hickey compiled this team for the 1976 *Our Games Annual*.

1. Tommy Daly *(Clare)*
2. Bobby Rackard *(Wexford)*
3. Nick O'Donnell *(Wexford)*
4. Jim Treacy *(Kilkenny)*
5. Jimmy Finn *(Tipperary)*
6. John Keane *(Waterford)*
7. Paddy Phelan *(Kilkenny)*
8. Mick Gill *(Galway)*
9. Lory Meagher *(Kilkenny)*
10. Eudie Coughlan *(Cork)*
11. Mick Mackey *(Limerick)*
12. Eddie Keher *(Kilkenny)*
13. Paddy Kenny *(Tipperary)*
14. Martin Kennedy *(Tipperary)*
15. Christy Ring *(Cork)*

Owen McCrohan's Team of Patricks

Former Kerry physio Owen McCrohan compiled these
two teams for a St Patrick's Day feature.

Team No 1

1. Paddy Cullen *(Dublin)*
2. Paddy Driscoll *(Cork)*
3. Paddy Prendergast *(Mayo)*
4. Paddy Bawn Brosnan *(Kerry)*
5. Páidí Ó Sé *(Kerry)*
6. Paddy Casey *(Offaly)*
7. Paudie Lynch *(Kerry)*
8. Paddy Kennedy *(Kerry)*
9. Paddy O'Brien *(Meath)*
10. Paudie Sheehy *(Kerry)*
11. Padraic Carney *(Mayo)*
12. Pat Spillane *(Kerry)*
13. Paddy Meegan *(Meath)*
14. Paddy Burke *(Kerry)*
15. Paddy Doherty *(Down)*

Team No 2

1. Paudie O'Mahony *(Kerry)*
2. Paddy McCormack *(Offaly)*
3. P.A. 'Weeshie' Murphy *(Cork)*
4. Paud O'Donoghue *(Kerry)*
5. P. J. Duke *(Cavan)*
6. Paddy Holden *(Dublin)*
7. Pat Reynolds *(Meath)*
8. Paddy McDonnell *(Dublin)*
9. Pat 'Aeroplane' O'Shea *(Kerry)*
10. Paddy Martin *(Kildare)*
11. Pat Griffin *(Kerry)*
12. Packie McGarty *(Leitrim)*
13. Padraig Joyce *(Galway)*
14. Paddy Moclair *(Mayo)*
15. Packie Boylan *(Cavan)*

Micheál Ó Muirchartaigh's Managers

In his autobiography *From Dun Sion to Croke Park*, Micheál Ó Muircheartaigh lists the greatest managers in the game with the previso that, 'I do not intend to rank them.'

Mick O'Dwyer *(Kerry)*

Kevin Heffernan *(Dublin)*

Seán Boylan *(Meath)*

Mickey Harte *(Tyrone)*

Brian Cody *(Kilkenny)*

Joe Kernan *(Armagh)*

Liam Griffin *(Wexford)*

Ger Loughnane *(Clare)*

Eugene McGee *(Offaly)*

John O'Mahony *(Mayo* and *Galway)*

Nick English *(Tipperary)*

Brian McEnniff *(Donegal)*

Páidí Ó Sé *(Kerry)*

Michael Babs Keating *(Tipperary)*

Michael O'Brien *(Tipperary)*

Micheál Ó Muircheartaigh's Greatest Hurling Team

'It would be easy to call the match a draw,' he says in his biography *From Dun Sion to Croke Park*.

1.   Tipperary 1968–75
2.   Kilkenny 1969–75

Liam Griffin's Teams of his Time

Liam Griffin coined the phrase 'the *Riverdance* of sport' to describe the hurling revival of the 1990s. He managed the successful Wexford team of 1996.

Hurling

1. Pat Nolan *(Oylegate, Wexford)*
2. Jimmy Brohan *(Cork)*
3. Brian Lohan *(Clare)*
4. Tommy McGarry *(Limerick)*
5. Seanie McMahon *(Clare)*
6. Billy Rackard *(Wexford)*
7. Jimmy Cullinane *(Clare)*
8. Ned Wheeler *(Wexford)*
9. Phil Grimes *(Waterford)*
10. Sean Clohessy *(Kilkenny)*
11. Padge Kehoe *(Wexford)*
12. Frankie Walsh *(Waterford)*
13. Oliver Hopper McGrath *(Wexford)*
14. Nick English *(Tipperary)*
15. D. J. Carey *(Kilkenny)*

Football

1. Johnny Geraghty *(Galway)*
2. Sean Turner *(Wexford)*
3. Noel Tierney *(Galway)*
4   Enda Colleran *(Galway)*
5. Pat Red Collier *(Meath)*
6. Kevin Moran *(Dublin)*
7. Martin O'Connell *(Meath)*
8. Jack O'Shea *(Kerry)*
9. Mick O'Connell *(Kerry)*
10. Eamonn O'Donoghue *(Kerry)*
11. Mattie McDonagh *(Galway)*
12. Pat Spillane *(Kerry)*
13. Mikey Sheehy *(Kerry)*
14. Jimmy Keaveney *(Dublin)*
15. Sean O'Neill *(Down)*

The Original All-Stars: The Invasion Team of 1888

Of the 54 who travelled, 17 stayed in America including world hammer record holder Jim Mitchell.

Athletes

Pat Davin *(Carrick, world long and high jump record older)*, Jim Mitchell *(Emly, world hammer throw record older)*, Dan Shanahan *(Kilfinane, world triple jump record holder)*, Pat T. Keoghan *(Dungarvan, standing jump champion)*, T. M. O'Connor *(Ballyclough, high jumper)*, William Phibbs *(Glenville, 880 champion)*, Mike and Jack Connery *(Staker Wallace Limerick, high jump and pole vault)*, Pat Looney *(Macroom, triple jump)*, Tim O'Mahoney *(Rosscarberry, 440 champion)*, William McCarthy *(Macroom, miler)*, J.C. Daly *(Borrisokane, former hammer record older)*, William Real *(Pallaskreen, hammer thrower)*, P. O'Donnell *(Carrick, hammer thrower)*, J. McCarthy *(Staker Wallace, sprinter)*, T. Barry *(Dungarvan, sprinter)*, D. Power *(Shanballymore, hurdler)*, J. Mooney *(Ballyhea, sprinter)*.

Hurlers

H. Burgess *(Dunleary, Dublin)*, J. Cordial *(Kinnitty, Offaly)*, F. Coughlan *(Kickhams, Dublin)*, Michael Curran *(Castlecomer, Kilkenny)*, J. Dunne *(Rahan, Offaly)*, J. Fitzgibbon *(Ogonelloe, Clare)*, John Fox *(Mooncoin, Kilkenny)*, T. Furlong *(Davitts, Dublin)*, James Grace *(Tullaroan, Kilkenny)*, J. Hayes *(Faughs, Dublin)*, M. Hickey *(Carrickbeg, Waterford)*, J McEvoy *(Knockroo, Laois)*, P. Minogue *(Tulla, Clare)*, P.J. Molohan *(Monasterevin, Kildare)*, P. Muleady *(Birr, Offaly)*, J. Nolan *(Donkerrin, Offaly)*, John O'Brien *(Moycarkey, Tipperary)*, Tom O'Grady *(Moycarkey, Tipperary)*, William Prendergast *(Clonmel, Tipperary)*, J. Rourke *(Kilbane, Clare)*, J. Royce *(Albert Hill, Wexford)*, P. Ryan *(Rathdowney, Laois)*, Thady Ryan *(Clonoulty, Tipperary)*, Jim Stapleton *(Thurles, Tipperary)*, P.P. Sutton *(Metropolitans, Dublin)*

Most All-Star Awards

The All-Stars scheme, voted by Gaelic writers each autumn, was instituted in 1963 and ran until 1967 under the auspices of *Gaelic Weekly* magazine, then resumed in 1971 as a sponsored awards scheme. A selection of the players who have won most, in their positions, reflects the controversies that have dogged the selection, such as when Brian Whelahan failed to win a place despite being made hurler of the year.

The delicacies of the system are reflected by the fact Whelahan has just 2 awards, despite being the only player of his era selected for the team of the millennium. Selectors had a tendency to shift players around to find a berth for more star players. The selection is not dictated solely by position. Larry Tompkins won more All-Star awards at centre-half forward (3) than Tommy Dowd, but Dowd won more overall. Martin Hanamy won 3 awards at left corner-back, but Jimmy Cooney won more overall.

Football

1.	John O'Leary *(Dublin)*	5
2.	Páidí Ó Sé *(Kerry)*	5
3.	John O'Keeffe *(Kerry)*	5
4.	Robbie Kelleher *(Dublin)*	4
5.	Tommy Drumm *(Dublin)*	4

6. Paddy Holden *(Dublin)* 4

   Tom Spillane *(Kerry)* 4

   Steven O'Brien *(Cork)* 4

   Kieran McGeeney *(Armagh)* 3

7. Martin O'Connell *(Meath)* 4

8. Jack O'Shea *(Kerry)* 6

9. Anthony Tohill *(Derry)* 4

10. Ger Power *(Kerry)* 6

11. Tommy Dowd *(Meath)* 3

12. Pat Spillane *(Kerry)* 9

13. Mike Sheehy *(Kerry)* 7

14. Peter Canavan *(Tyrone)* 5

15. John Egan *(Kerry)* 5

Hurling

1. Noel Skehan *(Kilkenny)* 7

2. Phil Fan Larkin *(Kilkenny)* 4

   Pat Henderson *(Kilkenny)* 4

3. Pat Hartigan *(Limerick)* 5

4. Martin Hanamy *(Offaly)* 3

5. Pete Finnerty *(Galway)* 5

6. Ger Henderson *(Kilkenny)* 5

7. Mick Roche *(Tipperary)* 4

   Denis Coughlan *(Cork)* 4

   Iggy Clarke *(Galway)* 4

8. Frank Cummins *(Kilkenny)* 5

9.	John Fenton *(Cork)*	4
10.	D.J. Carey *(Kilkenny)*	9
11.	Henry Shefflin *(Kilkenny)*	4
12.	Eddie Keher *(Kilkenny)*	9
13.	Jimmy Barry-Murphy *(Cork)*	5
14.	Joe McKenna *(Limerick)*	6
15.	Nicky English *(Tipperary)*	6

Women's Football

1.	Kathleen Curran *(Kerry)*	5
2.	Bridget Leen *(Kerry)*	5
3.	Connie Conway *(Laois)*	5
4.	Helena Lohan *(Mayo)*	4
5.	Anna Lisa Crotty *(Waterford)*	7
6.	Jenny Greenan *(Monaghan)*	6
7.	Edel Clarke *(Westmeath)*	5
8.	Christina Heffernan *(Mayo)*	6
9.	Mary J. Curran *(Kerry)*	11
10.	Aine Wall *(Waterford)*	8
11.	Marie Crotty *(Waterford)*	5
12.	Marina Barry *(Kerry)*	6
13.	Geraldine O'Ryan *(Waterford)*	5
14.	Sue Ramsbottom *(Laois)*	7
15.	Eileen Lawlor *(Kerry)*	5

All-Star Teams: Football

1963

Andy Phillips *(Wicklow)*, Gabriel Kelly *(Cavan)*, Noel Tierney *(Galway)*, Pa Connolly *(Kildare)*, Seamus Murphy *(Kerry)*, Paddy Holden *(Dublin)*, Martin Newell *(Galway)*, Mick Garrett *(Galway)*, Des Foley *(Dublin)*, Sean O'Neill *(Down)*, Mickey Whelan *(Dublin)*, Tom Browne *(Laois)*, Jimmy Whan *(Armagh)*, Tom Long *(Kerry)*, Pat Donnellan *(Galway)*

1964

Johnny Geraghty *(Galway)*, Gabriel Kelly *(Cavan)*, Noel Tierney *(Galway)*, Peter Darby *(Meath)*, Enda Colleran *(Galway)*, Paddy Holden *(Dublin)*, Frank Lynch *(Louth)*, Mick O'Connell *(Kerry)*, Mick Reynolds *(Galway)*, Cyril Dunne *(Galway)*, Mattie McDonagh *(Galway)*, Mickey Kearns *(Sligo)*, Sean O'Neill *(Down)*, Charlie Gallagher *(Cavan)*, Paddy Doherty *(Down)*

1965

Johnny Geraghty *(Galway)*, Enda Colleran *(Galway)*, Tom McCreesh *(Armagh)*, Bosco McDermott *(Galway)*, Donie O'Sullivan *(Kerry)*, Paddy Holden *(Dublin)*, Martin Newell *(Galway)*, Mick O'Connell *(Kerry)*, Des Foley *(Dublin)*, Cyril Dunne *(Galway)*, Mickey Kearns *(Sligo)*, Seamus Leydon *(Galway)*, Sean Murray *(Longford)*, Sean O'Neill *(Down)*, Paddy Doherty *(Down)*

1966

Johnny Geraghty *(Galway)*, Enda Colleran *(Galway)*,
Jack Quinn *(Meath)*, Peter Darby *(Meath)*, Pat Collier
(Meath), Mick Carolan *(Kildare)*, Brendan Barden
(Longford), Pat Donnellan *(Galway)*, Ray Carolan
(Cavan), Mickey Kearns *(Sligo)*, Mattie McDonagh
(Galway), Seamus Leydon *(Galway)*, Pat Dunny *(Kildare)*,
Con O'Sullivan *(Cork)*, John Keenan *(Galway)*

1967

Billy Morgan *(Cork)*, Gabriel Kelly *(Cavan)*, Jack Quinn
(Meath), Seamus O'Connor *(Mayo)*, Frank Cogan *(Cork)*,
Bertie Cunningham *(Meath)*, Pat Reynolds *(Meath)*, Mick
Burke *(Cork)*, Ray Carolan *(Cavan)*, Cyril Dunne
(Galway), Joe Langan *(Mayo)*, Joe Corcoran *(Mayo)*, Sean
O'Connell *(Derry)*, Con O'Sullivan *(Cork)*, Sean O'Neill
(Down)

1968–1970
No All-Star Teams

1971

P. J. Smyth *(Galway)*, Johnny Carey *(Mayo)*, Jack
Cosgrove (Galway), Donie O'Sullivan *(Kerry)*, Eugene
Mulligan *(Offaly)*, Nicholas Clavin *(Offaly)*, Pat Reynolds
(Meath), Liam Sammon *(Galway)*, Willie Bryan *(Offaly)*,
Tony McTague *(Offaly)*, Ray Cummins *(Cork)*, Mickey
Kearns *(Sligo)*, Andy McCallin *(Antrim)*, Sean O'Neill
(Down), Seamus Leydon *(Galway)*

1972

Martin Furlong *(Offaly)*, Mick Ryan *(Offaly)*, Paddy
McCormack *(Offaly)*, Donie O'Sullivan *(Kerry)*, Brian
McEniff *(Donegal)*, Tommy Joe Gilmore *(Galway)*,
Kevin Jer O'Sullivan *(Cork)*, Willie Bryan *(Offaly)*, Mick
O'Connoll *(Kerry)*, Johnny Cooney *(Offaly)*, Kevin
Kilmurray *(Offaly)*, Tony McTague *(Offaly)*, Mickey
Freyne *(Roscommon)*, Sean O'Neill *(Down)*, Paddy
Moriarty *(Armagh)*

1973

Billy Morgan *(Cork)*, Frank Cogan *(Cork)*, Mick Ryan
(Offaly), Brian Murphy *(Cork)*, Liam O'Neill *(Galway)*,
Tommy Joe Gilmore *(Galway)*, Kevin Jer O'Sullivan
(Cork), John O'Keeffe *(Kerry)*, Dinny Long *(Cork)*,
Johnny Cooney *(Offaly)*, Kevin Kilmurray *(Offaly)*, Liam
Sammon *(Galway)*, Jimmy Barry-Murphy *(Cork)*, Ray
Cummins *(Cork)*, Anthony McGurk *(Derry)*

297

1974

Paddy Cullen *(Dublin)*, Donal Monaghan *(Donegal)*,
Sean Doherty *(Dublin)*, Robbie Kelleher *(Dublin)*, Paddy
Reilly *(Dublin)*, Barnes Murphy *(Sligo)*, Johnny Hughes
(Galway), Dermot Earley *(Roscommon)*, Paudie Lynch
(Kerry), Tom Naughton *(Galway)*, Declan Barron *(Cork)*,
David Hickey *(Dublin)*, Jimmy Barry-Murphy *(Cork)*,
Jimmy Keaveney *(Dublin)*, Johnny Tobin *(Galway)*

1975

Paud O'Mahony *(Kerry)*, Gay O'Driscoll *(Dublin)*, John O'Keeffe *(Kerry)*, Robbie Kelleher *(Dublin)*, Peter Stevenson *(Derry)*, Anthony McGurk *(Derry)*, Ger Power *(Kerry)*, Dinny Long *(Cork)*, Colm McAlarney *(Down)*, Gerry McElhinney *(Derry)*, Ken Rennicks *(Meath)*, Mickey O'Sullivan *(Kerry)*, John Egan *(Kerry)* Matt Kerrigan *(Meath)*, Anton O'Toole *(Dublin)*

1976

Paddy Cullen *(Dublin)*, Ger O'Keeffe *(Kerry)*, John O'Keeffe *(Kerry)*, Brian Murphy *(Cork)*, Johnny Hughes *(Galway)*, Kevin Moran *(Dublin)*, Ger Power *(Kerry)*, Brian Mullins *(Dublin)*, Dave McCarthy *(Cork)*, Anton O'Toole *(Dublin)*, Tony Hanahoe *(Dublin)*, David Hickey *(Dublin)*, Bobby Doyle *(Dublin)*, Micky Sheehy *(Kerry)*, Pat Spillane *(Kerry)*

1977

Paddy Cullen *(Dublin)*, Gay O'Driscoll *(Dublin)*, Pat Lindsay *(Roscommon)*, Robbie Kelleher *(Dublin)*, Tommy Drumm *(Dublin)*, Paddy Moriarty *(Armagh)*, Pat O'Neill *(Dublin)*, Brian Mullins *(Dublin)*, Joe Kernan *(Armagh)*, Anton O'Toole *(Dublin)*, Jimmy Smith *(Armagh)*, Pat Spillane *(Kerry)*, Bobby Doyle *(Dublin)*, Jimmy Keaveney *(Dublin)*, John Egan *(Kerry)*

1978

Ollie Crinnigan *(Kildare)*, Harry Keegan *(Roscommon)*, John O'Keeffe *(Kerry)*, Robbie Kelleher *(Dublin)*, Tommy Drumm *(Dublin)*, Ollie Brady *(Cavan)*, Paudie Lynch *(Kerry)*, Colm

McAlarney *(Down)*, Connor *(Offaly)*, Ger Power *(Kerry)*, Declan Barron *(Cork)*, Pat Spillane *(Kerry)*, Micky Sheehy *(Kerry)*, Jimmy Keaveney *(Dublin)*, John Egan *(Kerry)*

1979

Paddy Cullen *(Dublin)*, Eugene Hughes *(Monaghan)*, John O'Keeffe *(Kerry)*, Tom Heneghan *(Roscommon)*, Tommy Drumm *(Dublin)*, Tim Kennelly *(Kerry)*, Danny Murray *(Roscommon)*, Dermot Earley *(Roscommon)*, Bernard Brogan *(Dublin)*, Ger Power *(Kerry)*, Sean Walsh *(Kerry)*, Pat Spillane *(Kerry)*, Micky Sheehy *(Kerry)*, Sean Lowry *(Offaly)*, Joe McGrath *(Mayo)*

1980

Charlie Nelligan *(Kerry)*, Harry Keegan *(Roscommon)*, Kevin Kehilly *(Cork)*, Gerry Connellan *(Roscommon)*, Kevin McCabe *(Tyrone)*, Tim Kennelly *(Kerry)*, Danny Murray *(Roscommon)*, Jack O'Shea *(Kerry)*, Colm McKinstry *(Armagh)*, Ger Power *(Kerry)*, Dinny Allen *(Cork)*, Pat Spillane *(Kerry)*, Matt Connor *(Offaly)*, Eoin Liston *(Kerry)*, John Egan *(Kerry)*

1981

Martin Furlong *(Offaly)*, Jimmy Deenihan *(Kerry)*, Paddy Kennedy *(Down)*, Paudie Lynch *(Kerry)*, Paudie O'Shea *(Kerry)*, Ritchie Connor *(Offaly)*, Seamus McHugh *(Galway)*, Jack O'Shea *(Kerry)*, Sean Walsh *(Kerry)*, Barry Brennan *(Galway)*, Denis Moran *(Kerry)*, Pat Spillane *(Kerry)*, Micky Sheehy *(Kerry)*, Eoin Liston *(Kerry)*, Brendan Lowry *(Offaly)*

1982

Martin Furlong *(Offaly)*, Mick Fitzgerald *(Offaly)*, Liam O'Connor *(Offaly)*, Kevin Kehily *(Cork)*, Paudie O'Shea *(Kerry)*, Sean Lowry *(Offaly)*, Liam Currams *(Offaly)*, Jack O'Shea *(Kerry)*, Padraig Dunne *(Offaly)*, Peter McGinnity *(Fermanagh)*, Joe Kernan *(Armagh)*, Matt Connor *(Offaly)*, Micky Sheehy *(Kerry)*, Eoin Liston *(Kerry)*, John Egan *(Kerry)*

1983

Martin Furlong *(Offaly)*, Paudie O'Shea *(Kerry)*, Stephen Kinneavy *(Galway)*, John Evans *(Cork)*, Pat Canavan *(Dublin)*, Tommy Drumm *(Dublin)*, Jimmy Kerrigan *(Cork)*, Jack O'Shea *(Kerry)*, Liam Austin *(Down)*, Barney Rock *(Dublin)*, Matt Connor *(Offaly)*, Greg Blaney *(Down)*, Martin McHugh *(Donegal)*, Colm O'Rourke *(Meath)*, Joe McNally *(Dublin)*

1984

John O'Leary *(Dublin)*, Paudie O'Shea *(Kerry)*, Mick Lyons *(Meath)*, Seamus McHugh *(Galway)*, Tommy Doyle *(Kerry)*, Tom Spillane *(Kerry)*, P. J. Buckley *(Dublin)*, Jack O'Shea *(Kerry)*, Eugene McKenna *(Tyrone)*, Barney Rock *(Dublin)*, Eoin Liston *(Kerry)*, Pat Spillane *(Kerry)*, Michael Sheehy *(Kerry)*, Frank McGuigan *(Tyrone)*, Dermot McNicholl *(Derry)*

1985

John O'Leary *(Dublin)*, Paudie O'Shea *(Kerry)*, Gerry Hargan *(Dublin)*, Mick Spillane *(Kerry)*, Tommy Doyle *(Kerry)*, Cathal Murray *(Monaghan)*, Dermot Flanagan *(Mayo)*, Jack O'Shea *(Kerry)*, Willie Joe Padden *(Mayo)*, Barney Rock

(Dublin), Tommy Conroy *(Dublin)*, Pat Spillane *(Kerry)*, Kevin McStay *(Mayo)*, Paul Earley *(Roscommon)*, Eugene Hughes *(Monaghan)*

1986

Charlie Nelligan *(Kerry)*, Harry Keegan *(Roscommon)*, Mick Lyons *(Meath)*, John Lynch *(Tyrone)*, Tommy Doyle *(Kerry)*, Tom Spillane *(Kerry)*, Colm Browne *(Laois)*, Plunkett Donaghy *(Tyrone)*, Liam Irwin *(Laois)*, Ray McCarron *(Monaghan)*, Eugene McKenna *(Tyrone)*, Pat Spillane *(Kerry)*, Micky Sheehy *(Kerry)*, Damian O'Hagan *(Tyrone)*, Ger Power *(Kerry)*

1987

Gerry McEntee *(Meath)*, John Kearns *(Cork)*, Robbie O'Malley *(Meath)*, Colman Corrigan *(Cork)*, Tony Scullion *(Derry)*, Niall Cahalane *(Cork)*, Tom Spillane *(Kerry)*, Ger Lynch *(Kerry)*, Brian McGilligan *(Derry)*, David Beggy *(Meath)*, Barry Tompkins *(Cork)*, Kieran Duff *(Dublin)*, Val Daly *(Galway)*, Brian Stafford *(Meath)*, Bernard Flynn *(Meath)*

1988

Paddy Linden *(Monaghan)*, Robbie O'Malley *(Meath)*, Colman Corrigan *(Cork)*, Mick Kennedy *(Dublin)*, Niall Cahalane *(Cork)*, Noel McCaffrey *(Dublin)*, Martin O'Connell *(Meath)*, Shea Fahy *(Cork)*, Liam Hayes *(Meath)*, Maurice Fitzgerald *(Kerry)*, Larry Tompkins *(Cork)*, Kieran Duff *(Dublin)*, Colm O'Rourke *(Meath)*, Brian Stafford *(Meath)*, Eugene Hughes *(Monaghan)*

1989

Gabriel Irwin *(Mayo)*, Jimmy Browne *(Mayo)*, Gerry Hargan *(Dublin)*, Dermot Flanagan *(Mayo)*, Connie Murphy *(Kerry)*, Conor Counihan *(Cork)*, Tony Davis *(Cork)*, Teddy McCarthy *(Cork)*, Willie Joe Padden *(Mayo)*, Dave Barry *(Cork)*, Larry Tompkins *(Cork)*, Noel Durkin *(Mayo)*, Paul McGrath *(Cork)*, Eugene McKenna *(Tyrone)*, Tony McManus *(Roscommon)*

1990

John Kearns *(Cork)*, Robbie O'Malley *(Meath)*, Steven O'Brien *(Cork)*, Terry Ferguson *(Meath)*, Michael Slocum *(Cork)*, Conor Counihan *(Cork)*, Martin O'Connell *(Meath)*, Shea Fahy *(Cork)*, Mickey Quinn *(Leitrim)*, David Beggy *(Meath)*, Val Daly *(Galway)*, Joyce McMullan *(Donegal)*, Paul McGrath *(Cork)*, Kevin O'Brien *(Wicklow)*, James McCartan *(Down)*

1991

Michael McQuillan *(Meath)*, Mick Deegan *(Dublin)*, Conor Deegan *(Down)*, Enon Gavin *(Roscommon)*, Tommy Carr *(Dublin)*, Keith Barr *(Dublin)*, Martin O'Connell *(Meath)*, Barry Breen *(Down)*, Martin Lynch *(Kildare)*, Ross Carr *(Down)*, Greg Blaney *(Down)*, Tommy Dowd *(Meath)*, Colm O'Rourke *(Meath)*, Brian Stafford *(Meath)*, Bernard Flynn *(Meath)*

1992

Gary Walsh *(Donegal)*, Seamus Clancy *(Clare)*, Matt Gallagher *(Donegal)*, Tony Scullion *(Derry)*, Paul Curran *(Dublin)*, Martin Gavigan *(Donegal)*, Eamon Heery

(Dublin), Anthony Molloy *(Donegal)*, T. J. Kilgallon
(Mayo), Anthony Tohill *(Derry)*, Martin McHugh
(Donegal), James McHugh *(Donegal)*, Tony Boyle
(Donegal), Vinny Murphy *(Dublin)*, Enda Gormley *(Derry)*

1993

John O'Leary *(Dublin)*, John Joe Doherty *(Donegal)*,
Dermot Deasy *(Dublin)*, Tony Scullion *(Derry)*, Johnny
McGurk *(Derry)*, Henry Downey *(Derry)*, Gary Coleman
(Derry), Anthony Tohill *(Derry)*, Brian McGilligan *(Derry)*,
Kevin O'Neill *(Mayo)*, Joe Kavanagh *(Cork)*, Charlie
Redmond *(Dublin)*, Colin Corkery *(Cork)*, Ger Houlihan
(Armagh), Enda Gormley *(Derry)*

1994

John O'Leary *(Dublin)*, Michael Magill *(Down)*, Seamus
Quinn *(Leitrim)*, Paul Higgins *(Down)*, Graham Geraghty
(Meath), Steven O'Brien *(Cork)*, D. J. Kane *(Down)*, Jack
Sheedy *(Dublin)*, Greg McCartan *(Down)*, Peter Canavan
(Tyrone), Greg Blaney *(Down)*, James McCartan *(Down)*,
Micky Linden *(Down)*, Tommy Dowd *(Meath)*, Charlie
Redmond *(Dublin)*

1995

John O'Leary *(Dublin)*, Tony Scullion *(Derry)*, Mark
O'Connor *(Cork)*, Fay Devlin *(Tyrone)*, Paul Curran
(Dublin), Keith Barr *(Dublin)*, Steven O'Brien *(Cork)*,
Brian Stynes *(Dublin)*, Anthony Tohill *(Derry)*, Jarleth
Fallon *(Galway)*, Dessie Farrell *(Dublin)*, Paul Clarke
(Dublin), Tommy Dowd *(Meath)*, Peter Canavan *(Tyrone)*,
Charlie Redmond *(Dublin)*

1996

Finbarr McConnell *(Tyrone)*, Kenneth Mortimer *(Mayo)*, Darren Fay *(Meath)*, Martin O'Connell *(Meath)*, Pat Holmes *(Mayo)*, James Nallen *(Mayo)*, Paul Curran *(Dublin)*, John McDermott *(Meath)*, Liam McHale *(Mayo)*, Trevor Giles *(Meath)*, Tommy Dowd *(Meath)*, James Horan *(Mayo)*, Joe Brolly *(Derry)*, Peter Canavan *(Tyrone)*, Maurice Fitzgerald *(Kerry)*

1997

Declan O'Keeffe *(Kerry)*, Kenneth Mortimer *(Mayo)*, Davy Dalton *(Kildare)*, Cathal Daly *(Offaly)*, Seamus Moynihan *(Kerry)*, Glen Ryan *(Kildare)*, Eamon Breen *(Kerry)*, Pat Fallon *(Mayo)*, Niall Buckley *(Kildare)*, Pa Laide *(Kerry)*, Trevor Giles *(Meath)*, Dermot McCabe *(Cavan)*, Joe Brolly *(Derry)*, Brendan Reilly *(Meath)*, Maurice Fitzgerald *(Kerry)*

1998

Martin McNamara *(Galway)*, Brian Lacey *(Kildare)*, Sean Martin Lockhard *(Derry)* , Tomas Mannion *(Galway)*, John Finn *(Kildare)*, Glen Ryan *(Kildare)*, Sean Og de Paor *(Galway)*, John McDermott *(Meath)*, Kevin Walsh *(Galway)*, Michael Donnellan *(Galway)*, Jarelth Fallon *(Galway)*, Dermot Earley *(Kildare)*, Karl O'Dwyer *(Kildare)*, Padraig Joyce *(Galway)*, Declan Browne *(Tipperary)*

1999

Kevin O'Dwyer *(Cork)*, Mark O'Reilly *(Meath)*, Darran Fay *(Meath)*, Anthony Lynch *(Cork)*, Ciaran O'Sullivan *(Cork)*, Kieran McGeeney *(Armagh)*, Paddy Reynolds *(Meath)*, John McDermott *(Meath)*, Ciaran Whealan *(Dublin)*, Diarmuid Marsden *(Armagh)*, Trevor Giles *(Meath)*, James Horan *(Mayo)*, Philip Clifford *(Cork)*, Graham Geraghty *(Meath)*, Ollie Murphy *(Meath)*

2000

Declan O'Keeffe *(Kerry)*, Kieran McKeever *(Derry)*, Seamus Moynihan *(Kerry)*, Michael McCarthy *(Kerry)*, Declan Meehan *(Galway)*, Kieran McGeeney *(Armagh)*, Anthony Rainbow *(Kildare)*, Anthony Tohill *(Derry)*, Dara Ó Sé *(Kerry)*, Michael Donnellan *(Galway)*, Liam Hassett *(Kerry)*, Oisin McConville *(Armagh)*, Mike Frank Russell *(Kerry)*, Padraig Joyce *(Galway)*, Derek Savage *(Galway)*

2001

Cormac Sullivan *(Meath)*, Kieran Fitzgerald *(Galway)*, Darren Fay *(Meath)*, Coman Goggins *(Dublin)*, Declan Meehan *(Galway)*, Francie Grehan *(Roscommon)*, Seán Óg de Paor *(Galway)*, Kevin Walsh *(Galway)*, Rory O'Connell *(Westmeath)*, Evan Kelly *(Meath)*, Stephen O'Neill *(Tyrone)*, Michael Donnellan *(Galway)*, Ollie Murphy *(Meath)*, Padraic Joyce *(Galway)*, John Crowley *(Kerry)*

2002

Stephen Cluxton *(Dublin)*, Enda McNulty *(Armagh)*, Paddy Christie *(Dublin)*, Anthony Lynch *(Cork)*, Aidan O'Rourke *(Armagh)*, Kieran McGeeney *(Armagh)*, Kevin Cassidy *(Donegal)*, Darragh Ó Sé *(Kerry)*, Paul McGrane *(Armagh)*, Stephen McDonnell *(Armagh)*, Eamonn O'Hara *(Sligo)*, Oisin McConville *(Armagh)*, Peter Canavan *(Tyrone)*, Ray Cosgrove *(Dublin)*, Colm Cooper *(Kerry)*

2003

Fergal Byron *(Laois)*, Francie Bellew *(Armagh)*, Cormac McAnallen *(Tyrone)*, Joe Higgins *(Laois)*, Conor Gormley *(Tyrone)*, Tom Kelly *(Laois)*, Philip Jordan *(Tyrone)*, Kevin Walsh *(Galway)*, Sean Cavanagh *(Tyrone)*, Brian Dooher *(Tyrone)*, Brian McGuigan *(Tyrone)*, Declan Browne *(Tipperary)*, Steven McDonnell *(Armagh)*, Peter Canavan *(Tyrone)*, Adrian Sweeney *(Donegal)*

2004

Diarmuid Murphy *(Kerry)*, Tom O'Sullivan *(Kerry)*, Barry Owens *(Fermanagh)*, Michael McCarthy *(Kerry)*, Tomás Ó Sé *(Kerry)*, James Nallen *(Mayo)*, John Keane *(Westmeath)*, Martin McGrath *(Fermanagh)*, Sean Cavanagh *(Tyrone)*, Paul Galvin *(Kerry)*, Ciaran McDonald *(Mayo)*, Dessie Dolan *(Westmeath)*, Colm Cooper *(Kerry)*, Enda Muldoon *(Derry)*, Matty Forde *(Wexford)*

306

All-Star Teams: Hurling

1963

Ollie Walsh *(Kilkenny)*, Tom Neville *(Wexford)*, Austin Flynn *(Waterford)*, John Doyle *(Tipperary)*, Seamus Cleere *(Kilkenny)*, Billy Rackard *(Wexford)*, Larry Guinan *(Waterford)*, Theo English *(Tipperary)*, Des Foley *(Dublin)*, Jimmy Doyle *(Tipperary)*, Mick Flannelly *(Waterford)*, Eddie Keher *(Kikenny)*, Liam Devaney *(Tipperary)*, Jimmy Smyth *(Clare)*, Phil Grimes *(Waterford)*

1964

Ollie Walsh *(Kilkenny)*, John Doyle *(Tipperary)*, Pa Dillon *(Kilkenny)*, Tom Neville *(Wexford)*, Seamus Cleere *(Kilkenny)*, Tony Wall *(Tipperary)*, Pat Henderson *(Kilkenny)*, Michael Roche *(Tipperary)*, Paddy Moran *(Kilkenny)*, Jimmy Doyle *(Tipperary)*, Michael Babs Keating *(Tipperary)*, Eddie Keher *(Kilkenny)*, Tom Walsh *(Kilkenny)*, John McKenna *(Tipperary)*, Donie Nealon *(Tipperary)*

1965

John O'Donogue *(Tipperary)*, Tom Neville *(Wexford)*, Austin Flynn *(Waterford)*, Kieran Carey *(Tipperary)*, Denis O'Riordan *(Cork)*, Tony Wall *(Tipperary)*, Jimmy Duggan *(Galway)*, Phil Wilson *(Wexford)*, Mick Roche *(Tipperary)*, Jimmy Doyle *(Tipperary)*, Pat Carroll *(Kilkenny)*, Pat Cronin *(Clare)*, Donie Nealon *(Tipperary)*, John McKenna *(Tipperary)*, Sean McLoughlin *(Tipperary)*

1966

Paddy Barry *(Cork)*, Pat Henderson *(Kilkenny)*, Austin Flynn *(Waterford)*, Denis Murphy *(Cork)*, Seamus Cleere *(Kilkenny)*, Kevin Long *(Limerick)*, Martin Coogan *(Kilkenny)*, Bernie Artigan *(Limerick)*, Theo English *(Tipperary)*, Sean Barry *(Cork)*, Eddie Keher *(Kilkenny)*, Pat Cronin *(Clare)*, Paddy Molly *(Offaly)*, John McKenna *(Tipperary)*, Mattie Fox *(Galway)*

1967

Ollie Walsh *(Kilkenny)*, Pat Henderson *(Kilkenny)*, Pa Dillon *(Kilkenny)*, Jim Treacy *(Kilkenny)*, Seamus Cleere *(Kilkenny)*, Jimmy Cullinan *(Clare)*, Len Gaynor *(Tipperary)*, Mick Roche *(Tipperary)*, Paddy Moran (Kilkenny), Eddie Keher *(Kilkenny)*, Tony Wall *(Tipperary)*, Pat Cronin *(Clare)*, Donie Nealon *(*Tipperary*)*, Tony Doran *(*Wexford*)*, Michael Babs Keating *(Tipperary)*

1968–1970

No All Star Teams

1971

Damien Martin *(Offaly)*, Tony Maher *(Cork)*, Pat Hartigan *(Limerick)*, Jim Treacy *(Kilkenny)*, Tadhg O'Connor *(Tipperary)*, Mick Roche *(Tipperary)*, Martin Coogan *(Kilkenny)*, John Connolly *(Galway)*, Frank Cummins *(Kilkenny)*, Francis Loughnane *(Tipperary)*, Michael Keating *(Tipperary)*, Eddie Keher *(Kilkenny)*, Mick Bermingham *(Dublin)*, Ray Cummins *(Cork)*, Eamonn Cregan *(Limerick)*

1972

Noel Skehan *(Kilkenny)*, Tony Maher *(Cork)*, Pat
Hartigan *(Limerick)*, Jim Treacy *(Kilkenny)*, Pat Lalor
(Kilkenny), Mick Jacob *(Wexford)*, Con Roche *(Cork)*,
Denis Coughlan *(Cork)*, Frank Cummins *(Kilkenny)*,
Francis Loughnane *(Tipperary)*, Pat Delaney *(Kilkenny)*,
Eddie Keher *(Kilkenny)*, Charlie McCarthy *(Cork)*, Ray
Cummins *(Cork)*, Eamon Cregan *(Limerick)*

1973

Noel Skehan *(Kilkenny)*, Phil Larkin *(Kilkenny)*, Pat
Hartigan *(Limerick)*, Jim O'Brien *(Limerick)*, Colm
Doran *(Wexford)*, Pat Henderson *(Kilkenny)*, Sean Foley
(Limerick), Liam O'Brien *(Kilkenny)*, Richie Bennis
(Limerick), Francis Loughnane *(Tipperary)*, Pat Delaney
(Kilkenny), Eamon Grimes *(Limerick)*, Martin Quigley
(Wexford), Kieran Purcell *(Kilkenny)*, Eddie Keher
(Kilkenny)

1974

Noel Skehan *(Kilkenny)*, Phil Larkin *(Kilkenny)*, Pat
Hartigan *(Limerick)*, John Horgan *(Cork)*, Ger
Loughnane *(Clare)*, Pat Henderson *(Kilkenny)*, Con
Roche *(Cork)*, Liam O'Brien *(Kilkenny)*, John Galvin
(Waterford), Joe McKenna *(Limerick)*, Martin Quigley
(Wexford), Mick Crotty *(Kilkenny)*, John Quigley
(Wexford), Kieran Purcell *(Kilkenny)*, Eddie Keher
(Kilkenny)

1975

Noel Skehan *(Kilkenny)*, Niall McInerney *(Galway)*, Pat
Hartigan *(Limerick)*, Brian Cody *(Kilkenny)*, Tadhg
O'Connor *(Tipperary)*, Sean Silke *(Galway)*, Iggy Clarke
(Galway), Liam O'Brien *(Kilkenny)*, Gerard McCarthy
(Cork), Martin Quigley *(Wexford)*, Joe McKenna
(Limerick), Eamon Grimes *(Limerick)*, Mick Brennan
(Kilkenny), Kieran Purcell *(Kilkenny)*, Eddie Keher
(Kilkenny)

1976

Noel Skehan *(Kilkenny)*, Phil Larkin *(Kilkenny)*, Willie
Murphy *(Wexford)*, John McMahon *(Clare)*, Joe
McDonagh *(Galway)*, Mick Jacob *(Wexford)*, Denis
Coughlan *(Cork)*, Frank Burke *(Galway)*, Pat Moylan
(Cork), Michael Malone *(Cork)*, Martin Quigley
(Wexford), Jimmy Barry-Murphy *(Cork)*, Mick Brennan
(Kilkenny), Tony Doran *(Wexford)*, Sean O'Leary *(Cork)*

1977

Seamus Durack *(Clare)*, John McMahon *(Clare)*, Martin
O'Doherty *(Cork)*, John Horgan *(Cork)*, Ger Loughnane
(Clare), Mick Jacob *(Wexford)*, Denis Coughlan *(Cork)*,
Tom Cashman *(Cork)*, M. Moroney *(Clare)*, Christy
Keogh *(Wexford)*, Jimmy Barry-Murphy *(Cork)*, P. J.
Molloy *(Galway)*, Charlie McCarthy *(Cork)*, Ray
Cummins *(Cork)*, Sean O'Leary *(Cork)*

1978

Seamus Durack *(Clare)*, Phil Larkin *(Kilkenny)*, Martin O'Doherty *(Cork)*, John Horgan *(Cork)*, Joe Hennessy *(Kilkenny)*, Ger Henderson *(Kilkenny)*, Denis Coughlan *(Cork)*, Tom Cashman *(Cork)*, Iggy Clarke *(Galway)*, Jimmy Barry-Murphy *(Cork)*, Noel Casey *(Clare)*, Colm Honan *(Clare)*, Charlie McCarthy *(Cork)*, Joe McKenna *(Limerick)*, Tommy Butler *(Tipperary)*

1979

Pat McLoughney *(Tipperary)*, Brian Murphy *(Cork)*, Martin O'Doherty *(Cork)*, Tadhg O'Connor *(Tipperary)*, Dermot McCurtain *(Cork)*, Ger Henderson *(Kilkenny)*, Iggy Clarke *(Galway)*, John Connolly *(Galway)*, Joe Hennessy *(Kilkenny)*, John Callinan *(Clare)*, Frank Burke *(Galway)*, Liam O'Brien *(Kilkenny)*, Mick Brennan *(Kilkenny)*, Joe McKenna *(Limerick)*, Ned Buggy *(Wexford)*

1980

Pat McLoughney *(Tipperary)*, Niall McInerney *(Galway)*, Leonard Enright *(Limerick)*, Jimmy Cooney *(Galway)*, Dermot McCurtain *(Cork)*, Sean Silke *(Galway)*, Iggy Clarke *(Galway)*, Joachim Kelly *(Offaly)*, Mossie Walsh *(Waterford)*, Joe Connolly *(Galway)*, Pat Horgan *(Cork)*, Pat Carroll *(Offaly)*, Bernie Forde *(Galway)*, Joe McKenna *(Limerick)*, Eamon Cregan *(Limerick)*

1981

Seamus Durack *(Clare)*, Brian Murphy *(Cork)*, Leonard Enright *(Limerick)*, Jimmy Cooney *(Galway)*, Liam O'Donoghue *(Limerick)*, Sean Stack *(Clare)*, Ger Coughlan *(Offaly)*, Steve Mahon *(Galway)*, Liam Currams *(Offaly)*, John Cullinan *(Clare)*, George O'Connor *(Wexford)*, Mark Corrigan *(Offaly)*, Pat Carroll *(Offaly)*, Joe McKenna *(Limerick)*, John Flaherty *(Offaly)*

1982

Noel Skehan *(Kilkenny)*, John Galvin *(Waterford)*, Brian Cody *(Kilkenny)*, Pat Fleury *(Offaly)*, Aidan Fogarty *(Offaly)*, Ger Henderson *(Kilkenny)*, Paddy Prendergast *(Kilkenny)*, Tim Crowley *(Cork)*, Frank Cummins *(Kilkenny)*, Tony O'Sullivan *(Cork)*, Pat Horgan *(Cork)*, Richie Power *(Kilkenny)*, Billy Fitzpatrick *(Kilkenny)*, Christy Heffernan *(Kilkenny)*, Jim Greene *(Waterford)*

1983

Noel Skehan *(Kilkenny)*, John Henderson *(Kilkenny)*, Leonard Enright *(Limerick)*, Dick O'Hara *(Kilkenny)*, Joe Hennessy *(Kilkenny)*, Ger Henderson *(Kilkenny)*, Tom Cashman *(Cork)*, John Fenton *(Cork)*, Frank Cummins *(Kilkenny)*, Nicky English *(Tipperary)*, Ger Fennelly *(Kilkenny)*, Noel Lane *(Galway)*, Billy Fitzpatrick *(Kilkenny)*, Jimmy Barry-Murphy *(Cork)*, Liam Fennelly *(Kilkenny)*

1984

Ger Cunningham *(Cork)*, Paudie Fitzmaurice *(Limerick)*, Eugene Coughlan *(Offaly)*, Pat Fleury *(Offaly)*, Joe Hennessy *(Kilkenny)*, John Crowley *(Cork)*, Dermot McCurtain *(Cork)*, John Fenton *(Cork)*, Joachim Kelly *(Offaly)*, Nicky English *(Tipperary)*, Kieran Brennan *(Kilkenny)*, Paddy Kelly *(Limerick)*, Tomás Mulcahy *(Cork)*, Noel Lane *(Galway)*, Sean O'Leary *(Cork)*

1985

Ger Cunningham *(Cork)*, Seamus Coen *(Galway)*, Eugene Coughlan *(Offaly)*, Sylvie Linnane *(Galway)*, Peter Finnerty *(Galway)*, Pat Delaney *(Offaly)*, Ger Coughlan *(Offaly)*, John Fenton *(Cork)*, Pat Critchley *(Laois)*, Nicky English *(Tipperary)*, Brendan Lynskey *(Galway)*, Joe Cooney *(Galway)*, Pat Cleary *(Offaly)*, Padraic Horan *(Offaly)*, Liam Fennelly *(Kilkenny)*

1986

Ger Cunningham *(Cork)*, Denis Mulcahy *(Cork)*, Conor Hayes *(Galway)*, Sylvie Linnane *(Galway)*, Peter Finnerty *(Galway)*, Tony Keady *(Galway)*, Bobby Ryan *(Tipperary)*, John Fenton *(Cork)*, Richie Power *(Kilkenny)*, Tony O'Sullivan *(Cork)*, Tomás Mulcahy *(Cork)*, Joe Cooney *(Galway)*, David Kilcoyne *(Westmeath)*, Jimmy Barry-Murphy *(Cork)*, Kevin Hennessy *(Cork)*

1987

Ken Hogan *(Tipperary)*, Joe Hennessy *(Kilkenny)*, Conor Hayes *(Galway)*, Ollie Kilkenny *(Galway)*, Peter Finnerty *(Galway)*, Ger Henderson *(Kilkenny)*, John Conran *(Wexford)*, Steve Mahon *(Galway)*, John Fenton *(Cork)*, Martin McGrath *(Galway)*, Joe Cooney *(Galway)*, Aidan Ryan *(Tipperary)*, Pat Fox *(Tipperary)*, Nicky English *(Tipperary)*, Liam Fennelly *(Kilkenny)*

1988

John Cummins *(Galway)*, Sylvie Linnane *(Galway)*, Conor Hayes *(Galway)* Martin Hanamy *(Offaly)* Peter Finnerty *(Galway)*, Tony Keady *(Galway)*, Bobby Ryan *(Tipperary)*, Colm Bonner *(Tipperary)*, George O'Connor *(Wexford)*, Declan Ryan *(Tipperary)*, Ciaran Barr *(Antrim)*, Martin Naughton *(Galway)*, Martin McGrath *(Galway)*, Nicky English *(Tipperary)*, Tony O'Sullivan *(Cork)*

1989

John Commins *(Galway)*, Aidan Fogarty *(Offaly)*, Eamon Cleary *(Wexford)*, Dessie Donnelly *(Antrim)*, Conal Bonner *(Tipperary)*, Bobby Ryan *(Tipperary)*, Sean Treacy *(Galway)*, Michael Coleman *(Galway)*, Declan Carr *(Tipperary)*, Eanna Ryan *(Galway)*, Joe Cooney *(Galway)*, Olcan McFetridge *(Antrim)*, Pat Fox *(Tipperary)*, Cormac Bonner *(Tipperary)*, Nicky English *(Tipperary)*

1990

Ger Cunningham *(Cork)*, John Considine *(Cork)*, Noel Sheehy *(Tipperary)*, Sean O Gorman *(Cork)*, Peter

Finnerty *(Galway)*, Jim Cashman *(Cork)*, Liam Dunne
(Wexford), Michael Coleman *(Galway)*, Johnny Pilkington
(Offaly), Michael Cleary *(Tipperary)*, Joe Cooney *(Galway)*,
Tony O'Sullivan *(Cork)*, Eamon Morrissey *(Kilkenny)*,
Brian McMahon *(Dublin)*, John Fitzgibbon *(Cork)*

1991

Michael Walsh *(Kilkenny)*, Paul Delaney *(Tipperary)*, Noel
Sheehy *(Tipperary)*, Sean Treacy *(Galway)*, Conal Bonner
(Tipperary), Jim Cashman *(Cork)*, Chris Casey *(Cork)*,
Terence McNaughton *(Antrim)*, John Leahy *(Tipperary)*,
Michael Cleary *(Tipperary)*, Gary Kirby *(Limerick)*, D. J.
Carey *(Kilkenny)*, Pat Fox *(Tipperary)*, Cormac Bonner
(Tipperary), John Fitzgibbon *(Cork)*

1992

Michael Walsh *(Kilkenny)*, Eddie O'Connor *(Kilkenny)*,
Sean O'Gorman *(Cork)*, Liam Simpson *(Kilkenny)*, Liam
Dunne *(Wexford)*, Pat O'Neill *(Kilkenny)*, Padraig Kelly
(Galway), Pat Malone *(Galway)*, Paul McKillen *(Antrim)*,
Martin Storey *(Wexford)*, John Power *(Kilkenny)*, D. J.
Carey *(Kilkenny)*, Michael Cleary *(Tipperary)*, Joe Rabbitte
(Galway), Barry Egan *(Cork)*

1993

Michael Walsh *(Kilkenny)*, Eddie O'Connor *(Kilkenny)*,
Sean O'Gorman *(Cork)*, Liam Simpson *(Kilkenny)*, Liam
Dunne *(Wexford)*, Pat O'Neill *(Kilkenny)*, Padraig Kelly
(Galway), Pat Malone *(Galway)*, Paul McKillen *(Antrim)*,

Martin Storey *(Wexford)*, John Power *(Kilkenny)*, D. J. Carey *(Kilkenny)*, Michael Cleary *(Tipperary)*, Joe Rabbitte *(Galway)*, Barry Egan *(Cork)*

1994
Joe Quaid *(Limerick)*, Anthony Daly *(Clare)*, Kevin Kinahan *(Offaly)*, Martin Hanamy *(Offaly)*, Dave Clarke *(Limerick)*, Hubert Rigney *(Offaly)*, Kevin Martin *(Offaly)*, Mike Houlihan *(Limerick)*, Ciaran Carey *(Limerick)*, Johnny Dooley *(Offaly)*, Gary Kirby *(Limerick)*, John Leahy *(Tipperary)*, Billy Dooley *(Offaly)*, D. J. Carey *(Kilkenny)*, Damien Quigley *(Limerick)*

1995
Davey Fitzgerald *(Clare)*, Kevin Kinahan *(Offaly)*, Brian Lohan *(Clare)*, Liam Doyle *(Clare)*, Brian Whelahan *(Offaly)*, Sean McMahon *(Clare)*, Anthony Daly *(Clare)*, Michael Coleman *(Galway)*, Ollie Baker *(Clare)*, Johnny Dooley *(Offaly)*, Gary Kirby *(Limerick)*, Jamesie O'Connor *(Clare)*, Billy Dooley *(Offaly)*, D. J. Carey *(Kilkenny)*, Ger O'Loughlin *(Clare)*

1996
Joe Quaid *(Limerick)*, Tom Helebert *(Galway)*, Brian Lohan *(Clare)*, Larry O'Gorman *(Wexford)*, Liam Dunne *(Wexford)*, Ciaran Carey *(Limerick)*, Mark Foley *(Limerick)*, Adrian Fenlon *(Wexford)*, Mike Houlihan *(Limerick)*, Rory McCarthy *(Wexford)*, Martin Storey *(Wexford)*, Larry Murphy *(Wexford)*, Liam Cahill *(Tipperary)*, Gary Kirby *(Limerick)*, Tom Dempsey *(Wexford)*

1997

Damien Fitzhenry *(Wexford)*, Paul Shelley *(Tipperary)*,
Brian Lohan *(Clare)*, Willie O'Connor *(Kilkenny)*, Liam
Doyle *(Clare)*, Sean McMahon *(Clare)*, Liam Keoghan
(Kilkenny), Colin Lynch *(Clare)*, Tommy Dunne
(Tipperary), Jamesie O'Connor *(Clare)*, Declan Ryan
(Tipperary), John Leahy *(Tipperary)*, Kevin Broderick
(Galway), Ger O'Loughlin *(Clare)*, D. J. Carey *(Kilkenny)*

1998

Stephen Byrne *(Offaly)*, Willie O'Connor *(Kilkenny)*,
Kevin Kinahan *(Offaly)*, Martin Hanamy *(Offaly)*,
Anthony Daly *(Clare)*, Sean McMahon *(Clare)*, Kevin
Martin *(Offaly)*, Tony Browne *(Waterford)*, Ollie Baker
(Clare), Michael Duignan *(Offaly)*, Martin Storey
(Wexford), Jamesie O'Connor *(Clare)*, Joe Dooley
(Offaly), Brian Whelahan *(Offaly)*, Charlie Carter
(Kilkenny)

1999

Donal Og Cusack *(Cork)*, Fergal Ryan *(Cork)*, Diarmuid
O'Sullivan *(Cork)*, Frank Lohan *(Clare)*, Brian Whelahan
(Offaly), Brian Corcoran *(Cork)*, Peter Barry *(Kilkenny)*,
Andy Comerford *(Kilkenny)*, Tommy Dunne *(Tipperary)*,
D. J. Carey *(Kilkenny)*, John Troy *(Offaly)*, Brian McEvoy
(Kilkenny), Sean McGrath *(Cork)*, Joe Deane *(Cork)*, Niall
Gilligan *(Clare)*

2000

Brendan Cummins *(Tipperary)*, Noel Hickey *(Kilkenny)*, Diarmuid O'Sullivan *(Cork)*, Willie O'Connor *(Kilkenny)*, John Carroll *(Tipperary)*, Eamonn Kennedy *(Kilkenny)*, Peter Barry *(Kilkenny)*, Johnny Dooley *(Offaly)*, Andy Comerford *(Kilkenny)*, Denis Byrne *(Kilkenny)*, Joe Rabbitte *(Galway)*, Henry Shefflin *(Kilkenny)*, Charlie Carter *(Kilkenny)*, D. J. Carey *(Kilkenny)*, Joe Deane *(Cork)*

2001

Brendan Cummins *(Tipperary)*, Darragh Ryan *(Wexford)*, Philip Maher *(Tipperary)*, Ollie Canning *(Galway)*, Eamonn Corcoran *(Tipperary)*, Liam Hodgins *(Galway)*, Mark Foley *(Limerick)*, Thomas Dunne *(Tipperary)*, Eddie Enright *(Tipperary)*, Mark O'Leary *(Tipperary)*, James O'Connor *(Clare)*, Kevin Broderick (Galway), Charlie Charter *(Kilkenny)*, Eugene Cloonan *(Galway)*, Eoin Kelly *(Tipperary)*

2002

Davy Fitzgerald *(Clare)*, Michael Kavanagh *(Kilkenny)*, Brian Lohan *(Clare)*, Philip Larkin *(Kilkenny)*, Fergal Hartley *(Waterford)*, Peter Barry *(Kilkenny)*, Paul Kelly *(Tipperary)*, Colin Lynch *(Clare)*, Derek Lyng *(Kilkenny)*, Eoin Kelly *(Waterford)*, Henry Shefflin *(Kilkenny)*, Ken McGrath *(Waterford)*, Eoin Kelly *(Tipperary)*, Martin Comerford *(Kilkenny)*, D. J. Carey *(Kilkenny)*

2003

Brendan Cummins *(Tipperary)*, Michael Kavanagh *(Kilkenny)*, Noel Hickey *(Kilkenny)*, Ollie Canning *(Galway)*, Seán Óg Ó hAilpín *(Cork)*, Ronan Curran *(Cork)*, J. J. Delaney *(Kilkenny)*, Derek Lyng *(Kilkenny)*, Tommy Walsh *(Kilkenny)*, John Mullane *(Waterford)*, Henry Shefflin *(Kilkenny)*, Eddie Brennan *(Kilkenny)*, Setanta Ó hAilpín *(Cork)*, Martin Comerford *(Kilkenny)*, Joe Deane *(Cork)*

2004

Damien Fitzhenry *(Wexford)*, Wayne Sherlock *(Cork)*, Diarmuid O'Sullivan *(Cork)*, Tommy Walsh *(Kilkenny)*, J. J. Delaney *(Kilkenny)*, Ronan Curran *(Cork)*, Seán Óg Ó hAilpín *(Cork)*, Ken McGrath *(Waterford)*, Jerry O'Connor *(Cork)*, Dan Shanahan *(Waterford)*, Niall McCarthy *(Cork)*, Henry Shefflin *(Kilkenny)*, Eoin Kelly *(Tipperary)*, Brian Corcoran *(Cork)*, Paul Flynn *(Waterford)*

All-Star Teams: Ladies Football

1980

Martina McGuire *(Cavan)*, Ann Maher *(Tipperary)*, Eileen O'Connor *(Kerry)*, Nuala Egan *(Roscommon)*, Bernadette Stankard *(Galway)*, Rose Duncan *(Offaly)*, Mary Troy *(Laois)*, Josie Stapleton *(Tipp)*, Ann Molloy *(Offaly)*, Elizabeth O'Brien *(Roscommon)*, Eileen Lawlor *(Kerry)*, Mary J. Curran *(Kerry)*, Lilian Gory *(Tipperary)*, Agnes Gorman *(Offaly)*, Rose Curley *(Meath)*

1981

Martina McGuire *(Cavan)*, Ann Maher *(Tipperary)*, Eileen O'Connor *(Kerry)*, Bridget Sheridan *(Cavan)*, Bernadette Stankard *(Galway)*, Rose Duncan *(Offaly)*, Bernie Dunne *(Offaly)*, Mary Twomey *(Kerry)*, Jean Dunne *(Offaly)*, Bridget Reynolds *(Offaly)*, Elizabeth O'Brien *(Roscommon)*, Mary J. Curran *(Kerry)*, Lilian Gory *(Tipperary)*, Deidre Quinn *(Leitrim)*, Patricia O'Brien *(Cavan)*

1982

Hilda O'Leary *(Kerry)*, Ann Molloy *(Offaly)*, Tracy Monahan *(Leitrim)*, Josie Briorty *(Cavan)*, Margaret Lawlor *(Kerry)*, Marion O'Shea *(Tipperary)*, Bernie Dunne *(Offaly)*, Mary Twomey *(Kerry)*, Jean Dunne *(Offaly)*, Claire Dolan *(Galway)*, Angela McCabe *(Cavan)*, Angie Hearne *(Wexford)*, Patricia O'Brien *(Cavan)*, Del Whyte *(Kerry)*, Bridget Reynolds *(Offaly)*

1983

Kathleen Kennedy *(Dublin)*, Agnes Gorman *(Offaly)*, Nora Foley *(Kerry)*, Tracy Monahan *(Leitrim)*, Claire Geraghty *(Galway)*, Rose Dunican *(Offaly)*, Jacinta Kehoe *(Wexford)*, Annette Walsh *(Kerry)*, Ann Cullen *(Offaly)*, Mary Dempsey *(Galway)*, Mary J. Curran *(Kerry)*, Deidre Quinn *(Leitrim)*, Bridget Reynolds *(Offaly)*, Mary Twomey *(Kerry)*, Eileen Lawlor *(Kerry)*

1984

Kathleen Kennedy *(Dublin)*, Bridget Leen *(Kerry)*, Christine Byrne *(Wexford)*, Connie Conway *(Laois)*, Marion Doherty *(Kerry)*, Jean Dunne *(Offaly)*, Edel Clarke *(Westmeath)*, Catherine Murphy *(Wexford)*, Mary J. Curran *(Kerry)*, Theresa Rafferty *(Galway)*, Eileen Lawlor *(Kerry)*, Meave Quinn *(Leitrim)*, Margaret Lawlor *(Kerry)*, Ann Whelan *(Wexford)*, Geraldine Wrynn *(Leitrim)*

1985

Kathleen Curran *(Kerry)*, Mary Rice *(Wexford)*, Connie Conway *(Laois)*, Joan Shannon *(Cork)*, Marion Doherty *(Kerry)*, Kathleen Murphy *(Laois)*, Edel Cullen *(Wexford)*, Meave Quinn *(Leitrim)*, Lil O'Sullivan *(Kerry)*, Sheila Conroy *(Laois)*, Mary J. Curran *(Kerry)*, Margaret Lawlor *(Kerry)*, Mary Conroy *(Laois)*, Del Whyte *(Kerry)*, Mairead O'Leary *(Cork)*

1986

Kathleen Curran *(Kerry)*, Mary Moore *(Wexford)*, Mary Thorpe *(Wexford)*, Nora Hallissey *(Kerry)*, Christine Harding *(Wexford)*, Anne White *(Wexford)*, Edel Clarke *(Westmeath)*, Mary J. Curran *(Kerry)*, Catherine Murphy *(Wexford)*, Angie Hearne *(Wexford)*, Marie Crotty *(Waterford)*, Marina Barry *(Kerry)*, Jo Glennon *(Westmeath)*, Del Whyte *(Kerry)*, Catherine Conroy *(Laois)*

1987

Kathleen Curran *(Kerry)*, Mary Moore *(Wexford)*, Del Whyte *(Kerry)*, Connie Conway *(Laois)*, Ann Fitzpatrick *(Waterford)*, Jo Glennon *(Westmeath)*, Mary Lane *(Kerry)*, Annette Walsh *(Kerry)*, Rita Dowling *(Laois)*, Marina Barry *(Kerry)*, Mary J Curran *(Kerry)*, Edel Clarke *(Westmeath)*, Kathleen Moore *(Wexford)*, Marie Crotty *(Waterford)*, Siobhan Dunne *(Wexford)*

1988

Kathleen Curran *(Kerry)*, Mary Moore *(Wexford)*, Connie Conway *(Laois)*, Dolores Tyrell *(Waterford)*, Mary Quinn *(Leitrim)*, June Whyte *(Waterford)*, Phil Curran *(Kerry)*, Mary J. Curran *(Kerry)*, Annette Walsh *(Kerry)*, Bridget Bradley *(Wexford)*, Mary Crotty *(Waterford)*, Eileen Lawlor *(Kerry)*, Sue Ramsbottom *(Laois)*, Bernie Ryan *(Waterford)*, Margeret Lawlor *(Kerry)*

1989

Theresa Furlong *(Wexford)*, Mary Moore *(Wexford)*, Phil Curran *(Kerry)*, Anne Dunford *(Waterford)*, Marion

Doherty *(Kerry)*, Kathleen Moore *(Wexford)*, Mary
Quinn *(Leitrim)*, Mary J. Curran *(Kerry)*, Annette Walsh
(Kerry), Aine Wall *(Waterford)*, Bernie Ryan *(Waterford)*,
Marina Barry *(Kerry)*, Sue Ramsbottom *(Laois)*, Angie
Hearne *(Wexford)*, Siobhan Dunne *(Wexford)*

1990

Mary Keane *(Clare)*, Bridget Leen *(Kerry)*, Connie
Conway *(Laois)*, Mary Mullery *(Galway)*, Marion
Doherty *(Kerry)*, Ann Fitzpatrick *(Waterford)*, Mary
Downey *(Laois)*, Amanda Donohoe *(Laois)*, Mary J.
Curran *(Kerry)*, Aine Wall *(Waterford)*, Katie Liston
(Kerry), Marie Ryan *(Waterford)*, Margaret Lawlor *(Kerry)*,
Sue Ramsbottom *(Laois)*, Eileen Lawlor *(Kerry)*

1991

Lulu Carroll *(Laois)*, Bridget Leen *(Kerry)*, Martina
O'Ryan *(Waterford)*, Anne Dunford *(Waterford)*, Mary
Gallagher *(Westmeath)*, Phil Curran *(Kerry)*, Anne
Fitzpatrick *(Waterford)*, Marie Crotty *(Waterford)*, Julie
Kavanagh *(Dublin)*, Marina Barry *(Kerry)*, Katie Liston
(Kerry), Michelle Donnelly *(Clare)*, Amanda Donohoe
(Laois), Aine Wall *(Waterford)*, Margaret Brennan *(Laois)*

1992

Bernie Deegan *(Laois)*, Bridget Leen *(Kerry)*, Martina
O'Ryan *(Waterford)*, June Whyte *(Waterford)*, Mary
Gallagher *(Westmeath)*, Mary Casey *(Laois)*, Marie
Gallagher *(Clare)*, Fionnuala Ruane *(Kerry)*, Bernie Ryan
(Waterford), Marina Barry *(Kerry)*, Geraldine O'Ryan

(Waterford), Edel Clarke *(Westmeath)*, Patricia Mimna *(London)*, Aine Wall *(Waterford)*, Pauline Mullen *(Mayo)*

1993
Bernie Deegan *(Laois)*, Margaret Buckley *(Cork)*, Bernie O'Neill *(Mayo)*, Katie Liston *(Kerry)*, Mary O'Gorman *(Wexford)*, Mary Casey *(Laois)*, Fionnuala Ruane *(Kerry)*, Denise Smith *(Dublin)*, Marie Fitzgerald *(Kerry)*, Patricia Mimna *(London)*, Mary J. Curran *(Kerry)*, Sinead Cullinane *(Clare)*, Marina Barry *(Kerry)*, Sue Ramsbottom *(Laois)*, Aine Wall *(Waterford)*

1994
Kathleen Curran *(Kerry)*, Bridget Leen *(Kerry)*, Martina O'Ryan *(Waterford)*, Margaret Phelan *(Laois)*, Diane O'Hora *(Mayo)*, Noirin Walsh *(Waterford)*, Edel Clarke *(Westmeath)*, Jenny Greenan *(Monaghan)*, Meave Quinn *(Leitrim)*, Marie Gallagher *(Clare)*, Sue Ramsbottom *(Laois)*, Catriona Casey *(Waterford)*, Fiona Crotty *(Waterford)*, Aine Wall *(Waterford)*, Tish Mimna *(London)*

1995
Anna Lisa Crotty *(Waterford)*, Regina Byrne *(Waterford)*, Bernie O'Neill *(Mayo)*, Cleona Walsh *(Waterford)*, Eileen Gill *(Westmeath)*, Fionnuala Ruane *(Kerry)*, Julianne Torpey *(Waterford)*, Jennifer Greenan *(Monaghan)*, Marie Fitzgerald *(Kerry)*, Fiona O'Driscoll *(Cork)*, Marie Crotty *(Waterford)*, Catriona Casey *(Waterford)*, Geraldine O'Ryan *(Waterford)*, Patricia Mullen *(Mayo)*, Geraldine O'Shea *(Kerry)*

1996

Anna Lisa Crotty *(Waterford)*, Maread Kelly *(Monaghan)*, Noirin Walsh *(Waterford)*, Margaret Phelan *(Laois)*, Brenda McAnespie *(Monaghan)*, Jenny Greenan *(Monaghan)*, Julianne Torpey *(Waterford)*, Christina Heffernan *(Mayo)*, Linda Farrelly *(Monaghan)*, Nicola Dunne *(Wicklow)*, Geraldine O'Shea *(Kerry)*, Anne Marie Curran *(Westmeath)*, Margaret Kerins *(Monaghan)*, Sue Ramsbottom *(Laois)*, Aine Wall *(Waterford)*

1997

Anna Lisa Crotty *(Waterford)*, Maread Kelly *(Monaghan)*, Noirin Walsh *(Waterford)*, Maread Kelly *(Monaghan)*, Moira McMahon *(Clare)*, Brenda McAnespie *(Monaghan)*, Julianne Torpey *(Waterford)*, Jenny Greenan *(Monaghan)*, Eithne Morrisey *(Clare)*, Christine O'Brien *(Meath)*, Angela Larkin *(Monaghan)*, Fiona Blessington *(Longford)*, Geraldine O'Ryan *(Waterford)*, Sue Ramsbottom *(Laois)*, Catriona Casey *(Waterford)*

1998

Patricia Bohan *(Leitrim)*, Eileen McIlvaney *(Monaghan)*, Siobhan O'Ryan *(Waterford)*, Noirin Walsh *(Waterford)*, Anna Lisa Crotty *(Waterford)*, Anne Marie Dennehy *(Meath)*, Niamh Kindlon *(Monaghan)*, Christin Heffernan *(Mayo)*, Jenny Greenan *(Monaghan)*, Margaret Kerins *(Monaghan)*, Edel Byrne *(Monaghan)*, Christine O'Brien *(Meath)*, Rebecca Hallihan *(Waterford)*, Aine Wall *(Waterford)*, Geraldine O'Ryan *(Waterford)*

1999

Denise Horan *(Mayo)*, Brenda McAnespie *(Monaghan)*, Siobhan O'Ryan *(Waterford)*, Marcella Heffernan *(Mayo)*, Anna Lisa Crotty *(Waterford)*, Mary Casey *(Laois)*, Assumpta Cullen *(Wexford)*, Christina Heffernan *(Mayo)*, Niamh McNelis *(Meath)*, Edel Byrne *(Monaghan)*, Fiona Blessington *(Longford)*, Catriona Casey *(Waterford)*, Christine O'Brien *(Meath)*, Eilish Gormley *(Tyrone)*, Geraldine O'Ryan *(Waterford)*

2000

Denise Horan *(Mayo)*, Marcella Heffernan *(Mayo)*, Helena Lohan *(Mayo)*, Olivia Condon *(Waterford)*, Claire McGarvey *(Tyrone)*, Martina O'Ryan *(Waterford)*, Lynda Donnelly *(Tyrone)*, Anna Lisa Crotty *(Waterford)*, Christina Heffernan *(Mayo)*, Fiona Blessington *(Longford)*, Lynnette Hughes *(Tyrone)*, Mary O'Donnell *(Waterford)*, Diane O'Hora *(Mayo)*, Eilish Gormley *(Tyrone)*, Cora Staunton *(Mayo)*

2001

Denise Horan *(Mayo)*, Noelle Comyns *(Clare)*, Anna Connolly *(Laois)*, Margaret Phelan *(Laois)*, Marcella Heffernan *(Mayo)*, Jenny Greenan *(Monaghan)*, Lorraine Muckian *(Louth)*, Christina Heffernan *(Mayo)*, Kathleen O'Reilly *(Laois)*, Louise Kelly *(Dublin)*, Majella Griffin *(Clare)*, Brianne Leahy *(Kildare)*, Sarah O'Connor *(Kerry)*, Eithne Morrissey *(Clare)*, Cora Staunton *(Mayo)*

2002

Suzanne Hughes *(Dublin)*, Donna Frost *(Waterford)*, Helena Lohan *(Mayo)*, Olivia Butler *(Waterford)*, Claire Egan *(Mayo)*, Jenny Greenan *(Monaghan)*, Julie Torpey *(Waterford)*, Christina Heffernan *(Mayo)*, Mary O'Donnell *(Waterford)*, Sile Nic Coitir *(Dublin)*, Niamh Kindlon *(Monaghan)*, Edel Byrne *(Monaghan)*, Orla Callan *(Monaghan)*, Geraldine O'Shea *(Kerry)*, Cora Staunton *(Mayo)*

2003

Andrea O Donoghue *(Kerry)*, Nuala O Se *(Mayo)*, Helena Lohan *(Mayo)*, Maria Kavanagh *(Dublin)*, Anna Lisa Crotty *(Waterford)*, Martina Farrell *(Dublin)*, Emer Flaherty *(Galway)*, Angie McNally *(Dublin)*, Mary O'Donnell *(Waterford)*, Lisa Cohill *(Galway)*, Christina Heffernan *(Mayo)*, Michelle McGing *(Mayo)*, Mary O'Rourke *(Waterford)*, Geraldine O'Shea *(Kerry)*, Kasey O'Driscoll *(Kerry)*

2004

Cliodhna O'Connor *(Dublin)*, Christine O'Reilly *(Monaghan)*, Ruth Stephens *(Galway)*, Helena Lohan *(Mayo)*, Rena Buckley *(Cork)*, Louise Keegan *(Dublin)*, Emer Flaherty *(Galway)*, Annette Clarke *(Galway)*, Claire Egan *(Mayo)*, Lisa Cohill *(Galway)*, Bernie Finlay *(Dublin)*, Valerie Mulcahy *(Cork)*, Mary Nevin *(Dublin)*, Geraldine O'Shea *(Kerry)*, Cora Staunton *(Mayo)*

All-Star Teams: Camogie

2004

Aoife Murray *(Cork)*, Suzanne Kelly *(Tipperary)*, Una O'Dwyer *(Tipperary)*, Aine Codd *(Wexford)*, Mary Leacy *(Wexford)*, Ciara Gaynor *(Tipperary)*, Therese Brophy *(Tipperary)*, Kate Kelly *(Wexford)*, Gemma O'Connor *(Cork)*, Jennifer O'Leary *(Cork)*, Mairin McAleenan *(Down)*, Claire Grogan *(Tipperary)*, Anne-Marie Hayes *(Galway)*, Deirdre Hughes *(Tipperary)*, Sinead Millea *(Kilkenny)*.

5

Hurling Finals

We shall never know which was the greatest hurling final of them all, but they have all contributed to the folklore of the games, mythologising the heroes and creating a rich contemporary iconography for an ancient game.

Hurling semi-finals too have thrown up some of the greatest games in recent times. Although film cameras recorded hurling matches as far back as 1910, there is no surviving newsreel film of matches before the 1930s, and only patchy coverage of games until the 1960s. Newspaper accounts are often contradictory, attendances and even scorers were not definitively recorded until the 1930s. It is, however, possible to recreate the sense of occasion in most of the finals from a variety of newspaper reports and oral and written retrospectives by some of the players, referees, officials and spectators who shared the excitement of hurling's most important occasions.

Edited Highlights: A 35-Minute History of the Hurling Championship

1887
Tipperary 1–1 (1) Galway 0–0 (0)
Birr c. 5,000

Thurles captain Jim Stapleton passed the ball to Tommy Healy of Coolcroo for the winning goal in the first All-Ireland final. When a Thurles man was injured by falling on his hurl and received facial injuries early in the game, Meelick sportingly withdrew one of their players to care for the wounded man. Thurles scored a point after 11 minutes and led by that score at half-time. Both teams togged out in nearby Cunningham's hotel (now the Wayside Inn), Meelick in green jerseys with white stripes and Thurles in green jerseys with stars 'artistically worked in the centre'.

1888
Cork v. Clare unresolved
Kilkenny Leinster champions

The GAA's organisational staff and 48 'invaders' went on a promotional tour of the United States, and 17 of the 'invaders' never came home.

1889
Dublin 5–1 Clare 1–6
Inchicore, c.1,500

Tulla from Clare, who played in their bare feet, led 1–5 to 1–0 at half-time. Heavy rain caused the slippery surface spoiled the match, despite being strewn with sawdust. William J. Spain of Nenagh, who scored 3 goals for Dublin, became the first dual All-Ireland medalist. Tulla missed star player Patrick Liddy through injury.

1890
Wexford 2–2 Cork 1–6 (unfinished)
Clonturk Park, c.1,000, Cork awarded match

The trouble started when a Cork player had his toe broken by a Wexford man's hurl and Aghabullogue captain, Dan Lane, took his men off the field. Referee John Sheehy of Limerick, and eventually the Central Council, backed Cork.

1891
Kerry 2–3 Wexford 1–5 (after extra-time)
Clonturk Park, c.2,000

Ballyduff played in their bare feet, wearing grey jumpers with a gold band, and in long trousers. Eight of the players were from Kilmoyley, who disbanded and re-registered with Ballyduff to win this match. Ballyduff had a point from Paddy 'Carr' Carroll after 5 minutes and another after 20 minutes to lead 0–2 to 0–1, added a goal midway through the second half and the sides were level 1–2 each at full-time. Kerry said Crossabeg's goal should not have been allowed as the ball had rebounded off a spectator and back across the goalline. The match finished in a melee.

1892
Cork 2–4 Dublin 1–1 (unfinished)
Clonturk Park, c.5,000

Redmonds selected 3 players from Blackrock and 2 from Aghabullogue as county selection teams were allowed for the first time. Referee Dan Fraher changed his mind after initially awarding the goal to Cork, and decreed the Central Council should decide the matter. But Dublin's Davitts had left the field and some had actually gone to work, where they were due at 1.30. Because Dublin players withdrew, Cork were awarded the championship.

1893
Cork 6–8 Kilkenny 0–2
Phoenix Park, c.1,000

Cork won on probably the most unsuitable field in hurling history after somebody neglected to get the grass cut at the original venue, Ashtown. The goalposts were uprooted and the whole jamboree set off for the Phoenix Park after a long delay.

1894
Cork 5–20 Dublin 2–0
Clonturk Park, c.2,000

Blackrock were, according to the *Freeman's Journal*, 'living in a district which might be called the home of hurling'. Only a row over the 1894 football championship prevented them entering the 1895 championship and chasing four-in-a-row.

1895
Tipperary 6–8 Kilkenny 1–10
Jones's Road, c.8,000

The first final at what is now Croke Park. Cork did not compete in the championship and Tipperary tore Kilkenny apart. Paddy Riordan of Drombane is said to have scored all but 1 point of Tipperary's total. Mick Coogan scored the goal for Kilkenny, who trailed 1–0 to 1–6 at half-time.

1896
Tipperary 8–14 Dublin 0–4
Jones's Road, c.3,500

Bill and Maurice Scanlon would not play for Dublin against their old Gaile and Tubberdora colleagues. Tipperary had a goal in the first minute in the most one-sided final in hurling history. At half-time, the score was 4–6 to 0–1, Tipperary having played with a piercing northeasterly wind.

1897
Limerick 3–4 Kilkenny 2–4
Tipperary, c.5,000

At half-time, Kilkenny led 2–4 to 1–1, but they failed to score in the second half while Limerick, who developed the art of hooking, had 2 goals early in the second half and the winning goal from a free after 52 minutes. Archbishop Croke was among the attendance who watched this curtain-raiser to the Croke Cup football tie between Cork and Tipperary.

1898
Tipperary 7–13 Kilkenny 3–10
Jones's Road, *c*.2,500

There was controversy over hand-passed scores, awarded to Tubberdora although illegal at the time. Kilkenny dominated for the first 23 minutes of the match. Mike Maher scored 3 second-half goals to give Tipperary a comfortable margin, while Bill Devane scored a remarkable point, kicking the ball over off the top of the goalpost.

1899
Tipperary 3–12 Wexford 1–4
Jones's Road, *c*.3,500

Tipperary were held for the first 15 minutes, led 2–6 to 1–3 at half-time and, until Wexford walked off the field with 10 minutes to go, as they could not find a substitute for an injured player.

1900
Tipperary 2–5 London 0–6
Jones's Road, *c*.8,000

The sides were level at 0–5 each with 8 minutes to go, and then London took the lead. Dan Horgan attempted a puck-out for London, the ball got stuck in a rut, and he conceded a free. Mike Maher took the free and a forward 'charge' carried the ball over the line. A weak puck-out led to another forward surge and Tipperary claimed the championship. Tipperary turned out in their various club colours for their one-sided 'home' final against Ardrahan of Galway.

1901

London 1–5 Cork 0–4

Jones's Road, c.1,000

London scored the winning goal 5 minutes from the end despite arriving off the boat on the morning of the game, instead of Saturday as expected. Cork never found their feet in a downpour against a team of 9 Corkmen, 4 from Limerick, 2 from Clare and 1 each from Kerry and Tipperary. Many Cork supporters, having paid 1/3 for a special train ticket from Cork, missed the game because the train was delayed behind a British troop carrier and arrived just in time to hear the result.

1902

Cork 3–13 London 0–0

Cork, c.10,000

Cork got revenge as they opened their new Athletic. In the 'home' final, Dublin's Andy Harty scored a last-minute equaliser to force a replay.

1903

Cork 3–16 London 1–1

Jones's Road, c.10,000

Cork's scoring hero was Andy 'Dooric' Buckley, credited with 6 goals, 7–4 or all 8 goals according to different reports of the 'home' final.

1904

Kilkenny 1–9 Cork 1–8

Carrick on Suir, c.10,000

Kilkenny won their first title thanks to Dick Doyle's first-half goal and a last-minute miracle save by Pat 'Fox' Maher.

1905
Cork 5–10 Kilkenny 3–13
Tipperary, c.6,000
Replay: Kilkenny 7–7 Cork 2–9
Dungarvan, c.9,000

The final was replayed because Cork goalkeeper Daniel McCarthy was a British army reservist and Kilkenny's Matt Gargan played with Waterford in the Munster championship before lining out against Cork. Jimmy Kelly scored a record-equalling 5–2 in the replay. Kilkenny scored their 7 goals in a 30-minute period. A puck-out by Cork goalkeeper, Jamesy Kelleher of Dungourney, is said to have hopped over the Kilkenny bar during the match.

1906
Tipperary 3–16 Dublin 3–8
Kilkenny, c.5,000

Dublin's Bill Leonard snatched the quickest goal in the history of All-Ireland hurling finals after just 5 seconds. Tipperary's Paddy Riordan got most of his team's scores. Eleven of the Dublin team were from Tipperary.

1907
Kilkenny 3–12 Cork 4–8
Dungarvan, 15,000

Kilkenny got the winning point from Jack Anthony but had to survive 2 Cork goal-hunts in the dying minutes. Jim Kelly got all 3 Kilkenny goals, the first within seconds of the start.

1908
Tipperary 2–5 Dublin 1–8
Jones's Road, c.6,000
Replay: Tipperary 3–15 Dublin 1–5
Athy, c.3,000

Tipperary had a goal from Hugh Shelly in the first half and 2 from Tony Carew midway through the second half to beat Dublin at Athy. They also drove the ball out of the Athy Agricultural Grounds enclosure twice. On the first occasion, it was some time before the ball was recovered and when it happened again minutes later, another long search 'dampened the ardour of the spectators'. Dublin earned their replay when Harry Boland and Bill Leonard combined for a goal in the last minute.

1909
Kilkenny 4–6 Tipperary 0–12
Cork, c.11,000

This was Tipperary's first defeat in a final, Kilkenny winning with a goal from Jimmy Kelly and 3 by Bill Hennebry. A selection row left Kilkenny short of substitutes, but Richard Grace replaced the injured Dick Doherty near the end.

1910
Wexford 7–0 Limerick 6–2
Jones's Road, 4,780

Nobody was quite sure about the new parallelogram rules. Limerick had a goal disallowed for 'square ball' at the end of each half. Wexford lost an 8th goal for the same offence. The crowd sat on chairs hired from the local.

1911
Kilkenny awarded, Limerick refused to play
(Alternative to final: Kilkenny 3–3 Tipperary
2–1 in Thurles)

Cork's lower park was water-logged so the final was
refixed for Thurles. A retreat in Limerick meant that
Limerick pulled out of the replay. A council meeting on 2
June gave Kilkenny the title by 6 votes to 5. Limerick beat
Kilkenny in a challenge later in the year.

1912
Kilkenny 2–1 Cork 1–3
Jones's Road, *c.*18,000

Sim Walton pulled on a long, dropping ball from Jimmy
Kelly for Kilkenny's first goal, then another long Matt
Gargan ball hopped past the goalkeeper after 13 minutes
and stopped just an inch inside the line. Spectators at
Jones's Road could pay 1/– or 6*d* for admittance, 2/– for a
balcony seat, or 2/6 for a sideline seat, receipts were a
record £589.

1913
Kilkenny 2–4 Tipperary 1–2
Jones's Road, *c.*15,000

Kilkenny led 1–4 to 1–1 at half-time through a Matt
Gargan goal and their only score of the second half was a
goal from Sim Walton 12 minutes from the end. Tipperary
scored just 1 point in the second half. This was the first
15-a-side final and Kilkenny's 7th title in 11 years – it
could have been more if Kilkenny had not opted out in
1908 in a row over custody of the Railway Shield.

1914
Clare 5–1 Laois 1–0
Croke Park, *c*.12,000

Clare had 3 goals from Jimmy Guerin, an opening goal from James Clancy, and a second half goal from Martin Moloney that hopped over the Laois goalkeeper's stick to the net for their first and only title.

1915
Laois 6–2 Cork 4–1
Croke Park, *c*.14,000

Laois won in a downpour, after trailing 2–2 to 3–0 at half-time, their winning goal came from John Carroll with 9 minutes to go. Some of the players wore their overcoats playing in the rain in the second half.

1916
Tipperary 5–4 Kilkenny 3–2
Croke Park, *c*.5,000

Tipperary came bouncing back from 5 points down for a famous victory. Tipperary's Tommy Shanahan and Kilkenny's Dick Grace were sent off by Waterford referee Willie Walsh. Hugh Shelley scored 3 of their goals.

1917
Dublin 5–4 Tipperary 4–2
Croke Park, *c*.11,500

Collegians Club sprang from nowhere to win the Dublin, Leinster and All-Ireland championships. Joe Phelan scored 3 of their goals in the final, Mick Neville and Brendan

Considine. Stephen Hackett of Toomevarra played for Tipperary. His brother Martin was on the Dublin team. Frank Burke came into the squad for the first of 5 dual medals.

1918
Limerick 9–5 Wexford 1–3
Croke Park c.12,000

Willie Gleeson scored 3 goals, Bob McConkey 2 as Limerick led 5–4 to 0–2 at half-time. Long ground strokes were a feature of the match, spoiled for spectators by bad light, particularly in the first half.

1919
Cork 6–4 Dublin 2–4
Croke Park, 14,300

Cork were coasting at half-time, Jimmy Kennedy having nabbed 4 goals and had 2 more disallowed for a 4–2 to 1–1 lead. It ended a 16-year barren spell and meant Cork traded in their old saffron and blue jerseys for their 'lucky' new red ones – more maroon than red. The old jerseys had been seized by British, so the County Board bought the jerseys second-hand from the defunct Father O'Leary Temperance Association team.

1920
Dublin 4–9 Cork 4–3
Croke Park, c.22,000

Dublin won with a 4-goal blitz from Joe Phelan, and 1 each from Jimmy Walsh and Mick Neville at the start of the second half.

1921
Limerick 8–5 Dublin 3–2
Croke Park, *c*.18,000

The new Liam McCarthy Cup was presented to Limerick captain Bob McConkey who got 3 goals in the first half and 4 in all. Tom McGrath (who had an opening goal disallowed) and Willie Gleeson got one each. McConkey may have had a hand in the other 2 scrambled goals.

1922
Kilkenny 4–2 Tipperary 2–6
Croke Park 26,119

Kilkenny were 3 points down with 3 minutes to go, then Paddy Donoghue and Dick Tobin scored the winning goals, and Tipperary recovered to attack, only for Dwan's final effort to pass precariously over the bar.

1923
Galway 7–3 Limerick 4–5
Croke Park, *c*.7,000

Mick Gill's tactic of dropping the ball into the square paid off for Galway, and Bernie Gibbs, Dick Morrissey and Leonard McGrath all got Galway goals. Limerick refused to play until all Civil War prisoners were released and were initially disqualified and the title awarded to Galway.

1924
Dublin 5–3 Galway 2–6
Croke Park, *c*.9,000

Dublin got back on level terms when Garret Howard drove the Galway goalkeeper 'into and under the net' and with the wind, the sun, and former Galway player Mick Gill (who had won a medal with Galway just 3 months earlier) on their side, they went on to win by 6 points. Aylward dropped the ball repeatedly into the Galway goalmouth in the manner Galway themselves had perfected. Dublin's non-playing captain Frank Wall became the only man to accept the McCarthy Cup without having played in the final.

1925
Tipperary 5–6 Galway 1–5
Croke Park, c.20,000

Tipperary started with a goal punched into the net by Paddy Power as he lay on the ground. Their goalkeeper Arthur O'Donnell's puck-out went the length of the field and led to a second goal. The heavier Galway team never recovered.

1926
Cork 4–6 Kilkenny 2–0
Croke Park, 26,829

Snow covered Croke Park for this final, played on 24 October. Cork led by a point at half-time. Pat 'Balty' Ahearne led the attack, and Cork had a new trainer: Jim Tough Barry, destined to train 13 Cork teams to win All-Irelands over a 40-year period.

1927
Dublin 4–8 Cork 1–3
Croke Park, 23,824

Dublin's 9 gardaí policed the Cork attack to lead 2–3 to 0–1 at half-time having played against wind and sun in the first

half. Cork came back in the third quarter but were foiled
by a great goalkeeping display by Tommy Daly.

1928
Cork 6–12 Galway 1–0
Croke Park, 15,259

Galway got a bye into the final without picking up a
hurley. Cork romped to the championship. Mick
Ahearne scored 2 goals, Paddy Ahearne scored 3 and
Paddy Delea 1 to make 6.

1929
Cork 4–9 Galway 1–3
Croke Park, c.14,000

Cork had a goal from Mick Ahearne after just 25
seconds to start another rout. It was 3–5 to 1–2 at half-
time. Eudie Coughlan and Mick Ahearne added goals
and Pat Ahearne got a 4th as Galway collapsed in the
second half.

1930
Tipperary 2–7 Dublin 1–3
Croke Park, 21,730

Goals at the end of the first half from Martin Kennedy
and John J. Callanan gave Tipp the edge. Tom Treacy's
bloodied bandaged head could be seen at the thick of the
action. Tipperary won a minor-junior-senior treble that
year.

1931
Cork 1–6 Kilkenny 1–6

Croke Park, 26,460

Replay: Cork 2–5 Kilkenny 2–5

Croke Park, 33,124

Replay: Cork 5–8 Kilkenny 3–4

Croke Park, 31,935

Best remembered for the swinging fortunes of the second game when Lory Meagher hit a magnificent 90-yard point. Kilkenny lost the inspirational Meagher for the last of a famous 3-game series and left the way clear for Cork's 7-point win. The first 2 games followed the same pattern: Cork led in both cases by 4 points at half-time, Kilkenny took the lead in both cases in the second half, and Cork's 2 late equalisers were scored by Pat 'Hawker' O'Grady and Paddy Delea respectively.

1932
Kilkenny 3–3 Clare 2–3

Croke Park, 34,392

Kilkenny won with goals by Matty Power, Martin White, and Lory Meagher direct from a line ball – a score legalised the previous year. Clare's Tull Considine scored 2 goals and was foiled of what would almost certainly have been a third Clare goal when he rounded full-back Peter O'Reilly. Martin Power hit the winning point.

1933
Kilkenny 1–7 Limerick 0–6

Croke Park, 45,176

Kilkenny won with a remarkably solo run goal by Johnny

Dunne 10 minutes from the end. The gates were closed 5 minutes before the start, locking out 5,000 people.

1934
Limerick 2–7 Dublin 3–4
Croke Park, 34,867
Replay: Limerick 5–2 Dublin 2–6
Croke Park, 30,250
Dave Clohessy got 2 goals in the drawn match and 4 in the replay to beat Dublin. Dublin managed to knock out 39-year-old Limerick veteran Bob McConkey twice during the drawn game.

1935
Kilkenny 2–5 Limerick 2–4
Croke Park, 46,591
In a downpour, Kilkenny ended Limerick's run of 31 matches without defeat. Kilkenny had a great second goal from Martin White with 13 minutes to go to lead by 5 points. Mick Mackey smashed a free to the net for Limerick, Cross got a point for Limerick from another free, but Kilkenny held on to win by the last point.

1936
Limerick 5–6 Kilkenny 1–5
Croke Park, 51,235
Jackie Power goals in the 4th and 22nd minutes set Limerick on course. Gerry McMahon, Dave Clohessy and Mick Mackey added goals in the second half, Mackey's solo-run goal was one of his best.

1937
Tipperary 3–11 Kilkenny 0–3
Killarney 43,638

Tipperary surprised even themselves with their runaway 17-point victory as Kilkenny inexplicably collapsed. Lory Meagher, who came on as a sub for his last match, got Kilkenny's only score in the second half. A builder's strike meant the Cusack Stand would not be completed in time for the final, so the match was shifted to the new FitzGerald Stadium in Killarney.

1938
Dublin 2–5 Waterford 1–6
Croke Park, 37,129

Declan Goode's 6th-minute goal gave Waterford a good start to their first appearance in the final, but first-half goals from Mick Flynn and Bill Loughnane won the match for Dublin. Jim Byrne to become the first ever Dublin-born player to win an All-Ireland hurling medal.

1939
Kilkenny 2–7 Cork 3–3
Croke Park, 39,302

The thunder and lightning final (when a spectacular thunderstorm lit up proceedings and doused spectators and players alike) exploded in the final minutes. Willy Campbell landed a long-range free in the net for a dramatic equalising goal for Cork. Then Terry Leahy whipped over the winning point for Kilkenny from a Paddy Phelan 70. It was played on the day World War II began.

1940
Limerick 3–7 Kilkenny 1–7
Croke Park, 49,260

Mick Mackey, switched to centre-field early in the second half, accepted the cup. Jackie Power scored the first goal, laid on the second for Dick Stokes and John Mackey scored the third.

1941
Cork 5–11 Dublin 0–6
Croke Park, 26,150

John Quirke's goal from a mighty Liam Murphy puck-out after 3 minutes started the rout. Ted O'Sullivan added another before half-time to end the game as a contest. A foot and mouth outbreak in Tipperary and Kilkenny disrupted the championship. When the delayed Munster final was played in October, Cork lost to Tipperary.

1942
Cork 2–14 Dublin 3–4
Croke Park, 27,313

Cork got their noses ahead 1–7 to 2–1 with a Johnny Quirke goal just before half-time. Just before the final whistle, Derry Beckett, kicked a second. Dublin missed several goal chances.

1943
Cork 5–16 Antrim 0–4
Croke Park, 48,843

A rout. At half-time, it was 3–11 to 0–2 and Cork had 2 further goals disallowed, just enough to keep them out of the record books. Antrim had sprung 2 of the biggest surprises in hurling history, beating Galway and Kilkenny on the tight, sloping Corrigan Park field.

1944
Cork 2–13 Dublin 1–2
Croke Park, 26,896

Cork were 6 points clear at half-time, 0–8 to 0–2, before national sprint silver medalist Joe Kelly added 2 second-half goals.

1945
Tipperary 5–6 Kilkenny 3–6
Croke Park, 69,459

Tipperary led 4–3 to 0–3 at half-time, then Kilkenny strung 3 goals together, the first from St Kieran's schoolboy Tim Maher, and forced 2 great saves from Tipperary's 5-foot goalkeeper Jimmy Maher. When the gates were shut, 5,000 fans were locked outside.

1946
Cork 7–5 Kilkenny 3–8
Croke Park, 64,415

Two goals in 2 minutes just before half-time put Cork in command. Christy Ring's classic solo-run goal from midfield gave Cork a 4-point lead. They then added 5 goals in the second half.

1947
Kilkenny 0–14 Cork 2–7
Croke Park, 61,510

Some describe this as the greatest hurling final ever. Jim Langton scored 0–3 and Terry Leahy 0–6, including the final 4 points, while Mossie O'Riordan and Joe Kelly shot goals for Cork that almost won them the match.

1948
Waterford 6–7 Dublin 4–2
Croke Park, 61,742
First-half goals from Willie Galvin and John Keane helped Waterford to a 9-point lead at half-time. Eddie Daly, Keane, Galvin and Christy Moylan added 4 in the second half.

1949
Tipperary 3–11 Laois 0–3
Croke Park, 67,168
Tipperary opened the floodgates with a Paddy Kennedy goal just before half-time. Jim Kennedy added 2 goals in the second half while Laois failed to score.

1950
Tipperary 1–9 Kilkenny 1–8
Croke Park, 67,629
Tipperary won a close, but uninteresting final. Paddy Kelly of Tipperary and Jimmy Kelly of Kilkenny exchanged goals in lost time at the end of the second half.

1951
Tipperary 7–7 Wexford 3–9
Croke Park, 68,515
Nicky Rackard's artistry was beaten off by Tipperary goalkeeper Tony Reddan with a series of great saves. Seamus Bannon, Tim Ryan and Paddy Kenny got the goals in the second quarter that did the damage for Tipperary.

1952
Cork 2–14 Dublin 0–7
Croke Park, 64,332

Cork had a goal in each half from Liam Dowling and won by 13 points after leading by 3 at half-time.

1953
Cork 3–3 Galway 0–8
Croke Park, 71,195

Controversy as Christy Ring was struck by a Galway hurler in retaliation for an ugly blow he had delivered into the face of Mick Burke. Joe Hartnett scored Cork's first goal, Ring had a glorious 60-yard goal, and Tom O'Sullivan got Cork's third after 9 minutes of lost time at the end.

1954
Cork 1–9 Wexford 1–6
Croke Park, 84,856

A record crowd came to see the competition between Christy Ring and Nicky Rackard, instead Johnny Clifford scored the winning goal with 4 minutes to go for Ring to collect a record 8th All-Ireland medal. Wexford led by 4 points with 17 minutes to go, they had lost full-back Nick O'Donnell with a shoulder injury early in the second half.

1955
Wexford 3–13 Galway 2–8
Croke Park, 72,854

Wexford got their title after 45 years with a Tim Flood

goal 9 minutes from the end. Galway were granted a bye into the final without playing a match. Two Galway goals from 18-year-old schoolboy Paddy Egan in a 4-minute spell between the 7th and 11th minutes meant Wexford trailed 2–5 to 2–3 at half-time.

1956
Wexford 2–14 Cork 2–8
Croke Park, 83,096

Nicky Rackard's goal with 2 minutes to go followed a save by goalkeeper Art Foley from Christy Ring seconds earlier. Ring had slammed a free into the net when Wexford led 1–9 to 0–5 with 18 minutes to go. Then Paddy Barry lost his marker with a great run and got an equalising goal with 11 minutes to go to set up a memorable finish. Wexford's other goal was scored by Padge Kehoe after just 3 minutes.

1957
Kilkenny 4–10 Waterford 3–12
Croke Park, 70,594

Waterford led by 6 points with 15 minutes to go. Then Billy Dwyer and Mick Kenny got goals, Sean Clohessy levelled and Kilkenny captain Mickey Kelly got the winning point – goalkeeper Dick Roche got his stick to the ball as it dropped over the crossbar. Ollie Walsh saved a last, dramatic free from Phil Grimes, having made 3 point-blank saves earlier on in the game. Actor John Gregson lined up with the Kilkenny team in the parade and scenes from the final were used in the film *Rooney*.

1958
Tipperary 4–9 Galway 2–5
Croke Park, 47,276

Tipperary scored 4 goals against the wind in the first half, from Larry Keane, man of the match Tony Wall, who sent a 70 untouched to the net, Liam Devaney, and Donie Nealon. After getting a bye to the final, Galway retired to the unhappy refuge of the Munster championship.

1959
Waterford 1–17 Kilkenny 5–5
Croke Park, 73,707
Replay: Waterford 3–12 Kilkenny 1–10
Croke Park, 77,285

Seamus Power scored Waterford's equalising goal with 90 seconds to go, deflected past the goalkeeper by Jim Walsh. Waterford won the replay with 3 first-half goals and a spectacular 8th point from captain Frank Walsh, scored from 50 yards out beside the touchline, to finish the game.

1960
Wexford 2–15 Tipperary 0–11
Croke Park, 77,154

Wexford won with goals from Mick Hassett and Oliver 'Hopper' McGrath at the beginning of each half. Wexford full-back Nick O'Donnell had a superb game. The crowd invaded the pitch with a minute to go, mistaking the final whistle, and when the disorder had cleared Tipperary continued with 12 men. A Bill Moloughney point for Tipp was not entered in the official records.

1961
Tipperary 0–16 Dublin 1–12
Croke Park, 67,866

A close run thing, Bill Jackson's goal 6 minutes after half-time inspired Dublin's first native hurling team. They led by 2 points with 13 minutes to go, and they might have drawn if Larry Shannon was not narrowly wide with a shot in the last minute. Jim Doyle scored 9 points for Tipperary. Tom Ryan and Lar Foley were sent off midway through the second half.

1962
Tipperary 3–10 Wexford 2–11
Croke Park, 75,039

Tom Moloughney and Sean Moloughney scored 2 goals for Tipperary in the first minute. Jimmy O'Brien scored a Wexford goal from 70 yards out at the start of the second half. Eventually, the match was decided by Tom Ryan's goal with 10 minutes to go after a great solo by John 'Mackey' McKenna.

1963
Kilkenny 4–17 Waterford 6–8
Croke Park, 73,123

Waterford came back from 11 points down to 2 points before Eddie Keher completed his personal total of 0–14 in the last minute.

355

1964
Tipperary 5–13 Kilkenny 2–8
Croke Park, 71,282

Tipperary toppled favourites Kilkenny with goals from John 'Mackey' McKenna, Sean McLoughlin and 3 from Donie Nealon. A 6th goal by John 'Mackey' McKenna was disallowed because the whistle had gone.

1965
Tipperary 2–16 Wexford 0–10
Croke Park, 67,498

Tipperary won comfortably with 2 unorthodox hand-passed goals from Sean McLoughlin and 7 points without reply in a last quarter.

1966
Cork 3–9 Kilkenny 1–10
Croke Park, 68,249

Cork ended a 12-year wait with 2 Colm Sheehan goals and a John O'Halloran free that struck the crossbar and bounced into the net. Kilkenny's goal from Eddie Keher came too late to save the day – an earlier goal by Tom Walsh had been disallowed.

1967
Kilkenny 3–8 Tipperary 2–7
Croke Park, 64,241

Kilkenny had goals at vital times from Paddy Moran, Martin Brennan, and Tom Walsh to lay to rest a 45-year Tipperary bogey.

1968
Wexford 5–8 Tipperary 3–12
Croke Park, 63,461

Eight points behind at half-time, Wexford had a Mick Jacob goal disallowed before Tony Doran struck 6 minutes after half-time. Late Sean McLoughlin and Michael 'Babs' Keating goals could not save tiring Tipperary.

1969
Kilkenny 2–15 Cork 2–9
Croke Park, 66,844

Kilkenny came from behind to win after Pat Delaney was stretchered off, scoring 5 points in the last 7 minutes.

1970
Cork 6–21 Wexford 5–10
Croke Park, 65,062

A record 64-point scoreline and lots of action as the final was extended to 80 minutes. Three goals from Eddie O'Brien, 1 each from Willie Walsh, Charlie Cullinane and Charlie McCarthy gave Cork a massive win.

1971
Tipperary 5–17 Kilkenny 5–14
Croke Park, 61,393

Tipperary relied on 2 freakish goals as Eddie Keher shot a record 2–11 for the losers. One passed through Ollie Walsh's legs, rebounded from the post and was landed in the net by Roger Ryan. Michael 'Babs' Keating discarded his boots and socks in the second half.

1972
Kilkenny 3–24 Cork 5–11
Croke Park, 66,137

Kilkenny came from 8 points down, had a magnificent a
Frank Cummins solo-run goal to equalise, and finished
with 7 points without reply. Noel Skehan saved 4 Cork
goal chances.

1973
Limerick 1–21 Kilkenny 1–14
Croke Park, 58,009

Mossie Dowling was credited with Limerick's vital goal 8
minutes after half-time in a downpour. After the goal,
Richie Bennis spearheaded the rampant Limerick attack for
a 7-point victory.

1974
Kilkenny 3–19 Limerick 1–13
Croke Park, 62,071

Limerick stormed 0–6 to 0–1 ahead in the first 11 minutes
before Kilkenny goals from Mick 'Cloney' Brennan, an
Eddie Keher penalty and a long Pat Delaney ball that
trickled past the goalkeeper turned the game.

1975
Kilkenny 2–22 Galway 2–10
Croke Park, 63,711

Galway took the lead with an 18th minute Frank Burke
goal, led 0–9 to 1–3 at half-time and, although P J. Qualter
scored a second Galway goal 6 minutes into the second

half, Eddie Keher's 2–7 kept Galway at bay. Kilkenny midfielder Liam 'Chunky' O'Brien, who scored 5 points, had 2 teeth extracted the day before the game. Fast-starting Galway had stunned Cork in the semi-final.

1976
Cork 2–21 Wexford 4–11
Croke Park, 62,684
Cork came back from 2 points down with 10 minutes to go with 3 points from Jimmy Barry-Murphy, 2 from Pat Moylan and a kicked effort from Ray Cummins.

1977
Cork 1–17 Wexford 3–8
Croke Park, 63,168

Seanie O'Leary scored Cork's goal as the game entered the last quarter and goalkeeper Martin Coleman brought off a match-clinching save from Christy Keogh to foil Wexford's comeback.

1978
Cork 1–15 Kilkenny 2–8
Croke Park, 64,155
Jimmy Barry-Murphy secured Cork's three-in-a-row with a goal 13 minutes from the end. Cork moved Tim Crowley back to midfield early in the second half.

1979
Kilkenny 2–12 Galway 1–8
Croke Park, 53,535

Galway took a 2 points lead with a goal from Noel Lane 12 minutes into the second half but failed to score again as Kilkenny won with 2 long-range goals, from Liam 'Chunky' O'Brien's 70 off the goalkeeper's chest and Mick 'Cloney' Brennan's 55-yard shot with 4 minutes to go.

1980
Galway 2–15 Limerick 3–9
Croke Park, 64,895

When Galway started with Bernie Forde and P. J. Molloy goals, led 2–7 to 1–5 at half-time and survived Joe McKenna's and Eamonn Cregan second-half goals, the celebrations surpassed anything ever seen in Croke Park. After 58 years of waiting, it took captain Joe Connolly 10 minutes to reach the rostrum, and several hours for the team bus to reach home the following night.

1981
Offaly 2–12 Galway 0–15
Croke Park, 71,348

Johnny Flaherty hand-passed Offaly's goal with 3 minutes to go. At the other end, goalkeeper Damien Martin batted out an almost certain Galway goal early in the second half. Flaherty supplied the pass for another vital goal by Pat Carroll after 14 minutes. Galway led by 6 points but failed to score in the final 23 minutes.

1982
Kilkenny 3–18 Cork 1–15
Croke Park 59,550

Christy Heffernan scored 2 goals in a 40-second spell 2 minutes before half-time and Ger Fennelly got Kilkenny's third goal 8 minutes into the second half.

1983
Kilkenny 2–14 Cork 2–12
Croke Park, 58,381

Kilkenny used a strong wind to dominate the first half. Richie Power scored their second goal 18 seconds into the second half. Newcomer Tomas Mulcahy and veteran Seanie O'Leary got the goals that brought Cork back to 2 points.

1984
Cork 3–16 Offaly 1–12
Thurles, 59,814

Cork held their final team-talk for the centenary final in Thurles in the local Ursuline Convent then won the match with second-half goals from Kevin Hennessy and Seanie O'Leary.

1985
Offaly 2–11 Galway 1–12
Croke Park, 61,451

Offaly's legitimate goals were scored by Pat Cleary 9 minutes before half-time and again within 22 seconds of the restart. Offaly's Joe Dooley denied he was in the square when his 55th-minute goal was disallowed. P. J. Molloy scored a memorable goal for Galway. Galway claimed another goal when a long Joe Cooney shot seemed to trickle over the line before it was cleared.

1986
Cork 4–13 Galway 2–15
Croke Park, 63,451
John Fenton, Tomas Mulcahy (twice) and Kevin Hennesy scored Cork's goals. Galway goalkeeper John Commins ran the length of the field to lash a penalty into the net. P. J. Molloy scored Galway's second goal a minute from the end.

1987
Galway 1–12 Kilkenny 0–9
Croke Park, 65,586
Substitute Noel Lane struck his winning goal off Kilkenny goalkeeper Kevin Fennelly with 7 minutes to go.

1988
Galway 1–15 Tipperary 0–14
Croke Park, 63,545
Once more Noel Lane scored the crucial goal and Galway held on against a strong wind in the second half. Tipperary's Nicholas English had a late penalty which he sent over the bar. With 2 minutes to go, Cormac Bonner's goal shot was parried by goalkeeper John Commins and sent out for a 70.

1989
Tipperary 4–24 Antrim 3–9
Croke Park, 65,496

Tipperary demolished Antrim, surprise semi-final
winners over Offaly. Galway, victims of the controversial
and demoralising suspension of Tony Keady were
beaten by Tipperary in the other semi-final.

1990
Cork 5–15 Galway 2–21
Croke Pk 63,954

Cork steamrolled back from 7 points down, inspired by
Tomas Mulcahy's goal. Galway had a superb first-half
display from Joe Cooney and a controversially
disallowed Eanna Ryan goal to remember.

1991
Tipperary 1–16 Kilkenny 0–15
Croke Park, 64,500

A controversial 20-metre free, mishit by Michael Cleary
landed in the Kilkenny net in the first half and they
never lost control afterwards, despite losing Cormac
Bonner and Nick English through injury.

1992
Kilkenny 3–10 Cork 1–12
Croke Park, 64,534

Kilkenny opted to play against the strong wind, entered
the second half 2 points behind thanks to a goal from
D. J. Carey 4 minutes before half time. John Power and
Michael Phelan added second-half goals.

1993
Kilkenny 2–17 Galway 1–15
Croke Pk 63,460

Galway fell 1–5 to 0–3 behind after 15 minutes but entered the final quarter a point ahead before P. J. Delaney slid the winning goal along the ground past the advancing goalkeeper. Galway's Liam Burke missed a great goal chance then the sides were level.

1994
Offaly 3–16 Limerick 2–13
Croke Park, 54,458

An explosive finish. Offaly trailed by 5 points with 4 minutes to go. Johnny Dooley was given the signal from the bench to go for a point but he decided to 'do something different' and the goal that resulted inspired 2–4 from Offaly in a 4-minute period.

364

1995
Clare 1–13 Offaly 2–8
Croke Park, 65,092

Ger Loughnane's team of bachelor hurlers won a thrilling final, inspired by a goal from substitute Eamonn Taaffe 4 minutes from the end. Johnny Dooley levelled for Offaly but Anthony Daly and Jamesie O'Connor scored winning points. Clare goalkeeper Davey Fitzgerald had dropped Michael Duignan's ball over his own line just before half-time, Johnny Pilkington got Offaly's other goal in the 48th minute.

1996
Wexford 1–13 Limerick 0–14
Croke Park, 65,849

Tom Dempsey's goal after 19 minutes was enough to give
Wexford an emotional victory, they led 1–8 to 0–10 at
half-time despite having Eamonn Scallan sent off and had
a 4-point lead whittled down to 2 as they hung for the last
20 minutes.

1997
Clare 0–20 Tipperary 2–13
Croke Park, 65,575

Clare conceded 2 goals in the last 10 minutes before a
classic late point from Jamesie O'Connor gave them a
historic victory in the first final between teams from the
same province. Tipperary's goals came from Liam
Cahill and a rebound goal from Eugene O'Neill.
Another Tipperary point in the 15th minutes had been
ruled wide and John Leahy missed a goal chance in the
last minute.

1998
Offaly 2–16 Kilkenny 1–13
Croke Park, 65,491

Offaly had lost the Leinster final and a controversial
replayed All-Ireland semi-final against Clare when they
came from behind to beat Kilkenny with the help of
goals from Joe Errity and a match-winning tap-in from
Brian Whelahan with 3 minutes to go. 'A game that

gave hurling aback to the hurlers,' GAA President Joe McDonagh commented afterwards.

1999
Cork 0–13; Kilkenny 0–12
Croke Park 62,989

Poor fare on a wet day. Jimmy Barry-Murphy's Cork team, with an average age of 22, swept from 4 points down in the last 15 minutes. Both teams shot 17 wides. Kilkenny felt they might have had a first-half penalty when John Power was pulled down.

2000
Kilkenny 5–15 Offaly 1–14

Croke Park, 61,493

D. J. Carey capitalised on a mistake after just 6 minutes to start the goalfest as Kilkenny won by 13. Carey scored 2–4 in all, sharing his second goal with Henry Shefflin (who added a second-half goal). The others were scored by Charlie Carter and sub Eddie Brennan in injury time. Offaly switched Brian Whelahan to full forward as they struggled to stay in touch.

2001
Tipperary 2–18 Galway 2–15
Croke Park, 68,515

Mark O'Leary's 2 goals, his second 4 minutes after half time, gave Tipperary the threshold to withstand Galway's attempted comeback. Galway's Fergal Healy hit the post twice. His goal cut the margin to 1 point with 9 minutes to go, but Tipperary outscored Galway 5–3 in those closing minutes.

2002
Kilkenny 2–20 Clare 0–19
Croke Park, 76,254

Kilkenny won easily thanks to goals from D. J. Carey after just 3 minutes and Henry Shefflin – they scored 2–13 between them. Clare cut the margin back to 3 points at the start of the second half but missed 2 goal chances.

2003
Kilkenny 1–14 Cork 1–11
Croke Park, 79,383

Favourites Kilkenny never led by more than 4 points and only secured victory with Martin Comerford's goal with 5 minutes to go. Setanta Ó hAilpín had scored Cork's equalising goal at the start of the last quarter.

2004
Cork 0–17 Kilkenny 0–9
Croke Park, 78,212

Niall McCarthy made up for missed chances 12 months earlier with 2 equalising points and the scores which pushed Cork ahead as they scored 9 points without replay in the final 23 minutes.

2005

Cork 1–21 Galway 1–16

Croke Park, 81,136

Ben O'Connor's 16th-minute goal laid the way for Cork's
30th championship title, and they held their nerve when a
goal from Damien Hayes brought Galway to within a
point with 21 minutes to go. Disappointed Galway,
victors over Kilkenny in a classic semi-final, didn't score
for the last 10 minutes.

6

Football Finals

Hurling has managed to capture most of the mythology for itself, but history lies heavy over Croke Park during the September Sunday each year when the All-Ireland football championship is decided.

The football final championship took 20 years to find a home and settle into its own date on the calendar (the 4th Sunday in September, moved to the third Sunday between 1979 and 1997) and its own home in north Dublin. There is some scratchy newsreel of matches as far back as 1914, uncovered by the GAA's greatest film maker Louis Marcus, but we have only oral tradition and newspaper reports to give us a picture of what happened until the 1960s. It may be that the best games really were played before television. As late at the 1950s one of the spectators at the 1894 final was claiming it was still the greatest football match ever played.

From unpromising beginnings, the All-Ireland football final has grown to become the most important and best attended event in Irish sporting culture.

Edited Highlights: A 35-Minute History of the Football Championship

1887

Limerick 1-4 Louth 0-3
Clonskeagh, c.7,000

William J. Spain, later to win a hurling medal with Dublin, scores the winning goal for Commercials, which outweighs any number of points under the rules of the time. It came 11 minutes into the second half after a long dribbling run from his own 21-yard line by McNamara, and a 3-man hand-passing movement. Referee John Cullinane had just been released from jail for his activity in the Land War.

1888

Tipperary, Kilkenny and Monaghan

No players on the football teams left in the championship were involved in the United States tour that almost bankrupted the infant GAA. The Leinster final is not played until a week after the 'invaders' had left.

1889

Tipperary 3–6 Queen's County 0-0
Inchicore, c.1,500

This was a semi-final, as Connacht and Ulster had been drawn in the other semi-final, and Tipperary technically got a walkover in the All-Ireland final. Bohercrowe of Tipperary kicked an early goal and led 1–5 to nil at half-time. A 4th Tipperary goal is 'rightly disallowed' as the ball had crossed the line and there were 'one or two scenes' as the 'match is characterised by entirely too much roughness'. Every altercation was accompanied by a crowd invasion.

1890
Cork 2–4 Wexford 0–1
Clonturk Park, c.1,000

The final was hastily arranged at a special meeting of the Central Council the previous Monday at Limerick Junction. Wexford Blues and Whites are short 4 of their team, and miss a great goal chance to fall 1–3 to 0–1 behind Midleton at half-time. Then comes a stop–start second half: 13 minutes of play, 8 minutes seeking a sub for an injured player, 3 minutes more play, 7 minutes of delay as a Corkman was injured near the sidelines, 3 minutes later a Wexford goal then a second goal. A proposed replay is cancelled because of a fair in Midleton.

373

1891
Dublin 2–1 Cork 1–9
Clonturk Park, c.2,000

Guinness brewery team Young Irelands, who dominated Dublin football in the 1890s, were never officially awarded the title. Cork champions, Clondrohid, were declared winners on the field of play. Three hours after the game, the referee said he had disallowed Clondrohid's second goal because a Corkman had picked the ball off the ground. At the time, a goal outweighed any number of points, so Dublin were the winners and were awarded the title when Cork refused to travel for a replay fixed for Thurles. By the time of a further replay in September 1894, Clondrohid had disbanded. Dublin defended their 2–1 to 0–2 half-time lead in unique fashion: massing their 21 players across the goal. Teams were reduced to 17 a side a year later.

1892
Dublin 1–4 Kerry 0–3
Clonturk Park, c.5,000

A defensive mistake let Young Irelands in for the winning goal with 10 minutes to go after Killorglin dominated the second half. 'The crowd encroached on the pitch when Kerry look like scoring,' the *Freeman's Journal* reported. Kerry captain J. P. O'Sullivan is already has a 120-yard champion hurdler and decathlete.

1893
Wexford 1–1 Cork 0–2
Phoenix Park, c.1,000

The final was never finished. Cork scored the first point after 15 minutes of hard defending. Wexford then responded with a rushed goal. Cork had a point from a free at the start of the second half, won the ball from a kick-out and, when the goalkeeper cleared it to the sideline a melee began and the crowd invaded the field. Cork refused to play on when the referee tried to get the teams to resume with substitutes to replace the casualties of the riot.

1894
Dublin 0–6 Cork 1–1
Clonturk Park, c.2,000
Replay: Cork 1–2 Dublin 0–5
Thurles (unfinished) c.10,000
Dublin awarded championship

Cork champions Nils Desperandum earned a replay when
the Dublin Young Ireland's goalkeeper missed the ball
completely, mainly due to having to play 'with a Corkman
hanging around his neck'. The replay is 'very fair until the
last 10 of 15 minutes when the throng in their enthusiasm
broke in and as 12 of the Young Ireland's players were
assaulted by some Cork supporters and the feeling of the
crowd getting somewhat heated, disorder then reigning
supreme, the Young Irelands refused to continue'. When
the Central Council awarded the championship to Dublin,
Cork withdrew from the GAA for 12 months and took
parts of Limerick and Waterford with them.

1895
Tipperary 0–4 Meath 0–3
Jones's Road, c.8,000

Willie Ryan scored all of Arravale Rover's 4 points, kicking
1 ball into the air, racing after it, catching it and launching
the equalising score, and scoring the winner from a free
with 7 minutes to go. The referee wrote to the papers
admitting a mistake: one of Tipperary's points should not
have been allowed because it is scored from inside the 21-
yard line, but Navan O'Mahoneys did not demand a replay.

1896

Limerick 1–5 Dublin 0–7
Jones's Road, c.3,500

Another win for Commercials. Bill Murphy scored the winning goal, now worth 3 points, after which the heavier Limerickmen fell back to defend their lead, so deep that 'the Dublin goalkeeper was playing in the centre of the field where his presence was often not needed'. Dublin lost by a point, having spent too much energy looking for goals after a 50 by the Young Ireland's captain George Roche grazed the crossbar.

1897

Dublin 2–6 Cork 0–2
Jones's Road, c.4,000

Dunmanway arrived at 2 a.m. in the city and found that nobody had booked them into a hotel. They wandered the streets until 4 a.m. when they gained admittance to a hotel in Amiens Street. William Guiry scored both goals for the Kickhams, a team of drapers — seven worked in Clery's, four in Arnotts, and one each in Todd's and the Henry Street warehouse.

1898

8 April 1900 Dublin 2–8 Waterford 0–4
Tipperary, c.1,000

Two goals from Joe Ledwidge helped new Dublin champions Geraldines defeat Waterford's Erin's Hopes, who are not even undisputed county champions because there were 2 rival boards in Waterford at the time.

1899
Dublin 1–10 Cork 0–6
Jones's Road, *c.*2,000

After Joe Ledwidge shot Dublin Geraldines to a 1–7 to 0–2 half-time lead Tom Irwin, Fermoy's cricketing and rugby-playing star, inspired a short-lived Cork comeback in the second half.

1900
Tipperary 3–7 London 0–2
Jones's Road, *c.*2,000

Tipperary selected 5 'moving quarrymen' for the final, players who had played against them in the All-Ireland semi-final (including Jack Shea who had been sent off in the match). Tipp went on to beat Galway and the first London football team to compete in a final as Britain had been declared a province of Ireland at the previous Congress. London arrived at 2 a.m. on the Sunday morning and had just a few hours sleep in the North Star hotel before the match.

1901
Dublin 0–14 London 0–2
Jones's Road, *c.*2,000

Dan Holland from Ringsend club Isles of the Sea resigned not just the captaincy, but his place on the Dublin team to David 'Gush' Brady of Dolphins, before Dublin beat Cork in the home final. Dublin's Lord Mayor had a reception for the team in the Mansion House after they beat London easily in the final.

377

1902
Dublin 2–8 London 0–4
Cork, c.10,000

Cork's Lower Park was opened for the final, when Bray Emmetts, a Wicklow club representing Dublin, led 2–6 to nil at half-time and relaxed in the second half. Dublin's Pat 'Cocker' Daly is the star of their victory over Tipperary in the home final. A delay in the second half enabled Tipperary to find a sub for an injured player but 'did not help the state of the ground, already considerably diminished in width by the spectators'.

1903
Kerry 0–11 London 0–3
Jones's Road, c.10,000

Kerry beat London easily after the home final between Kerry and Kildare had to be played 3 times, breaking all attendance records. The first day, Kildare's goal by Joyce Conlan led to a 15-minute dispute with Kerry claiming that the ball had been played behind the spectators. Then a Dick Fitzgerald goal with 2 minutes to go led to another crowd invasion when the umpires disagreed whether or not Kildare goalkeeper, Jack Fitzgerald, was over the line when he stopped the ball. Kildare saved first replay with a great Jack Connolly goal 4 minutes from the end, followed by an inspirational save by goalkeeper Jack Fitzgerald from Kerry's Jim 'Thady' O'Gorman, after which the referee announced that Kerry had won but realised his mistake and announced a draw. Third-time around, Kerry won by 0–8 to 0–2, scoring 5 points without reply in the second half included one from an extraordinarily acute angle by Dick Fitzgerald.

1904
Kerry 0–5 Dublin 0–2
Cork, c.10.000

Kerry led by 4 points to 2 at half-time and Dick Fitzgerald got their second-half point to retain the title, despite having had no organised training. Such was the excitement that poor J. T. Sullivan was left unattended in the dressing room for the duration of the game after he was forced to retire through injury.

1905
Kildare 1–7 Kerry 0–5
Thurles, c.15,000

Kerry won the toss and chose to play against the breeze. Kildare led 0–6 to 0–1 at half-time and didn't lose the lead again. Joe Rafferty's 'deft punching' caused havoc at centre-field and Kildare got the game's only goal when Jack Connolly hit the crossbar, only to power his own rebound over the line 'after a few minutes of life-and-death struggle'. The telephone was used for the first time to send the result back to ecstatic Kildare.

1906
Dublin 0–5 Cork 0–4
Athy, c.8,000

Dublin came from behind to win with points from Kelly and Walsh, having trailed 3 points to 2 at half-time. Cork's team may have included Basil McClear, stationed as a cadet officer in Fermoy, who reputedly played in this match under a false name wearing his rugby cap – he was capped 15 times for Ireland.

1907
Dublin 0–6 Cork 0–2
Tipperary, 5,000

Dublin's train was delayed on the way to Tipperary, causing the match to start late for the second time in 7 years. The winning point was scored by Kilkennyman Dr Pierce Grace.

1908
Dublin 1–10 London 0–4
Jones's Road, c.10,000

Dublin beat London easily despite having a man sent off after 25 minutes (the player was not named in match reports to save him embarrassment). In the last 'home' final, a 30-yard point from Pat 'Cocker' Daly sent Dublin narrowly ahead of Kerry 0–3 to 0–2 at half-time, followed by a 5-point spree in the second half.

1909
Kerry 1–9 Louth 0–6
Jones's Road, c.16,000

The ball passed through 4 players without touching the ground before Kerry's brilliant last point by Johnny Skinner. Maurice McCarthy had Kerry's goal and Joe Quinn missed a chance of a goal for Louth in the first half.

1910
Louth walkover from Kerry

Consternation as the All-Ireland final is cancelled at 24 hours notice because of a row over railway tickets between Kerry and the Great Southern and Western Railway Company. The title is awarded to Louth. One Central Council delegate wanted Kerry suspended for 5 years for bringing the association into disrepute.

1911
Cork 6–6 Antrim 1–2
Jones's Road, *c.*11,000

Ulster's first final – and they got the first goal of a one-sided final. Charlie Paye replied, Billy Mackessy followed with a goal at the start of the second half, and then Cork piled in 4 goals in the last quarter, including 2 more from Mackessy. Some commentators claimed that one of Cork's 6 goals should have been a point.

1912
Louth 1–7 Antrim 1–2
Jones's Road, *c.*13,000

Antrim led by 2 points with 15 minutes to go, but Jack Bannon, Johnny Brennan, Paddy Reilly and Stephen Fitzsimons got 4 points for a Louth victory. Kerry blamed a wedding the day before for their shock semi-final defeat against Antrim, despite Antrim's full-back being sent off 5 minutes after half-time.

1913
Kerry 2–2 Wexford 0–3
Croke Park, *c.*17,000

Kerry's star Pat O'Shea from Castlegregory, earned a new nickname to go with the times – 'Aeroplane' O'Shea –

381

from opponent Jim Doyle. Kerry captain Dick Fitzgerald scored a goal and a point in the first half, had another goal disallowed and the opening points of the second half, before Johnny Skinner wrapped up the title with a goal.

1914
Kerry 1-3 Wexford 0-6
Croke Park, c.13,000

Replay: Kerry 2-3 Wexford 0-6
Croke Park, c.20,000

Wexford lost the lead twice. They were 6 points to 1 ahead in the first match when, seconds after the restart, Paddy Breen took Dick Fitzgerald's pass for a Kerry goal. Dick Fitzgerald's last-minute point earned a replay. Wexford led 6 points to nil in the replay, but Paddy Breen (again) started the second half with another Kerry goal, Johnny Mahoney piled in another straight from the kick-out, Dick Fitzgerald kicked 2 points and Skinner a third. Kerry become outright winners of the Railway Cup, having won the All-Ireland twice in succession.

1915
Wexford 2-4 Kerry 2-1
Croke Park, c.27,000

Wexford became champions at the third attempt to collect a new Railway Cup. Dick Fitzgerald hit the post in the first half, hit the crossbar in the second half, then charged the goalie into the net for a Kerry goal. In reply, Jim Byrne kicked 2 points and finished one of his characteristic long runs with a goal.

1916
Wexford 2–4 Mayo 1–2
Croke Park, *c.***3,000**

The rebellion and subsequent martial law meant the match was not played until the Sunday before Christmas. Overnight frost left the pitch extremely hard, despite the fact straw had been spread. At 2 o'clock it was pronounced playable, allowing Wexford to win the second Railway Cup outright. John O'Kennedy snatched 2 first-half goals and sent to Gus O'Kennedy for a third. During the match, Mayo's goalkeeper placed his hat against the net behind the goal.

1917
Wexford 0–9 Clare 0–5
Croke Park *c.***6,500**

Jim Byrne's sharp-shooting helped Wexford to an easy victory after Aidan Doyle had a goal disallowed. Clare's hurling star 'Tull' Considine broke through but was tripped from behind with the goal at his mercy. Poor Clare had another goal disallowed.

1918
Wexford 0–5 Tipperary 0–4
Croke Park, *c.***12,000**

The flu epidemic meant that final was not played until February 1919 when Wexford won four-in-a-row thanks to points from Jim Byrne, Tom Pierce, Jim Redmond and Gus O'Kennedy. At the other end, Gus McCarthy was inches wide with a last-minute 30-yard free. Tipperary also claimed the ball bobbed across the line before a Wexford back scooped it away. Tipperary could not train for the match in the aftermath of the Soloheadbeg shootings.

1919

Kildare 2–5 Galway 0–1

Croke Park, c.32,000

New high-fielding star Larry Stanley led Kildare to victory with the help of goals from 1903 survivor, Frank 'Joyce' Conlan after 17 minutes and a 39th minute goal from Jim O'Connor, who tipped a Mick Sammon 50 to the net. Sammon was later the referee on Bloody Sunday.

1920

Tipperary 1–6 Dublin 1–2

Croke Park, c.17,000

Tipperary were waiting to play the All-Ireland semi-final when they lined out in the challenge match that became 'Bloody Sunday' and lost their captain, Michael Hogan. It was June 1922 before the final could be played. Dan Breen started the match by throwing in the ball. Frank Burke, another hero of the revolution, scored a magnificent 30-yard goal for Dublin but Tipperary came back to equalise after 48 minutes and win with a Mick Arrigan point and a Tom Powell goal.

1921

Dublin 1–9 Mayo 0–2

Croke Park, c.16,000

Dublin had the game sewn up when Bill Fitzsimmons scored a late goal, having led 0–4 to 0–1 at half-time. Mayo

point-scorer and sprinter Sean Lavin was one of the first to
perfect the hand-to-toe technique, and represented Ireland at
the 1924 Olympics.

1922
Dublin 0–6 Galway 0–4
Croke Park, 11,792
Dublin captain Paddy Carey scored the last point from a 50.
Joe Synnott, Paddy McDonnell and Frank Burke, Pearse's
successor as headmaster in St Enda's, also scored before
Martin Walsh and Leonard McGrath gave Galway a brief lead.

1923
Dublin 1–5 Kerry 1–3
Croke Park, c.18,500
Extraordinary Civil War atonement in Kerry who organised a
selection match between their Pro and Anti-Treaty players.
Free Stater Con Brosnan scored from 50 yards to give Kerry a
1–2 to 0–1 half-time lead, and anti-treatyite John Joe Sheehy
added a second-half point before Dublin won with a goal
from P. J. Kirwan and points from Paddy McDonnell, Jack
Murphy and Joe Stynes, an uncle of Jim and Brian and
another Republican (who dropped a bag of revolvers he was
carrying on the terrace on Bloody Sunday).

1924
Kerry 0–4 Dublin 0–3
Croke Park, 28,844
Con Brosnan scored the winning point after John Baily had
a goal disallowed for 'whistle gone'. Spectators paid 5

shillings to sit in the newly erected wooden Hogan Stand, named after the Tipperary footballer who died on Bloody Sunday. A new scoreboard on the railway wall was used for the first time.

1925
Galway walk over

Galway were champions for 2 weeks before anyone knew, awarded the title after midnight at a Central Council meeting when delegates from Mayo had safely gone home. When Kerry beat Cavan in the semi-final both teams are disqualified because of confusion over a new county of residence 'declaration' rule. Mayo beat Wexford in the other semi-final and then lost the Connacht final to Galway. The embarrassed Council organised an 'in lieu' competition that had no real credibility because Kerry refused to compete.

1926
Kerry 1–3 Kildare 0–6
Croke Park, 37,500

Replay: Kerry 1–4 Kildare 0–4
Croke Park, 35,500

Bill Gorman scored a 59th-minute equaliser for Kerry to force a draw. Kildare's Larry Stanley was marked out of the game by Phil Sullivan. In the replay, Tom O'Mahoney scored Kerry's wining second-half goal as Kildare hit the woodwork 3 times. Jack Murphy of Kerry, centre half-back the first day, died of pneumonia before the replay.

1927
Kildare 0–5 Kerry 0–3
Croke Park, 36,529

Kildare trailed by 3 points to nil early in the game but
Tom Keogh, Paul Doyle, Bill 'Squires' Gannon, Joe
Curtis and Doyle again scored the points to restore Lily
White pride. Kerry broke through with 5 minutes to go
but this time John Joe Sheehy hit the post.

1928
Kildare 2–6 Cavan 2–5
Croke Park, 24,700

The Sam Maguire Cup was awarded for the first time as
Kildare took their last All-Ireland. Cavan claimed Paddy
Loughlin's winning goal was thrown to the net, it
provoked a retaliatory goal from Patsy Devlin before
Bill Mangan scored the winning point for Kildare.

1929
Kerry 1–8 Kildare 1–5
Croke Park, 43,839

Ned Sweeney's first-half goal, shot in off the upright
after a Jackie Ryan free, was enough for Kerry to
survive a rattling second-half comeback by Kildare
that kept the record attendance on their feet to the
end. John Joe Sheehy and Paul Doyle scored 5 points
each in a duel of free-taking. Paddy Martin of Kildare
landed a 30-yard drop-kick in the net at the start of
the second half.

1930
Kerry 3–11 Monaghan 0–2
Croke Park, 33,280

Kerry hammered Monaghan without their goalkeeper touching the ball once during the game. Ironically Peter McConnon opened the scoring for Monaghan, who shocked Kildare in the semi-final. John Joe Landers, Ned Sweeney and John Joe Sheehy scored Kerry's goals.

1931
Kerry 1–11 Kildare 0–8
Croke Park, 42,350

A good second-quarter performance put Kildare 0–6 to 0–4 ahead at half-time, then a series of switches helped Kerry take an 0–10 to 0–7 lead before a mix-up between goalkeeper and full-back allowed Paul Russell's long shot to drop into the Kildare net.

1932
Kerry 2–7 Mayo 2–4
Croke Park, 25,816

Mayo took a 3-point lead at half-time but Kerry's Bill Landers struck on the restart and Jim Forde's goal with only 4 minutes to go was Mayo's only score in the second half. Kerry's Eamonn Fitzgerald was at the Los Angeles Olympics where he finished 4th in the triple jump.

1933
Cavan 2–5 Galway 1–4
Croke Park, 45,188

Ulster got its first title when Louis Blessing put Jim Smith's free into the net after 22 minutes, and sent a pass to 'Son' Magee for the second goal just before half-time. Despite blinding rain, a record crowd showed up and 5,000 were locked out when the gates were closed 20 minutes before the start.

1934
Galway 3–5 Dublin 1–9
Croke Park, 36,143

Connacht's first title won on the field, thanks to 2 first-half goals from 23-year-old Kerry-born UCG/NUIG student Michael Ferriter and a third from Martin Kelly at the start of the second half. Dublin's team was led by Clare-born champion sprinter George Comerford.

1935
Cavan 3–6 Kildare 2–5
Croke Park, 50,380

Revenge for Cavan as Packie Boylan scored 24th and 31st minute goals and Tom O'Reilly a third in the second half. Kildare lost centre half-back Jack Higgins through injury and the county divided in a row over why their goalkeeper had been dropped. Tom Mulhall and Mick Geraghty scored Kildare's goals.

1936

Mayo 4-11 Laois 0-5
Croke Park, 50,168

A great midfield display by Mayo's Paddy Flannelly set up Paddy Munnelly for goals in the 10th and 12th minutes. They had 2 more in the second half from Paddy Moclair in the 40th minute and Munnelly again after 4 minutes of injury time. Laois midfielder Bill Delaney, 1 of 4 brothers on the team, limped through the game with 2 broken bones in his foot.

1937

Kerry 2-5 Cavan 1-8
Croke Park, 52,325
Replay: Kerry 4-4 Cavan 1-7
Croke Park, 51,234

Four Kerry goals secured victory, Timmy O'Leary scored the first after 12 minutes, Miko Doyle got the second 6 minutes after half-time, O'Leary the third 12 minutes into the second half, and John Joe Landers the 4th after 28 minutes. The radio commentator didn't notice Packie Boylan's would-be winning point was disallowed for throwing the first day and mistakenly told the nation Cavan had won.

1938

Galway 3-3 Kerry 2-6
Croke Park, 68,950
Replay: Galway 2-4 Kerry 0-7
Croke Park, 47,851

Kerry were beaten in replay for the first time: a free was

awarded to Kerry, a Galway man stood too close to the ball, and when the referee whistled again the crowd invaded. They managed to clear the field but Kerry finished the match without their complement of 15 because some of their players had gone to the dressing room. One of those to get a run was Joe Keohane, who had watched the rest of the final from the stand, dressed in his Sunday suit. The first day there were complaints from Kerry that the final whistle went early and a would-be winning point by John Joe Landers was disallowed.

1939
Kerry 2–5 Meath 2–3
Croke Park, 46,828

Newcomer Dan Spring, father of 1980s Tánaiste Dick, scored Kerry's 2 goals to beat Meath. Meath's replied with one of the best goals in GAA history from Mattie Gilsenan just before half-time. They had another goal from Jim Clarke midway through the second half but, having kicked 11 wides, they lost by 2 points in the end.

1940
Kerry 0–7 Galway 1–3
Croke Park, 60,821

Jimmy Duggan's goal from a John 'Tull' Dunne free just before half-time set the game alight but Kerry sub Paddy 'Bawn' Brosnan changed the course of the second half. Galway were awarded 38 frees to Kerry's 24, just over a free a minute.

1941
Kerry 1-8 Galway 0-7
Croke Park, 45,512

Kerry secured three-in-a-row with a goal from Tom 'Gega' O'Connor and 2 Murt Kelly points. Transport shortages restricted the attendance, with 11,000 coming by turf-fired train and 2 hardy Kerrymen arriving by tandem from Killarney.

1942
Dublin 1-10 Galway 1-8
Croke Park, 37,105

Paddy O'Connor's 10th-minute goal kept Dublin in touch at half-time, and they come back from 3 points down with late points from a Tommy Banks 50 and Matt Fletcher.

1943
Roscommon 1-6 Cavan 1-6
Croke Park, 68,023
Replay: Roscommon 2-7 Cavan 2-2
Croke Park, 47,193

A brilliant draw was followed by a bad-tempered replay. Roscommon won their first title with goals by Frank Kinlough after 10 minutes and Jack McQuillan after 12 minutes. Cavan fought back to 2 points behind despite having Joe Stafford sent off for a blow on Owensie Hoare, 2 Cavan players tried to prevent the umpire signalling Phelim Murray's winning point, another Cavan player felled the referee with a blow, the crowd invaded, it took several minutes to restart the game and the referee was attacked again after the final whistle.

1944
Roscommon 1–9 Kerry 2–4
Croke Park, 79,245

Roscommon took their second title. Frankie Kinlough
scored the vital goal from John Joe Nerney's pass after
11 minutes. Kerry managed to go 2 points ahead before
Donal Keenan scored 2 points to equalise with 5
minutes to go and Kinlough and Keenan slotted over 2
winning points.

1945
Cork 2–5 Cavan 0–7
Croke Park, 67,329

Cork ended 34 years in the wilderness and gave Jack
Lynch the 5th of 6 All-Ireland medals in succession,
the others were in hurling. The goals were from Mick
Tubridy (6 minutes) and Derry Beckett (1 minute from
the end).

1946
Kerry 2–4 Roscommon 1–7
Croke Park, 75,771
Replay: Kerry 2–8 Roscommon 0–10
Croke Park, 65,661

Roscommon lost Jimmy Murray 14 minutes from the
end of the drawn final. They still led by 6 points with 3
minutes to go in that final and it might have been more
– 3 Donal Keenan shots rebounded off the woodwork.
Kerry snatched a draw with goals from Paddy Burke
and Tom Gega O'Connor. In the replay, Kerry came
back from behind again, Paddy Burke took a Gega

O'Connor pass to score their winning goal and O'Connor bundled over a second goal in a last-minute melee.

1947
Cavan 2-11 Kerry 2-7
Polo Grounds, New York 34,491

Slow starting Cavan fell 8 points behind in a final staged in New York's Polo Grounds, after Batt Garvey and Eddie Dowling goals for Kerry. Then a 6-man move led to T. P. O'Reilly getting 1 back for Cavan, and Pete Donohue, nicknamed 'the Babe Ruth of Gaelic football', added 4 points in each half. Commentator Micheál Ó Hehir appealed over the airwaves to the New York telecommunications people not to cut off the commentary to the ears of excited fans at home.

1948
Cavan 4-5 Mayo 4-4
Croke Park, 74,645

Cavan won the big wind final with a late point from Peter Donohue, having led by 3–2 to nil, they allowed Mayo to come back to equalise. In the first half, Tony Tighe got 2 goals, Victor Sherlock another and Tom Byrne had a goal disallowed. Mick Higgins got a 4th early in the second half. Mayo had goals from Peter Solan and 2 from Tom Acton before Pádraig Carney scored the first-ever penalty in an All-Ireland final.

1949
Meath 1–10 Cavan 1–6
Croke Park, 79,460

Bill Halfpenny scored Meath's second-half goal. Mick Higgins got a goal in reply but Cavan relied too heavily on Peter Donohue's contribution of 6 points, 5 from frees. Jim Kearney, who had played on the 1939 All-Ireland final team, comes out of retirement to help Meath at midfield.

1950
Mayo 2–5 Louth 1–6
Croke Park, 76,174

Mayo snatched the title with a freak goal 5 minutes from the end. Sean Boyle tried to clear, Sean Flanagan charged the ball down and ran 20 yards to score. Mick Mulderrig added a point and Louth's dreams lay in tatters. Peter Solan and Nick Roe exchanged goals in the first half.

1951
Mayo 2–8 Meath 0–9
Croke Park, 78,201

Two first-half goals from Tom Langan and Joe Gilvarry and 3 points in the last 5 minutes from 'flying doctor' Padraig Carney gave Mayo another title, Mick Flanagan almost had a third at the start of the second half.

1952

Sept 28 Cavan 2-4 Meath 1-7
Croke Park, 64,200

Replay: Cavan 0-9 Meath 0-5
Croke Park, 62,515

A strange equalising point saved Cavan: Edwin Carolan chased a ball that appeared to go over the end-line, kicked it across the goal. It hit the far post and rebounded over the bar. While Paddy Meegan missed 3 frees, he should have scored in the replay, Mick Higgins scored 5 and another 2 from play for a 4-point win. Meath's Peter McDermott missed a great chance towards the end when he shot wide with only the goalkeeper to beat.

1953

Kerry 0-13 Armagh 1-6
Croke Park, 86,155

Six minutes from the end Bill McCorry missed a penalty for Armagh as Kerry came from 2 points down. Armagh lost Sean Quinn through injury and had to play with 3 different goalkeepers at different stages of the game. Mal McEvoy got their first-half goal from long range.

1954

Meath 1-13 Kerry 1-7
Croke Park, 75,276

Tom Moriarty's 20th-minute goal sealed victory for Meath when Peter McDermott's shot was saved by the goalkeeper but rebounded. John Sheehan got Kerry's first-half goal, 2 minutes before half-time, when he lashed out with his boot after missing a high ball.

1955
Kerry 0–12 Dublin 1–6
Croke Park, 87,102

Dublin were hot favourites, but points from Tadhgie
Lyne and 2 spectacular second-half saves from fair-
haired Jerome O'Shea gave Kerry a 6-point lead. Then
Ollie Freaney got a Dublin goal 5 minutes from the end,
and Kerry held on in the last 4 minutes in the face of
Dublin's final, desperate onslaught.

1956
Galway 2–13 Cork 3–7
Croke Park, 70,772

The terrible twins went into history: Frankie Stockwell
scored 2–5 and had another goal disallowed. Sean Purcell
sent in the line ball for the first goal and the punched
pass which gave Stockwell the second. For Cork, a
deflected shot was tipped in by Johnny Creedon, another
was sent to the net from 20 yards by Niall Kelleher and
Denis Kelleher's shot, which had been half-stopped,
trickled across the line.

1957
Louth 1–9 Cork 1–7
Croke Park, 72,732

Ireland's smallest county beat Ireland's biggest when
Kevin Beahan's line ball was punched to the net by Sean
Cunningham 5 minutes from the end. A long Nealy
Duggan lob ended in the Louth net before half-time.

1958
Dublin 2–12 Derry 1–9
Croke Park, 73,371

Derry shocked Kerry in the semi-final and almost did the same to Dublin in the final. The Dublin goalkeeper had saved brilliantly twice when Owen Gribben eventually scored. Two minutes later, the full-back slipped, and Paddy Farnan was left with a clear run for a goal. Johnny Joyce got Dublin's second at the end.

1959
Kerry 3–7 Galway 1–4
Croke Park, 85,897

After Kerry won convincingly with 3 goals: a punched Tom Long ball forced into the net by Dan McAuliffe, a dropped ball by goalkeeper Jimmy Farrell with Dan McAuliffe thundered in on top of him, and a third from substitute Garry McMahon, who slipped as he sent to the net 5 minutes from the end. Captain Mick O'Connell left the cup in the dressing room.

1960
Down 2–10 Kerry 0–8
Croke Park, 87,768

Down's famous first. Dan McCartan turned the game 11 minutes into the second half when he took Kevin Mussen's line-ball and sent in a high 40-yard lob which the goalkeeper dropped over the line. Two minutes later, Paddy Doherty was pulled down in the square. He scored the penalty to put Down 6 points up and change GAA history.

1961
Down 3–6 Offaly 2–8
Croke Park, 90,556

Down started badly. Mick Casey took a Har Donnelly pass and sent in a dropping ball from 20 yards out that arched into the Down net and Peter Daly snatched a second from a defensive mistake before Down recovered. Offaly then had a penalty request turned down as they lost their 6-point lead. Down got 3 goals of their own from James McCartan (11th minute), Sean O'Neill (23rd) and Ben Morgan (30th).

1962
Kerry 1–12 Roscommon 1–4
Croke Park, 75,771

Perhaps the worst final of all. Garry McMahon got Kerry's only goal after 35 seconds, punched to the net after 2 defenders let a Mick O'Connell free fall to him unmarked. Jim Lucey fielded the kick-out and Timmy O'Sullivan had Kerry's first point within seconds. Roscommon's goal failed to lift the game, a 20th-minute penalty from Don Feeley.

1963
Dublin 1–9 Galway 0–10
Croke Park, 87,106

Des Ferguson came out of retirement to help Dublin win. Nine minutes into the second half, Brian McDonald sends a line-ball to the goal-mouth, it is touched on by Simon Bohan, and Gerry Davey scored the winning goal as 6 defenders and 4 attackers fought for possession in the parallelogram. Galway managed to cut the margin back to 1 point near the end, but John Timmons finished the game with a Dublin point. The referee seemed to award a penalty to Galway then changed his mind.

1964
Galway 0–15 Kerry 0–10
Croke Park, 76,498

The fist was king as 4 of Galway's points were punched over the bar. Galway took a 4-point lead in the first 10 minutes and Cyril Dunne got 9 of their 15 points to hold it. Mick O'Connell scored 7 for Kerry. After John Donnellan collected the cup, he learned his father had died watching the game in the grandstand.

1965
Galway 0–12 Kerry 0–9
Croke Park, 77,735

Galway had their lead against Kerry cut back to just 1 point with 20 minutes to go but won by 3 as Pat Donnellan curtailed Mick O'Connell. Derry O'Shea (Kerry) and John Donnellan (Galway) were sent off and John O'Shea followed them off minutes later.

1966
Galway 1–10 Meath 0–7
Croke Park, 71,569

A long clearance found Mattie McDonagh unmarked at the edge of the square for a 21st-minute goal. Galway led 1–6 to 0–1 at half-time and win a three-in-a-row by 6.

1967
Meath 1–9 Cork 0–9
Croke Park, 70,343

Cork had a 3-point to 1 lead at the end of a terrible first half.
Six minutes later, Terry Kearns slipped unnoticed behind the
backline to punch Matt Kerrigan's centre to the net from 5 yards
out. Cork's last-minute goal chance was pulled back because
Con O'Sullivan's short free to Flor Hayes was too short.

1968
Down 2–12 Kerry 1–13
Croke Park, 71,294

Down have never lost a final. Sean O'Neill got the inside of
his boot to a rebounding ball for a goal after 6 minutes. John
Murphy stuck another following confusion in the Kerry
goalmouth. Brendan Lynch's goal from a close-in free in the
59th minute came too late to make a difference.

1969
Kerry 0–10 Offaly 0–7
Croke Park, 67,828

Kerry's converted goalkeeper Johnny Culloty had 2 great
first-half saves and another at the start of the second half.
Meanwhile Kerry kept a 3-point half-time lead as Offaly
sharp-shooter Tony McTague hit the post twice.

1970
Kerry 2–19 Meath 0–18
Croke Park, 71,775

The final went to 80 minutes and Kerry won an exciting
match. Din Joe Crowley's goal 4 minutes from the end sealed

what manager Tadhgie Lyne described as Kerry's answer to the Gormanston professors, and their blackboard tactics'. Kerry had seen their 8-point lead cut back to 3.

1971
Offaly 1-14 Galway 2-8
Croke Park, 70,789

Offaly's first. They switched Nicholas Clavin to partner Willie Bryan after half-time. A goal from Murt Connor gave Offaly the lead, Seamus Leyden scored an equalising second goal for Galway, and Offaly got 3 more points for a famous victory.

1972
Offaly 1-13 Kerry 1-13
Croke Park, 72,032
Replay: Offaly 1-19 Kerry 0-13
Croke Park, 66,136

Offaly eventually broke down Kerry's resistance with a goal after 48 minutes of the replay when Pat Fenning's long speculative ball hopped over the line without a Kerry defender touching it. It was Kerry's heaviest All-Ireland defeat ever. Offaly captain Tony McTague scored 10 points in the replay and 6 in the drawn match. Noel Cooney (Offaly) and Brendan Lynch (Kerry) exchanged goals in the drawn match.

1973
Cork 3-17 Galway 2-13
Croke Park, 73,308

Cork teenager Jimmy Barry-Murphy scored the first of 2 goals after just 2 minutes to give Cork the initiative. Jimmy

Barrett scored the third after switching to left half-forward.

1974
Dublin 0–14 Galway 1–6
Croke Park, 71,898

Galway led 1–4 to 0–5 at half-time through a punched goal from the edge of the parallelogram. But Dublin's hour had come, Paddy Cullen saved Liam Sammon's 52nd minute penalty. Kevin Heffernan's boys took the lead 17 minutes into the second half and Dublin ran out easy winners cheered by a new army of denim clad supporters on Hill 16.

1975
Kerry 2–12 Dublin 0–11
Croke Pk 66,346

In the rain, a new reign began. Dublin's defence slipped to let John Egan in after 3 minutes, and substitute Ger O'Driscoll got the second goal for a surprise win for Kerry and manager Mick O'Dwyer.

1976
Dublin 3–8 Kerry 0–10
Croke Park, 73,588

Dublin returned with a new hero, Kevin Moran careered through the Kerry defence, took a return pass from Bernard Brogan and sent a shot screaming narrowly wide to set the pace for a fast, thrilling match. John McCarthy finished a 5-man move for their first goal after 15 minutes. Jimmy Keaveney sent a penalty into the top corner at the start of the second half, and Brian Mullins side-footed the third with 12 minutes to go.

1977
Dublin 5-12 Armagh 3-6
Croke Park, 66,542

Dublin brushed Kerry aside in a classic semi-final, then beat Armagh easily. Jimmy Keaveney scored 2–6, his first goal after just 90 seconds, the second 2 minutes into the second half. Bobby Doyle (13th minute), John McCarthy (33rd minute) and Doyle again (60th minute) were Dublin's other goalscorers. Paddy Moriarty scored from the first of 2 penalties. When Armagh needed more goals Sean Devlin hit the post and Moriarty missed a second penalty.

1978
Kerry 5-11 Dublin 0-9
Croke Park, 71,503

Remembered for Mickey Sheehy's famous 32nd-minute goal sent over the head of a frantic Paddy Cullen, caught off his line disputing a refereeing decision. New 6 foot 3 full-forward Eoin Liston unveiled his fist for 3 second-half goals. Pat Spillane played all over the field, including goalkeeper for a short spell after Charlie Nelligan was sent off with Dublin's John McCarthy in the 57th minute.

1979
Kerry 3-13 Dublin 1-8
Croke Park 72,185

Starting without Ger Power, losing John O'Keeffe and having Páidí Ó Sé sent off did not deter Kerry, who crushed Dublin with a shattering Mike Sheehy goal after 10 minutes, another Sheehy penalty after 56 minutes, and a third from John Egan 8 minutes from the end. Jim Ronayne's controversial 46th minute handpassed goal is Dublin's only reward.

1980
Kerry 1–9 Roscommon 1–6
Croke Park, 63,854

Kerry got a scare and fell 5 points behind to Roscommon in the first 12 minutes after their full-back slipped and Tony O'Connor raced in for a Roscommon goal after just 35 seconds. A hand-passed Mikey Sheehy goal brought Kerry back on level terms at half-time and eventually the Liston-less Kerry won a ragged 64-free final by 3 points. Roscommon tried 3 different free-takers as missed chances mounted.

1981
Kerry 1–12 Offaly 0–8
Croke Park, 61,489

Seven Kerry players combined for a great quick-passing goal through Deenihan, Kennelly, Doyle, Liston, Egan, to Sheehy, and eventually Jack O'Shea who shot from 14 yards to the net.

1982
Offaly 1–15 Kerry 0–17
Croke Park, 62,309

Offaly smashed the five-in-a-row dream with 2 minutes to go. Substitute Seamus Darby had entered the play almost unnoticed, wing-back Tommy Doyle appeared to be nudged as he prepared to collect and Darby shot past stranded goalkeeper Nelligan. Kerry in disarray could not organise their counter-attack. Martin Furlong had saved a 53rd minute penalty.

1983
Dublin 1-10 Galway 1-8
Croke Park, 71,988

Barney Rock scored an opportunist 11th-minute goal, after a fluffed kick-out. Brian Mullins, Ray Hazley and Ciaran Duff of Dublin and Tomas Tierney of Galway are all sent off, a record.

1984
Kerry 0-14 Dublin 1-6
Croke Park, 68,365

Kerry controlled the centenary final. Only 2 Dublin forwards score, including Barney Rock with a 43rd-minute goal.

1985
Kerry 2-12 Dublin 2-8
Croke Park, 69,389

Kerry seized the initiative with a Jack O'Shea penalty goal after 11 minutes and led by 9 points at half-time. Kerry nerves were steadied by Timmy O'Dowd's breakaway goal when Dublin come storming back with 2 goals from Joe McNally.

1986
Kerry 2-15 Tyrone 1-10
Croke Park, 68,628

Peter Quinn's goal, 45 seconds into the second half, sent Tyrone 6 points clear, and a miskicked penalty from Kevin McCabe 3 minutes later put them 7 ahead. Man-of-the-match

Pat Spillane then ran 50 yards for a 41st-minute handpassed goal and Ger Power cantered through to give Mike Sheehy a second goal after 49 minutes, and Kerry eventually won by 8 points.

1987
Meath 1–14 Cork 0–11
Croke Park, 68,431

Colm O'Rourke deservedly scored Meath's 25th-minute winning goal. Seven minutes earlier Cork had a goal chance blocked by Mick Lyons when Jimmy Kerrigan seemed through for a 7-point lead. Instead, it was Meath who led 1–6 to 0–8 at half-time, and Larry Tompkins sent 6 of his 8 free kicks wide in the second half.

1988
Meath 0–12 Cork 1–9
Croke Park, 65,000
Replay: Meath 0–13 Cork 0–12
Croke Park, 64,069

A controversial final. After 7 minutes Gerry McEntee was sent off and Meath, down to 14 men, held on for a 1-point win. Cork scored the only goal of the 2 meetings after 3 minutes of the drawn final, when Teddy McCarthy finished a Dinny Allen-Paul McGrath move. Brian Stafford scored the equaliser from a controversial free.

1989
Cork 0–17 Mayo 1–11
Croke Park, 65,519

Substitute Anthony Finnerty got the only goal of the

game after 38 minutes to give Mayo a brief lead. Teddy McCarthy took control as Mayo failed to score in the final 19 minutes.

1990
Cork 0-11 Meath 0-9
Croke Park, 65,723

Shay Fahy controlled midfield and Teddy McCarthy became the first player to win All-Ireland hurling and football medals in the same year, despite Colm O'Neill of Cork being sent off before half-time.

1991
Down 1-16 Meath 1-14
Croke Park, 64,500

Meath, who had beaten Dublin in a famous 4-match epic, fell 11 points behind Down who had a 50th-minute goal from Barry Breen. Then Dublin nearly caught up again with the help of a spectacular Liam Hayes solo run goal, before losing by 2 points.

1992
Donegal 0-18 Dublin 0-14
Croke Park, 64,547

Donegal's running game made history as Tony Boyle popped over the points and Charlie Redmond missed a Dublin penalty.

1993
Derry 1-14 Cork 2-8
Croke Park, 64,500

Seamus Downey scored the winning goal and Enda Gormley

popped over 6 points for Derry. Cork's Tony Davis was harshly sent off.

1994
Down 1–12 Dublin 0–13
Croke Park, 58,684
Rampant Mickey Linden fed James MacCartan for the winning goal.

1995
Dublin 1–10 Tyrone 0–12
Croke Park, 65,000
Charlie Redmond scored the winning goal, then failed to leave the field for a minute after he was sent off. At the end, Peter Canavan, scorer of 11 points for Tyrone, was judged to have handled the ball on the ground and Sean McLoughlin had an equaliser disallowed for Tyrone.

1996
Meath 0–12 Mayo 1–9
Croke Park, 65,898
Replay: Meath 2–9 Mayo1–11
Croke Park, 65,802
Mayo lost a 6-point lead to a late Colm Coyle equaliser, then lost a replay they might have drawn. Brendan Reilly scored Meath's winner after Mayo's James Horan scored a 66th-minute equaliser. Trevor Giles (34th-minute penalty) and Tommy Dowd from a quick free in the 60th minute, got Meath goals in a replay best remembered for the chaotic punch-up which led to Liam McHale and Colm Coyle being sent off.

1997

Kerry 0-13 Mayo 1-7

Croke Park, 65,601

Maurice Fitzgerald scored 9 points and a player of the year award as Mayo scored 1-2 in 2 minutes but failed to score in the last 20.

1998

Galway 1-14 Kildare 1-10

Croke Park, 65,886

Sam went back to Connacht after 32 years thanks to Pádraig Joyce's goal at the start of the second half and some magnificent finishing by Ja Fallon. Dermot Earley had scored Kildare's goal to give his side a 1-5 to 0-5 half-time lead.

1999

Meath 1-11 Cork 1-8

Croke Park, 63,276

Ollie Murphy's first-half goal spoiled Cork's hopes of another double. Meath held their nerve after Graham Geraghty missed a penalty at the start of the second half and Joe Kavanagh responded with a goal that gave Cork a brief lead.

2000

Galway 0-14 Kerry 0-14

Croke Park, 63,349

Replay: Kerry 0-17 Galway 1-10

Croke Park, 64,094

A disputed free gave Kerry the lead with 17 minutes to go.

Galway worked the ball the length of the field for Declan Meehan's memorable early goal but lost Kevin Walsh to injury after 19 minutes. Galway had come from 7 points down to draw the first game as both sides missed easy chances.

2001
Galway 0–17 Meath 0–8
Croke Park, 70,482

Padraig Joyce scored 8 points in a row as Galway became the first 'back-door' champions, overwhelming Meath in the second half after Nigel Nestor was sent off. Meath had demolished Kerry in the All-Ireland semi-final.

2002
Armagh 1–12 Kerry 0–14
Croke Park, 79,500

Oisin McConville's 55th-minute goal gave Armagh an emotional victory in a match that appeared lost at half-time, when Armagh trailed by 4 points, faced the wind, had lost John McEntee to concussion and McConville had missed a 34th minute penalty. Kerry failed to score in the final 17 minutes.

2003
Tyrone 0–12 Armagh 0–9
Croke Park, 79,394

Brian Dooher played superbly. Peter Canavan overcame injury to guide Tyrone to their first title, reappearing for the final 10 minutes. Tyrone had 3 missed goal chances in a dour match that produced 10 yellow cards. Armagh

had Diarmaid Marsden sent off in the 56th minute and
Steven McDonnell's goal shot spectacularly blocked by
Conor Gormley. Within months of Tyrone's victory,
their young star Cormac McAnallen had died.

2004
Kerry 1–20 Mayo 2–9
Croke Park, 79,749

Colm 'Gooch' Cooper's 25th-minute goal put the match
beyond Mayo's reach, despite an early goal from Alan
Dillon. Michael Conroy scored a consolation goal for
Mayo in injury time.

2005
Tyrone 1–16 Kerry 2–10
Croke Park, 82,112

Brian Dooher's emotional eight-minute victory speech
paid tribute to his predecessor, Cormac MacAnallen,
who had died 18 months earlier, a tragic victim of adult
sudden death syndrome. Tyrone recovered from Daire
Ó Cinnéide's 6th-minute goal to get one of their own
from Peter Canavan just before half-time. Kerry's
comeback, inspired by Tomás Ó Sé's 57th-minute goal,
enlivened the best final for a decade.

7

Club Championship

How quickly time flies. It seems like only yesterday that teams were 21-a-side, players hurled for an hour before the ball was thrown-in and the club championship was played in Croke Park on a Friday night in case anybody found out about it. Come to think of it, that *was* only yesterday.

The GAA championships devised in 1887 was an ambitious project. Each of the association's 635 clubs would play off in their county championship, and then the winning clubs would go forward to the All-Ireland championship. This system meant inter-county competitions could start only after the county championships were finished, and eventually proved too cumbersome.

Until 1892, club teams represented counties in the GAA championship, and after 1895 one-club teams became increasingly rare. GAA records, and the inscriptions on early trophies, list the names of the champion clubs who, until 1919, were responsible for picking the county team. The practice still continues in many counties whereby the champion club nominates the captain of the county team for the following year's championship. It has led to some odd situations when the county champion club has no player on the county team, or one inexperienced player who ends up with the captaincy by default.

Action Replay: the Club Championship

Football

1971
East Kerry 5–9 Bryansford 2–7
Croke Park, c.200

A tiny attendance saw a divisional team, drawn from 5 different clubs, win the new club shield, racing 10 points ahead in the first 10 minutes and holding their lead with 2 goals from Dan Kavanagh and Denis Coffey. Within 2 years, divisional teams were excluded, causing problems for Kerry for many years.

1972
Bellaghy 0–15 UCC 1–11
Croke Park, c.300

The sides are level 5 times in the second half before Wolfe Tones from Derry won with late points from Frankie O'Loane and Brendan Cassidy on a Friday night in Croke Park. East Kerry hadn't returned the shield so there was no presentation.

1973
Nemo Rangers 2–11 St Vincent's 2–11
Portlaoise, c.3,000
Replay: Nemo Rangers 4–6 St Vincent's 0–10
Thurles, c.2,000

Scores were level 6 times before Jimmy Keaveney's pointed free forced a replay, which Nemo won through goals from Jimmy Barrett and Billy Cogan just before half-time, and Liam Goode and Seamus Coughlan in the second half.

1974
UCD 1–6 Lurgan Clan Na Gael 1–6
Croke Park, *c*.6,000
Replay: UCD 0–14 Lurgan Clan Na Gael 1–4
UCD, *c*.12,000

Eugene McGee's UCD were saved by a late point from Cavan's Ollie Leddy in a match graced by live television and an early attempt at a St Patrick's weekend slot for the championship (the final was staged on the day after Patrick's Day). The disappointing replay served as curtain-raiser to the Sligo–Roscommon league semi-final.

1975
UCD 1–11 Nemo Rangers 0–12
Croke Park, *c*.5,000

A great first-half goal from Mayo-man J. P. Kean kept UCD in touch but they still trailed by 4 points entering the final quarter. Fitness told as they secured victory with points from Jackie and Barry Walsh (Kerry) and Dublin's Pat O'Neill.

1976
St Vincent's 4–10 Roscommon Gaels 0–5
Portlaoise, *c*.4,000

The match was already won when 2 goals from Tony Hanahoe and a point from Jimmy Keaveney completed a Dublin three-in-a-row. UCD's great Dublin rivals had won the Dublin championship by default because the final clashed with examinations.

1977
Austin Stacks 1–13 Ballerin 2–7
Croke Park, 8,971

Footballing poet and son of 1920s star J. J. Barrett coached Tralee club Stacks to victory despite 2 first-half goals from the Derry club. Mikey Sheehy scored the winning points: an acute line-ball and a 45-yard free.

1978
Thomond College 2–14 St Johns 1–3
Croke Park, c.3,000

Limerick's title, but no Limerickman on the college team that beat Andy McCallin's Johns with goals from Kerryman Pat Spillane (his brother Mick was also on the team) and Sligoman Mick Kilcoyne. Galwayman Brian Talty contested midfield against Fermanaghman Pater McGinnity. En route to the final, Thomond fought 4 of the greatest matches in early club championship history with Austin Stacks for the Munster title, eventually winning with the help of a cheeky Pat Spillane goal. Thomond hadn't entered the Limerick championship the previous year but were inspired by UCD success.

1979
Nemo Rangers 2–9 Scotstown 1–3
Croke Park, 4,443

Swirling snow spoiled a St Patrick's Day final that ranks

with 1995 as the coldest ever, Frank Cogan emerged from the white to play a proverbial blinder.

1980
St Finbarr's 3–9 Ballinasloe 0–8
Tipperary, c.3,000

Five years after winning a hurling title, Barrs became the first and only club to double up thanks to Jimmy Barry-Murphy, who set up all 3 goals for Jamesie O'Callaghan and Finny O'Mahony. They became the first club to win the hurling–football double in Cork the same year.

1981
St Finbarr's 1–8 Walterstown 0–6
Croke Park, 4,066

Substitute Jim Barry brought the title back to Cork with a last-minute goal from Dave Barry in a match spoiled by missed chances and confusion over the new hand-pass rule.

1982
Nemo Rangers 6–11 Garrymore 1–8
Ennis, 3,600

The biggest winning margin in a club final as Denis Allen (scorer of 2–2 before he retired injured in the first half) powered Nemo to an outstanding win. Allen's first goal came after 50 seconds, Timmy Dalton scored 2 and Ephram Fitzgerald a 5th to give an extraordinary half-time score of 5–6 to 0–1. Charlie Murphy scored the 6th after 42 minutes.

1983

Portlaoise 0–12 Clan Na Gael 2–0
Cloughjordan, c.4,000

Portlaoise, inspired by defenders Jimmy Bergin and Michael Lillis, shot 20 wides as their south Roscommon opposition collapsed – the Clann depended on a lucky break and a penalty for their 2 goals.

1984

Nemo Rangers 2–10 Walterstown 0–5
Athlone, c.4,000

Nemo's fourth as Denis Allen engineered 2 Ephie Fitzgerald second-half goals on a weekend in which the GAA staged semi-finals and final at adjacent venues.

1985

Castleisland 2–2 St Vincents 0–7
Tipperary, c.4,000

The most dramatic finish of the decade as Donie Buckley despatched Willie O'Connor's line ball to the Dublin net for a 58th-minute winning goal.

1986

Burren 1–10 Castleisland 1–6
Croke Park, 10,176

John Treanor's 42nd-minute goal secured the title for one of Ireland's most progressive clubs – they staged the first floodlit GAA match on their Mourne playing field in 1975.

1987
St Finbarr's 0–10 Clan Na Gael 0–7
Croke Park, 9,550

A 5th title (2 hurling and 3 football) for the Barrs in terrible weather as Patrick's Day becomes the established date for the final.

1988
Burren 1–9 Clan Na Gael 0–8
Croke Park, c.7,000

Tony McArdle's 6th-minute goal and 4 points in the last 6 minutes brought the cup north again. Tommy McGovern led the rendition of 'Mountains of Mourne' from the podium.

1989
Nemo Rangers 1–13 Clan Na Gael 1–3
Croke Park, 9,158

Eoin O'Mahoney's free-taking left the Roscommon champions with three-in-a-row lost.

1990
Baltinglass 2–7 Clan na Gael 0–7
Croke Park, 15,708

Wicklow All-Star Kevin O'Brien set up Con Murphy for 2 first-half goals and an incredible 4th defeat in a final for the Roscommon champions.

1991

Lavey 2–9 Salthill 0–10

Croke Park, 8,316

Brian McCormack's 38th-minute goal sealed victory to St Mary's parish (2 townlands, Gulladuff and Mayogall, and about 1,300 people) and provided an emotional farewell for 43-year-old Anthony McGurk, one of 7 brothers to feature when he came on as a sub.

1992

Killarney Crokes 1–11 Thomas Davis 0–13

Croke Park, 13,885

One of the great finals as Pat O'Shea's 13th-minute goal was sufficient to beat Killarney's Tallaght opponents.

1993

O'Donovan Rossa 1–12 Éire Óg 3–6

Croke Park, 21,714

Replay: O'Donovan Rossa 1–7 Éire Óg 0–8 Limerick, 25,000

Class and controversy meet. The Skibbereen club team, 33/1 outsiders at the start of the Cork championship, survivde an ugly semi-final encounter with Lavey, and drew one of the greatest finals of all with Éire Óg where Mick McCarthy scored a record-equalling 1–8. His equalising point coming after it appeared an Éire Óg player had been fouled. They finally won the replay when Éire Óg's Joe Hayden had a winning goal disallowed 3 minutes into injury time.

1994
Nemo Rangers 3–11 Castlebar Mitchels 0–8
Croke Park, 13,392

The quickest goal in club final history, from Stephen Calnan after 10 seconds, set Nemo up for a 6th title, and a 5th medal each for Jimmy Kerrigan and Tim Dalton.

1995
Kilmacud Crokes 0–8 Bellaghy 0–5
Croke Park, 18,544

Mick Pender saved Karl Diamond's penalty and won the title for Tommy Lyons's south Dublin team on a day that rivals 1979 as the coldest in club final history.

1996
Laune Rangers 4–5 Eire Og 0–11
Croke Park, 21,986

Killorglin won with goals from Gerry Murphy after 3 minutes, a sparkling Billy O'Shea goal and a dubious penalty converted by Tommy Byrne before half-time and a 4th in the 53rd minute from Billy O'Sullivan.

1997
Crossmaglen 2–13, Knockmore 0–11
Croke Park, 34,852

Crossmaglen forgot the 28-year occupation of half their pitch by the British army for a day as Oisín McConville saw a long ball drop through the goalkeeper fingers and into the net. Jim McConville added a second to give

Cross a 2–5 to 0–6 lead at half-time, and the Mayo champions failed in the struggle to get back into the match.

1998
Corofin 0–15, Erin's Isle 0–10
Croke Park, 36,545

Level with 8 minutes to go, the tiny village from north Galway defeated the Finglas 'Parish' with points from Gerry Burke, Eddie Steede, Shane Conlisk and Derek Reilly (2). Three great saves from Martin MacNamara keep Corofin in the game at crucial stages while captain Ray Silke set another record: the longest speech.

1999
Crossmaglen 0–9 Ballina 0–8
Croke Park, 40,106

Crossmaglen took 19 minutes to score, equalised with 13 minutes to go, fell behind and won with 2 points from Oisin McConville and John McEntee as Ballina kicked 16 wides.

2000
Crossmaglen 1–14 Na Fianna 0–12
Croke Park, 31,965

The south Armagh team disregarded the risk of a replay and booked their Canaries holiday for the day after the final. They lost an 8-point lead against their north Dublin opposition before winning with 3 points in the last 5 minutes. Oisin McConville scored the pivotal goal 5 minutes into the second half and also hit the post.

2001

Crossmolina 0–16 Nemo Rangers 1–12

Croke Park, 20,025

A second-half comeback inspired by Kieran McDonald won a title for Mayo at last, despite a late Colin Corkery goal that cut their lead from 4 points to one. Corkery missed another chance for a draw. Foot and mouth disease delayed the final until Easter.

2002

Ballinderry 2–10 Nemo Rangers 0–9

Thurles, 16,112 (excluding children)

Gerard Cassidy's goal with 12 minutes to go sent the cup to Derry. Declan Bateson's goal after 21 minutes gave them the lead they never lost. The finals moved to Thurles because of reconstruction at Croker.

2003

Nemo Rangers 0–14 Crossmolina 1–9

Croke Park, 26,235

Colin Corkery won the 'battle of the White Boots' against Kieran McDonald, kicking 6 points while Joe Keane got Crossmolina's 20th-minute goal.

2004

Caltra 0–13 An Gaeltacht 0–12

Croke Park, 38,500

Michael Meehan scored 6 points, and his brother Noel 5 before accepting the cup and singing 'Oh, Flower of Caltra', to the air of the Scottish anthem. Caltra pulled ahead in the last 10 minutes after Aodán MacGearailt might have had 2 goals while the GAA apologised for not having enough turnstiles open – they expected 20,000.

2005
Ballina Stephenites 1–12 Portlaoise 2–8
Croke Park, 31,236

Ballina ferociously defended a 1-point lead for 4 minutes after Liam Brady's 68th-minute winning point. Hughes scored the pivotal goal 6 minutes after half-time, despite 2 well-timed Portlaoise goals from Kevin Fitzpatrick, including a harsh first-half penalty. Ballina's David Brady had lost 6 finals in Croke Park.

Hurling

1971
Roscrea 4–5 St Rynagh's 2–5
Birr, c.1,000

Francis Loughnane's Roscrea beat Banagher with the help of outstanding solo-run goals from Joe Cunningham and Joe Tynan. The first inter-club final, concluded a few days before the Christmas of 1971, shared a launch venue with the first inter-county hurling final, also a club affair won by a Tipperary side, 83 years earlier.

1972
Blackrock 5–13 Rathnure 6–9
Waterford, c.1,500

Pat Moylan's goal 74 minutes from the end secured a gripping victory for the Cork city club over their Wexford rivals, while John Rothwell and Dan Quigley exchanged 2 goals each in the first half, Dave Prendergast scored 2 for Rock in the second.

1973
Glen Rovers 2–18 St Rynagh's 2–8
Croke Park, c.500

Tom Buckley and Red Crowley inspired a Cork victory over Banagher in a tough final. Although the semi-finals were staged in May, the final was not played until 9 December 1973 due to a dispute.

427

1974

Blackrock 2-14 Rathnure 3-11
Croke Park, c.6,000

Replay: Blackrock 3-8 Rathnure 1-9
Dungarvan, c.3,000

A rousing draw caused the first club final to be staged on Patrick's Day to be hailed as a success and an adequate replacement for the ailing Railway Cup. Yet it took a further 11 years to establish the fixture. Superb late goals from Donal Collins and Eamonn O'Donoghue secured Rock's second title in the replay.

1975

St Finbarr's 3-8 Fenians 1-6
Croke Park, c.3,000

A Cork three-in-a-row for different clubs as goals in the last quarter from Jimmy Barry-Murphy, Jerry O'Shea and Charlie Cullinane defeated Kilkenny's champions.

1976

James Stephens 2-10 Blackrock 2-4
Thurles, c.3,000

Five points down at half-time, the George Leahy trained and Fan Larkin captained 'village' from Kilkenny city came storming back in the second half.

1977

Glen Rovers 2-12 Camross 0-8
Thurles, c.4,000

Christy Ring's old club had 9 survivors from 1973 as Patsy Harte, Red Crowley and Pat O'Doherty secured their second title against the plucky Laois champions, inspired by the Cuddy family.

1978
St Finbarr's 2–7 Rathnure 0–9
Thurles, c.3,000

Wexford's Rathnure led 0–8 to 0–1 at half-time thanks to a gale-force wind, but Barry Wiley scored an equaliser with 10 minutes to go, and Jimmy Barry-Murphy's goal from a rebound sealed another title for Cork.

1979
Blackrock 5–7 Ballyhale Shamrocks 5–5 Thurles, c.3,000

Two first-half Ray Cummins' goals in rapid succession gave Blackrock a narrow lead, while Tom Lyon's 5th goal secured Cork's second three-in-a-row with 3 different clubs. But only just.

1980
Castlegar 1–11 Ballycastle 1–8
Navan, c.4,000

Galway against Antrim to usher in a new decade. A brotherly All-Ireland sent 5 Connollys into action against 6 Donnellys. Olcan McLaverty's first-half goal failed to ignite Ballycastle then, 5 minutes into the second half, Liam Mulryan turned Joe Connolly's pass into the net. Ballycastle cut the Galway lead back to a point, then Gerry Connolly scored a point and Joe Connolly put a penalty over the bar for Galway's first title. Breathtaking.

1981

Ballyhale Shamrocks 1-15 St Finbarr's 1-11
Thurles, c.3,000

More brothers. Seven Fennellys (Liam getting the goal 14 minutes into the second half) helped a parish of 260 houses defeat Jimmy Barry-Murphy's star-studded Barrs from Cork after the sides were level 5 times in the first half. Barry-Murphy's 54th-minute goal came too late to secure the hurling–football double Barrs so nearly achieved in 1981.

1982

James Stephens 3-13 Mount Sion 3-8
Thurles, 6,300

Kilkenny's 'village' had 12 of their 1976 team as they staged another second-half comeback, this time from 7 points. John McCormack scored all 3 goals in the 34th, 49th and 54th minutes and Billy Walton scored 10 points to thwart John Dalton, Jim Greene and colleagues from the Waterford city club.

1983

Loughgiel 1-8 St Rynagh's 2-5
Croke Park, c.3,000
Replay: Loughgiel 2-12 St Rynagh's 1-12
Casement Park, 10,000

A historic first victory for Antrim, secured by goals from Brendan Laverty and Aidan McCarry in each half. Padraig Horan had missed a late free the first day, after a superb display Loughgiel's stocky captain and goalkeeper

Niall Patterson kept Loughgiel in the match against a
Banagher team still reeling from a controversial semi-final
encounter with Kiltormer.

1984
Ballyhale Shamrocks 1–10 Gort 1–10
Birr, c.3,000
Replay: Ballyhale Shamrocks 1–10 Gort 0–7
Thurles, c.3,000
Dermot Fennelly's 59th-minute point earned Kilkenny
champions Ballyhale a draw, Ger Fennelly's first-half goal
won the replay. Although the GAA organised semi-finals
and final on the same weekend, it was June before the
championship was completed

1985
St Martin's 2–9 Castlegar 3–6
Croke Park, c.4,000
Replay: St Martin's 1–13 Castlegar 1–10
Thurles, c.3,000
Tom Moran scored 2 goals the first day and inspired
victory on the second for the Kilkenny champions. In the
drawn match, St Martin's were foiled by a late goal for the
Galway city team – by Kilkenny man Martin O'Shea.

1986
Kilruane McDonaghs 1–15 Buffers Alley 2–10
Croke Park, 10,176
Five rallying points from Jim Williams helped Len
Gaynor's Tipperary champions to a 2-point victory over
their Wexford rivals.

1987

Borrisileigh 2-9 Rathnure 0-9
Croke Park, 9,550

Philip Kenny and Aidan Ryan's first-half goals brought the title to North Tipp on the day after St Patrick's Day, for another Wexford defeat.

1988

Midleton 3-8 Athenry 0-9
Croke Park, c.3,000

Kevin Hennessy's 2 early goals and a kicked goal from Colm O'Neill 2 minutes from the end secured Midleton and Cork victory just in time for John Fenton's retirement.

1989

Buffers Alley 2-12 Rossa 0-12
Croke Park, 9,158

Rossa's 5-point lead was hauled back with a Seamus O'Leary goal, and Kilmuckridge/Monamolin club won a medal for 43-year-old full forward Tony Doran. Only for goalkeeper Henry Butler the cup could have gone to Belfast.

1990

Ballyhale Shamrocks 1-16 Ballybrown 0-16
Croke Park, 15,708

Ballybrown led by 6 points before Ger Fennelly's 24th-minute goal. The margin was 4 points at half-time, then a second-half surge gave Ballyhale a third title against the Limerick champions.

1991
Glenmore 1–13 Patrickswell 0–12
Croke Park, 8,316

Christy Heffernan's 33rd-minute goal, characteristically booted to the net, brought victory to a small south Kilkenny club on the Wexford border, just a few years out of junior ranks, against Limerick's second successive finalists.

1992
Kiltormer 0–15 Birr 1–8
Thurles, 13,855

Tommy Lally trained Galway's Kiltormer to success, despite losing Ollie Kilkenny and Brendan Dervan for the final. Kiltormer's semi-final saga goes into club championship history, they played 3 matches against the Bonners' club, Cashel King Cormacs, before a goal from substitute Tony Furey secured their place in the final.

1993
Sarsfields 1–17 Kilmallock 2–7
Croke Park, 21,714

Despite conceding goals at the beginning of each half, Martin Conneely's Galway champions secured their title against the Limerick champions after a long Joe Cooney free ended up in the net 5 minutes from the end.

1994

Sarsfields 1–14 Toomevara 3–6
Croke Park, 13,392

History as Galway club Sarsfields retained their title through the free-taking of Aidan Donoghue. Goals in the 13th, 29th and 44th minutes gave Toomevara a 3-point lead before Sarsfields equalised an acute angle 65th-minute goal from Michael Kenny, again from Joe Cooney's pass.

1995

Birr 0–9 Dunloy 0–9
Croke Park, 18,544

Replay: Birr 3–13 Dunloy 2–3
Croke Park, 6,395

Tony McGrath justly scored Dunloy's equaliser 8 seconds into injury-time, his team had led for 52 minutes in dreadful conditions. Birr dominated the replay after Paul Murphy and Oisin O'Neill goals in the 1st and 3rd minutes gave them an unprecedented 2–7 to nil half-time lead.

1996

Sixmilebridge 5–10 Dunloy 2–8
Croke Park, 21,986

Two David Chaplin goals inspired the Bridge to a famous victory over the Antrim champions within months of Clare's historic All-Ireland.

1997
Athenry 0–14 Wolfe Tones 1–8
Croke Park, 34,852

Nine points from teenager Eugene Cloonan gave
Galway champions St Mary's the title, while Derek
Collins of the Shannon town club, scorer of a 4th-
minute goal, missed the opportunity of a second
immediately after half-time.

1998
Birr 1–13 Sarsfields 0–9
Croke Park, 36,545

Birr had 5 Under-21s in action and took command
immediately when Paul Carroll set up Darren Hanniffy
for a 5th-minute goal. Brian Whelahan won man of the
match, while captain Joe Errity paid tribute to his father
Tom, who had died watching Birr in the semi-final.

1999
St Joseph's 2–14 Rathnure 0–8
Croke Park, 40,106

Ennis suburban side St Joseph's Doora-Barefield took
Clare's second title with goals from Andrew Whelan in
the 12th-minute and Lorcan Hassett in injury time,
effectively killing off the Wexford challenge with 4
unanswered points before half-time.

2000
Athenry 0-16, St Joseph's 0-12
Croke Park, 31,965

A double point-blank save by Michael Crimmins from Colm Mullen and 2 points from Eugene Cloonan, the first from a penalty, brought Athenry success and the chorus of a famous song from Hill 16 on a day when Joe Rabbitte was outstanding.

2001
Athenry 3-24 Graigue-Ballycallan 2-19
Semple Stadium, 20,025

Joe Rabbitte's kicked goal just before half-time in extra time helped Athenry regain a title they had virtually lost, having led the Kilkenny champions by 5 points with 17 minutes to go before Adrian Ronan set to work on their lead. Graigue qualified for the final because Davey Fitzgerald missed a last-minute Sixmilebridge penalty on a day Semple Stadium's crossbars were a foot too low.

2002
Birr 2-10 Clarinbridge 1-5
Thurles, 16,112 (excluding children)

Birr took control with a Declan Pilkington goal after 30 seconds, brother Johnny added another and Brian Whelahan inspired a victory for his brother Simon (captain) and father Pat Joe (manager). Miserable weather kept the Thurles attendance low while Croke Park was being developed.

2003

Birr 1–19 Dunloy 0–11
Croke Park, 26,235

Declan Pilkington got another match-winning goal.
Alastair Elliot's 11th minute goal chance was cleared off
the line by John Paul O'Meara, although the Antrim
champions cut the lead to 3 points early in the second
half.

2004

Newtownshandrum 0–17 Dunloy 1–6
Croke Park, 38,500

Ben O'Connor scored 10 points to set up a surprise
victory for a small north Cork parish and another
disappointment for brave Antrim opposition, despite a
penalty goal from goalkeeper Gareth McGhee.

2005

James Stephens 0–19 Athenry 0–14
Croke Park, 31,236

Eoin Larkin scored 9 points for the 'village' from
Kilkenny, Eugene Cloonan scored 6 for Athenry, who
led briefly at the start of the second half.

437